Dedicated to Timothy Shaw, a true friend and inspiration

Papa Marcel
mon grand père

Pierre Koffmann
Memories of Gascony

Pierre Koffmann with Timothy Shaw
Foreword by Richard Vines
Photography by Laura Edwards

MITCHELL BEAZLEY

Sur le capot de la
Citroen de mon père

Contents

6   Foreword

8   Prologue

14   Introduction

20   Spring

92   Summer

156 Autumn

228 Winter

296 Epilogue

300 Index

304 Acknowledgements

Foreword by Richard Vines, Bloomberg

PIERRE KOFFMANN WOULD rather be in his restaurant than at a party and in a kitchen rather than in the dining room. When he can be persuaded to attend a social event, you may see him standing in a corner, talking with old friends rather than trying to make new ones. Networking doesn't come into it.

For someone who is tall and physically imposing, Pierre is self-effacing away from the stove. The humble background he describes in these pages has not rubbed off. If he hadn't become a chef he says he might have become a train driver. It's as if he feels out of place consuming cocktails and canapés. While taking pride in his own achievements, he sees himself as a cook.

When Pierre moved to the UK more than forty years ago, only a privileged few had tasted the haute cuisine presented by the Roux brothers, for whom Pierre worked. His skills, even then, were outstanding and he quickly rose to become head chef at the Waterside Inn. He might easily have built his career around such sophisticated gastronomy, but he didn't. He always says he likes to cook the kind of food he likes to eat. The food he likes most is inspired by the meals prepared by his mother and grandmother in south-west France more than half a century ago.

He opened La Tante Claire in 1977 and gave Londoners the big flavours of Gascony. Pierre had access to high-quality ingredients, he refined the cooking techniques and he improved the presentation, yet the dishes owed as much to his childhood as they did to his training and professional experience. Rusticity met gastronomy and it was a happy marriage.

Three Michelin stars followed. Pierre helped train a generation of British chefs, including Marco Pierre White, Gordon Ramsay, Tom Aikens, Tom Kitchin and Jason Atherton. He's commanding in the kitchen and his protégés still talk about the toughness of the chef they came to call 'the Bear.' He was quiet and completely focused but demanded perfection. After the death of his wife Annie, he closed La Tante Claire in 2003 and tried to settle into retirement.

Memories of his dishes lived on among his customers, while young food lovers could only hear about his food. When Pierre returned to the stove to open a temporary restaurant on the roof of Selfridges in 2009, it was like a veteran pop star going back on the road. The original plan was for the venue to run for about a week and it ended up continuing for two months.

He is matter-of-fact about his signature creation of pig's trotter stuffed with sweetbreads and morels. It's a dish that appears on menus as far away as Australia and was in constant demand when he opened his restaurant Koffmann's at The Berkeley Hotel in London in 2010. He says he can't understand why other chefs don't do something else, maybe with pigs' tails, rather than copying him. But he knows the importance of his creation.

'It's going to be written on my gravestone,' he says. 'Pig's trotter.'

Prologue

THIS IS A BOOK about my childhood, and it grew out of the gratitude and affection I have always felt for my maternal grandparents, Camille and Marcel Cadeillan, and out of my memories of their colourful and eccentric characters and the visits I used to make as a boy to their farm in a small village in central Gascony. My grandparents were peasant farmers, and the book tells of the seasons, of animals and crops, and of ploughing and harvesting; but above all it tells of the country food and the cooking of my grandmother. It describes the ducks and hares which we roasted on spits before the wide log fire in her kitchen; the endless soups and *garbures* she made in her thick iron pot; her jams, preserves and *confits*; the *poule au pot* we ate at harvest lunches in the summer and the quails wrapped in vine leaves or cooked over hot, glowing embers.

The stories centre on my grandparents' farm at Saint Puy, situated in the heart of Gascony in the *département* of the Gers. I was born in Tarbes, and so, by background and culture, I am a Gascon. Traditionally, the name of Gascony has always referred to a large square section of south-west France fitted in between the Garonne and the Pyrenees, bordered on one side by the old province of Languedoc and on the other by the Atlantic. But my own private Gascony is far smaller than that – it is, to me, the village of Saint Puy and the beautiful countryside which immediately surrounds it.

My grandmother's cooking was an important element in my boyhood memories, and was also important to me later. Like many other Frenchmen I have retained all my life the taste of the food I ate as a child, the food cooked by a near member of the family who is almost always a mother or a grandmother. In my own case my grandmother's cooking was the typical peasant cooking of the Gers. The peasants lived on whatever farm produce was instantly available during the different seasons of the year, and therefore their ingredients were always extremely fresh. Vegetables and fruit were combined with poultry, especially chickens and ducks, or with any meat that was left over for home consumption after an animal had been slaughtered. Freshwater fish and game were prized occasional items on the menu, and in the winter we ate a lot of *confits*, or preserved meats, and *conserves* of vegetables and fruit. My grandparents had no sea fish, very little beef, since they usually sold most of the meat which came from their own cows, and no cheese, for the Gers is not a cheese-producing region. Only on very rare occasions would any food be bought from a shop, a procedure which my grandmother regarded as being unnecessarily extravagant.

Compared to the cooking of the classical *haute cuisine* tradition, country cooking is comparatively simple, and in terms of ingredients, restricted. In the south-west it was based on duck and goose fat, which always retained the special, distinctive taste of the *confit* which had been cooked in it; soup, bread and chicken were staple dishes at most meals; and the wine my grandparents drank was simply what they made every year from their own grapes. There were no great sauces poured over meat to hide it and disguise it; there was no *fonds de veau*, or *fumet de poisson*, nor any attempt to present elaborately decorated dishes – but everything we ate was of excellent quality. Everything had its own natural taste, a taste which in many instances, such as that of poultry, pigeons, guinea fowl or pork, cannot even be imagined by people who only buy their food from modern shops and supermarkets, even specialized ones.

This book is not, however, a comprehensive account of the regional cooking of the whole of Gascony. All the recipes which come into the story are there because they were the ones I knew as a boy, and because they are the ones I remember best and enjoyed the most. They are not terribly complicated; many of them are quite straightforward, though their apparent simplicity is deceptive. Country cooking is founded on sympathy. It is only done well when it is done with deep instinctive feeling; and it is done best (though this is not of course essential) if you have been familiar with it all your life. Here I tell you how I became familiar with it myself, and in doing so I hope to paint an intimate picture of a unique place and its people.

When I think of the contrast between regional peasant cooking and the grandiose restaurant tradition of the 19th-century, and when I reflect on my own aims at La Tante Claire, I find it interesting to put it all into some sort of historical perspective. Over a period of some four hundred years the development of French *haute cuisine* centred around a dialogue between those who wished to honour the natural taste of original ingredients and those who wished to disguise these tastes and to replace them with complex artificial flavours of their own fabrication. Certain chefs and cookery writers of the 17th-century started the reaction against the spiced cuisine of the middle ages and the Renaissance; others in the 18th-century continued it and tried to evolve a lighter style of cooking which emphasized natural flavours, a style which even then was called *la cuisine moderne* and *la nouvelle cuisine*. But the battle between original simplicity and sophisticated elaboration was never really resolved, though in the tradition of *haute cuisine* the elaborators tended usually to have the upper hand.

Running parallel with the tradition of court cooking and the *grande cuisine*, there had, however, always existed another tradition, that of the *cuisine du terroir* – the country cooking followed by generations of peasants in the many different regions of France. Here the ideals of the 18th-century 'innovators' were in fact practised unthinkingly and quite naturally, since the peasants were obliged to use whatever ingredients came immediately to hand and their food and its flavour was therefore always fresh and unspoiled. Of course it is true that the repertoire of regional cooking was frequently a source of inspiration for the masters of 19th-century *grande cuisine*, but those 'honest local dishes' which appeared at the sumptuous banquets of the Second Empire and the *Belle Epoque* were in appearance and presentation far more aristocratic than countrified. Although the great chefs of the period exploited the country tradition whenever it suited them, they showed very little interest in real regional cooking in its genuine, natural surroundings.

Authentic regional dishes were encountered for the first time by the Parisian public when a Provençal restaurant was opened in the capital shortly before the Revolution. The number of such restaurants grew slowly during the 19th-century; but it was not until the 20th-century that the increasing availability of the motor car, together with studies of French country cooking by writers like Curnonsky and the annual Michelin restaurant guide, encouraged tourists to discover and appreciate the delicious local dishes which could be found in villages and provincial towns all over France. Gradually this regional, traditional style of peasant cooking grew up as an important alternative to the *grande cuisine* of the great restaurants.

It is with this particular stage in the history of French cooking that I feel very much at home. Though I was trained in the tradition of the *grande cuisine*, my real inspiration has always been the cooking of the Gers which I learned and appreciated at my grandparents' farm. Over twenty-five years at La Tante Claire I always cooked in my own way and in my own style; it never once changed, and has always been fundamentally related to country cooking. Certain things at the restaurant were not, of course, quite the same as they were at the farm. The presentation of the food was much more sophisticated, and the general range of ingredients and dishes was more extensive than my grandmother's could ever have been. We used, for example, lobster and turbot, which she would never have thought of buying; we had more beef dishes than she would have been able to provide; and we used such luxuries as truffles, which, again, were quite outside her range. But otherwise, if you looked at our restaurant menu, I think you would see how very close most of the dishes were to the recipes I remember and describe in this book.

Whereas, in the past, the masters of the *grande cuisine* raided regional cooking and carried off its dishes like prisoners to be dressed up and trained in foreign ways, nowadays the situation is reversed, due to some extent to improvements in refrigeration over the last twenty years which have enabled restaurant kitchens to keep ingredients fresh for far longer periods. Regional dishes start to command more and more of the chef's respect, and he uses his training in the techniques of *haute cuisine* to serve them with ever increasing fidelity rather than to transform them.

In recent years a lot has been said about the claims of *nouvelle cuisine* to be the great renewer of the French culinary tradition, but for me its contribution in this respect can only be subordinate to the more fundamental and long-standing part played by the rediscovery of regional cooking; my approach to *nouvelle cuisine* has therefore always been critically selective. At Koffmann's at The Berkeley I use its techniques in the preparation of fish and vegetables (where methods are similar to those in traditional Italian or Chinese cooking) but never for meat or game. Our decorative presentation of the food is also influenced by *nouvelle cuisine*, since in a restaurant it is very important that food should be as attractive to the eye as it is exciting to the palate.

Regional cooking, on the other hand, is intended for a totally different setting; it is enjoyed at home, round the family table, and smart presentation does not matter. It is, as we say, *la cuisine de l'amitié*, and the essential things are the good taste of the food and the warm, friendly atmosphere of the home. In this way *nouvelle cuisine*, eaten formally by diners at a restaurant, has little to do with the *cuisine du terroir* which, as I have explained, is the creative base of my own cooking. Personally I would always prefer a good, robust *poule au pot* to a contrived, even if fashionable, *tartare de thon au coulis de fraises*.

Comparing some of the more artificial exaggerations of *nouvelle cuisine* to the country cooking I knew as a boy always seems to me to be rather like dressing Marie Antoinette up as a shepherdess and then comparing her to a real farmer's wife looking after a real-life flock of sheep. Nothing can take the place of the regional peasant tradition in cooking. Although it is unchanging it never ceases to be vigorously alive. Nowhere else can you find a real *choucroute* or a real cassoulet or a real *bouillabaisse*, if these are the dishes you like and if you know them really well. Food fashions may come and go, but French country cooking will always remain, and it will always inspire us.

Mes grands-parents
maternels.

Introduction

THE GASCON VILLAGE of Saint Puy stands on a high shoulder of land overlooking the valley of the Gèle, about half-way between the two towns of Fleurance and Condom, in the very heart of south-western France. Its walls of corn-coloured stone and its red roofs climb gently up the hill towards the castle, an 18th-century manor house built above mediaeval fortifications, from which immense views stretch out in all directions over the surrounding countryside. Below the castle, the church of Our Lady, with its square tower and its wide, unexpectedly low-pitched roof, looms over the village like a stone galleon anchored in a diminutive harbour made of houses and streets.

Next to the church, if you peer over what is left of the walls of the 13th-century *bastide* or fortified town, you discover another magnificent view to the south, right across the river valley, which leads the eye on towards fold after bluish fold of distant, ensuing hills. When the Romans captured this town from the Gauls they called it, not surprisingly, Summum Podium, 'the high place', and this is how it has been known ever since, even though in the middle ages the Latin words somehow assumed the corrupted form of Sempuy, and this was later changed again into the modern name of Saint Puy.

Downhill, to the south-east, the main road leads away in the direction of Fleurance. Just outside the village, on the right-hand side of the road, there is a single-storey farmhouse called the Oratoire, which was, thirty-five or so years ago, when I first knew it, the farm of my maternal grandparents, Marcel and Camille Cadeillan. I was born in 1948 at Tarbes, an important provincial town at the foot of the Pyrenees, but though my childhood was therefore mostly an urban one, my school holidays were spent with my grandparents at their farm, about fifty miles to the north of Tarbes. These holidays played an immensely important part in my life between the ages of about five and eighteen. Even after that, I still used to visit the village, and in 1972 I was married there. By then I had really got to know the life and the work of the Gascon peasants and farmers in a way which would have been impossible in a town.

The aroma of wood smoke, the comfortable, pervading smell of animals, the sight of chickens roasting on a spit in front of a log fire, the rituals of harvest, the natural cycles of sowing and reaping, of birth and slaughter, are all things which are simple enough in themselves, but they are very precious to me, and I would never otherwise have known them. They have become a part of me, and have stayed with me all my life. But, above all, I got to know and love my two grandparents, *Mamie* and *Papa Marcel*, as I used to call them: this book is really about them and their farm and the village, and about the meals which my grandmother used to cook, which with their unforgettable, traditional character and the atmosphere of the country kitchen in which they were eaten were to have such a far-reaching influence on my life.

I have always found it difficult to imagine my grandparents as young people. Although they had great affection for each other, their two characters were so utterly different and often so completely opposed that whenever I wonder to myself how it was that they first met and what drew them together, I realize that I am approaching a mystery to which only they themselves held the secret answer.

When I first knew them, I was a small boy, and to my eyes they seemed amazingly, incredibly old. When I was ten, for example, Marcel was actually only sixty and Camille fifty-four; but at sixty, a peasant who has worked in the fields all his life is truly an old man, worn out with toil, whose active years are over. So I suppose it was natural for a child to think him ancient. I often noticed that the young cooks at La Tante Claire seemed to regard me as quite elderly but I was just over forty at the time and felt about twenty-five. My grandparents lived alone at the farm, so there was no one to bridge the gap between their generation and that of myself, my brother and my two sisters; but they adapted themselves kindly and generously to our noisy, high-spirited invasions, and to all the extra cooking and housework these entailed for Camille.

My grandfather, Marcel Cadeillan, was born at the Oratoire on 21st August 1898, exactly fifty years to the day before my own arrival in the world in 1948. His father, Pierre Cadeillan, was over six feet tall, and in a country where men tended to be rather short, he was looked on as an absolute giant. I was christened Pierre after him, and I think I may have inherited something else from him as well as his name, because, out of all my family, I am the tallest.

Marcel's father died before I was born, but his mother lived on until she was about eighty, and I can just remember her sitting by the kitchen fire, old and silent, and always dressed in black. Whether Pierre Cadeillan bought the farm or whether he inherited it I do not know, but it was there that Marcel, an only child, grew up, working the land and leading the cows, amid all the traditional scenes and customs which are so well illustrated in old, pre-1914 postcards.

By the time I knew him, the overriding purpose of Marcel's life was pleasure. He was a born hunter, and he knew no greater bliss than to be out in the fields with a gun and a bag of ferrets or a fishing rod, or to be looking for mushrooms, or setting traps for ortolans, or catching eels or netting crayfish. Any other activity, unless it was sitting with his friends in the little café in the market place, struck him, I think, as a regrettable even if unavoidable waste of time. He was of medium height and thick set, and had a teasing, humorous twinkle about his face and a quick, jaunty little twitch of his shoulders whenever he came out with some favourite joke or anecdote. With men whom he did not know well Marcel was often shy, but with people he liked, or with women, whom he always adored, he positively scintillated with happiness. On the other hand, he could be unbelievably obstinate if you annoyed him, or tried to make him do something he disliked, or if you persisted too long in discussing some disagreeable topic. On such occasions his jaws would clamp together like a vice; he would stop talking resolutely and remain gloweringly silent until the conversation was finally obliged to take a more pleasant turn.

But it would be wrong to think that Marcel had not worked very hard at the farm when he was younger. Every peasant worked extremely hard in those days. At first my grandfather had been responsible for all the heavy work at the Oratoire; even when he was older he never missed the harvest, when he worked as much and as long as everybody else. Of course he had always loved shooting and fishing and convivial occasions; but at the time I knew him there were two things, apart from his age, which affected him greatly and which made him gradually lose all interest in the farm. The lack of a son meant that there was no one to carry on the farm after his death, and this was an important psychological factor in a peasant family. Secondly, the revolutionary advances made in post-war agricultural technology and mechanization left him stranded in a world he could not cope with or understand. All his life he had farmed at the pace of a pair of cows. With cows he had ploughed, sown, reaped and carted; and the appearance of tractors, new chemical fertilizers, new varieties of crops, and in the 1960s the first combine harvesters left him bewildered and solitary. More and more he took to shooting and fishing, to eluding Camille's commands and instructions, and to spending time with his cronies at the café.

My grandmother's family name was Daris, and she was born in 1904 at Béraut, another old fortified village in the Gèle valley, about four miles to the north-west of Saint Puy. She was about the same height as Marcel; her face was still handsome, and she had quiet eyes which gave you a feeling of calm, instinctive good sense, an intuitive thoughtfulness which always seemed to me to be a sort of wisdom. Her hair was absolutely white and she wore it drawn into a tight bun at the back of her head. In the morning I used to watch with fascination the quick, deft movements of her hands as she transformed the long silver strands into that neat bun, and in a mere thirty seconds changed one human being miraculously into another. I was often told that when she was young Camille was the prettiest girl in the village; even in later life she was always neat and smart, and went regularly to the local hairdresser. She never dressed in black like the other women of Saint Puy, but always wore bright, light colours and clean white aprons which she embroidered herself with green and red borders and rows of little flowers.

Though she had no formal education, Camille was naturally intelligent. She could talk with anyone and always have an interesting conversation. She was never malicious and never repeated gossip, for which she was much liked and respected in the village. She would talk sensibly about the happenings of everyday life, and consequently she was irritated by Marcel's never-ending jokes and stories, his *bêtises*, as she used to call them; though this was only one of the many ways in which my grandfather's free and easy habits annoyed and pained her. Like all the peasants of the Gers, my grandparents always spoke to each other in patois, although they spoke French to us.

The farm of the Oratoire was the largest in the village, and it extended over about a hundred acres on either side of the Fleurance road. Most of the arable land was used for growing wheat and maize; large fields of vines, edged by a line of poplar trees, stretched away from the back of the house until they reached the old, sunken track which led down to the mill of Marin and the river Gèle and to the low range of hills beyond. On the other side of the road there were fruit trees, melon fields and more vines.

Surrounded by trees, and built beside the road on sloping ground about five hundred yards out of the village, the house was long and low, and had a pitched roof of red tiles. It was of local stone and had been built in two different stages. The right-hand part was the barn, and the other, older half with its neat arrangement of windows and door contained the kitchen, dining room and bedroom. Behind the house a dirt road led steeply down to a large, level stretch of land, near Camille's garden, where there were outbuildings and sheds. Here the whole of the bottom storey was given over to animals, poultry, tools, carts, machines and all the general impedimenta of a busy, working farm.

We had five annual school holidays. There were *Mardi gras* and Easter in spring; the two full months of the *grandes vacances* in summer; a week for *Toussaint* in autumn; and the Christmas holidays in winter. All of these, over a period of some ten or twelve years, I spent with Marcel and Camille at the farm; and, as time went on, they became for me symbols of the four seasons. People who live in towns always like to think of the year in terms of seasons, although in fact peasants like my grandparents never do. Instead they measure their year by the regularly recurring phases of the moon. Ancient tradition had always associated sowing and procreation with the rising of the moon, ripeness with its fullness, and gathering and picking with its wane; for in this way the universal rhythms of nature could not be offended or countered.

Every year Camille hung up a Post Office calendar in her kitchen. It was bright with coloured pictures, and feast days and holidays were marked in red. It also showed the exact dates of the phases of the moon throughout the year, and it was according to these that my grandmother pencilled in the days on which all the more important activities of the farm should take place. I remember that the moon must be rising when ducks' eggs were put under hens to be hatched; that trees were cut down at full moon, otherwise the wood would never be of the best quality; and that there were other vital phases for the making of children, to determine whether you would have a boy or a girl.

I am really, as I have said, a townsman. I was born in Tarbes, and have spent over forty years of my life in London, so I tend to think rather more about the seasons than about the moon; but, each time I do, I think of them in terms of life on a Gascon farm glimpsed within the temporal framework of my school holidays.

Ma sœur Nicole et moi,
photo de classe

Spring

In the warm sunshine of early spring the
landscape was still wintry. Later the vines
became green with buds and the fruit trees
came into blossom. We ate traditional pancakes
and sweets at *Mardi gras* and a paschal lamb at
Easter. With the spring vegetables came the
first trout, the first wild mushrooms, and snails
which we caught at night and grilled on the
kitchen fire.

THE FIRST HOLIDAY of the year was the seven or eight days we had in February for *Mardi gras*; the second was the fortnight we had for Easter, which usually fell in April. For Marcel and Camille February was still a wintry time, even if the weather was bright and warm, a month when the work on the farm still consisted of distant preparations for haymaking and harvest yet to come. There might be some crops still to be sown on land which had been first ploughed in September; machines and tools had to be seen to; the trunks of the vines were sprayed with insecticide; and it was a good period in which to carry out any necessary building work. For us children, this first holiday of the year was a time when we sat round the open wood fire of the farm kitchen, ate Camille's various *confits* and *conserves*, and looked forward to the festivities of *Mardi gras*.

Holidays always started on a Sunday. Saturday night at Tarbes was full of excitement and preparations, and on Sunday morning my father would drive us in the car all the way to Saint Puy. This was in the early years, between about 1953 and 1958, when, besides myself, there might be my two sisters and my brother all squeezed into the car together. When I was a bit older I would go by bus from Tarbes to Auch or Fleurance, where I would be met by Monsieur Capuron, my godfather and uncle by marriage, who kept the village grocery shop and was also mayor of Saint Puy and captain of the local fire brigade; he would drive me to my grandparents' farm. When I was eighteen, and the proud owner of my first car, I was independent and could travel as I liked.

If we had come from the south by the Auch road, we would cross the little river Gèle at the bottom of the hill and see the red roofs of Saint Puy and the church tower on the crest above us. We turned right near the *salle des fêtes* and the *boulangerie* of Monsieur Trille and in a few moments passed the tall line of poplar trees which marked the boundary of the farm. On the right of the road lay the farmhouse in front of which Camille always stood anxiously waiting for us. She had recognized the sound of the engine of my father's car a few moments before and had come to see us safely past the cross which stood about a quarter of a mile up the hill, at the junction with the Lectoure road; this was a dangerous point which my grandmother regarded as the worst accident black-spot in the entire *département*.

On arrival we all scrambled out of the car and rushed into the big, square kitchen to a turmoil of welcomes and kisses. I was always happy to embrace

Camille, but I found that kissing Marcel's prickly stubble was rather painful! As it was a Sunday morning, when no work was done in the fields and there were only the animals and poultry to feed, both my grandparents would be there waiting for us. As soon as the greetings were finished, Camille went to the cupboard in the dining room where she kept her aperitifs and *eaux-de-vie*, brought out a bottle of her special *remontant* (pick-me-up) and poured out a glass for everyone, including the children. Then, to eat with it, she would cut off a few slices from the hams and sausages hanging from the beams or inside the great fireplace.

My grandmother disapproved of alcoholic drinks, never drank any armagnac (though she was an expert at telling the exact place of origin of any blend just by its smell) and only very occasionally had a glass of wine. It was one of Marcel's lifelong tasks to circumvent this stern attitude. My grandmother's *remontant*, however, was quite a powerful drink, and everyone looked forward to it and enjoyed it. We never really understood why Camille regarded it as being almost as mild as a glass of orange juice, and ideal to give to small children tired out by what she thought was a very long journey.

We drank this aperitif at the beginning of every holiday, but Camille actually made it rather later in the year with the leaves from the walnut trees growing at the Oratoire. By local tradition the best time to pick walnut leaves is at the feast of Saint John, on 24th June, and Camille always used the leaves taken from the very tip of the branch, which she said had the best flavour. If she had to use leaves from another part of the tree, she always doubled the number she put into the aperitif, which she made in a big, red earthenware pot. She liked to make her aperitifs and *eaux-de-vie* in quite large quantities, as she thought they infused better and tasted better that way. Of course, it is perfectly possible to prepare smaller quantities.

Apéritif aux Feuilles de Noyer

WALNUT LEAF APERITIF

50 walnut leaves
40 g/1½oz bitter orange peel
1 l/1¾pt armagnac
1 kg/2¼lb caster sugar
5 l/8¾pt red wine

Put all the ingredients into a glass jar of approximately 8.5 l/15 pt capacity. Leave to macerate for 8 days, stirring well about twice a day to dissolve the sugar.

Strain the contents of the jar through a sieve, and bottle it. Cork the bottles, and keep them in a cool place for three months. If you can bear to wait that long before drinking a glass of this aperitif, your patience will be well rewarded.

We would usually arrive at the Oratoire about 11 o'clock, by which time the cooking of Sunday lunch, normally the best meal of the week, would already be well advanced. Two large chickens would be turning on the spit above the open wood fire, one for us and one for my uncle and aunt who were tied to their grocer's shop on a busy Sunday morning and could not do their own cooking. Inside the chickens Camille always put some *chapons*, pieces of bread which she had rubbed with garlic; these soaked up the juices of the bird so that they swelled during roasting.

She would also put the round end of a loaf of bread, called a *quignon*, rubbed with garlic, into the neck of the chicken, and she would fix the gizzard under one of the wings, so as not to waste it and to give the bird a better flavour. Marcel was in charge of turning the spit on Sundays. He would crouch down beside the fire, and every so often give the chicken a quarter- or a half-turn, and lock the spit into a different notch. If the delicious smell of the roasting birds began to make us children feel too desperately hungry, we were allowed to ask Marcel to cut off some bits of the trussing string; we would then chew and suck these bits of string impregnated with the juicy, salty chicken taste which made them, I think, the best chewing gum I have ever had.

As soon as the chickens were cooked enough, Marcel would slip quietly away, get on his *mobilette* (a motorized bicycle), and ride up to Dassain's café under the wide stone arches near the market hall to enjoy a quick aperitif or glass of wine with his friends before returning to the farm in time for lunch. One of his favourite drinks was an appropriately named dark-coloured aperitif called *goudron*, which means tar. He was the only person in the village who ever drank this brew, but a bottle was always kept specially for him behind the bar at the café. He also had his own special glass there, which no one else was allowed to touch. He always insisted on using only that glass as any other, he said, made his lips break out in spots.

Meanwhile, my uncle would arrive in his car, take his chicken (which Camille always put in a large basket covered with a neat white cloth) and leave in exchange a generous selection of *gâteaux* and *pâtisseries* which were a present from his grocery shop. My aunt, whom I called *Marraine* (godmother), did not make these cakes herself but bought them for the shop every Sunday from a *pâtissier* in the next village.

Lunch was punctually at noon. Marcel was always very strict about this. Invariably, like every other meal at the Oratoire, it started with a soup; this was followed by the main dish of roast chicken, then came the sweets and cakes, which were not of course at all typical of the local cooking but which delighted us and rounded off Sunday lunch with a treat. There were always plenty of these cakes because, in old age, my grandfather developed a very sweet tooth and insisted on having plenty of sugary delicacies. With the meal Marcel and my father, if he stayed to eat with us, would drink a bottle of *gros rouge*, the ordinary local red wine.

The soup, on a Sunday in February, would still be one of the thick winter varieties, such as a *soupe aux haricots* or a *soupe à pain trempé* or a *garbure*. A *garbure* can be made in many different ways, but here are two ways in which Camille would prepare it in the big iron pot which hung above the open fire. The first *garbure* is for an ordinary lunch.

Garbure de Gascogne

VEGETABLE SOUP WITH PRESERVED GOOSE—SERVES 8

20 g/³⁄₄ oz goose fat
5 garlic cloves, chopped
1 kg/2¼ lb potatoes
20–25 cabbage leaves
1 turnip, chopped
1 preserved goose wing or leg (see Confit de canard, *page 263)*
salt and freshly ground pepper

In a large saucepan, bring 3 l/5½ pt salted water to the boil. Put in the goose fat and garlic. Cut up any very large potatoes and add the potatoes to the pan. Continue to boil while preparing the cabbage.

Wash the cabbage leaves, cut out the central core and lay the leaves on top of each other in a thick pile. Roll it up very tightly, as if you were rolling a newspaper for posting and, using a sharp knife, shred the cabbage as finely as possible. Put the shredded cabbage and chopped turnip into the saucepan and cook for about 40 minutes. Add the preserved goose and continue to cook until the potatoes have disintegrated and the soup is thick enough for a wooden spoon to stand upright in it. Season to taste.

Either serve the *garbure* as a single complete dish, or serve the thick vegetable soup first and the preserved goose as a second course. In this case, add some whole potatoes and extra goose to the *garbure* about 20 minutes before the end of the cooking time.

Camille's other recipe for *garbure* took longer to prepare, so it was served on more important occasions or when there were more guests. This version is always eaten as a single dish, served in a large soup plate, and is accompanied by coarse salt, gherkins, ground pepper and a vinaigrette.

Garbure de Fête

CAMILLE'S SPECIAL GARBURE—SERVES 8

100 g/4 oz onions, cut into 8

100 g/4 oz goose fat

100 g/4 oz bayonne ham, cut into chunks

500 g/1 lb 2 oz salt pork or beef, cut into chunks

1 bouquet garni

10 garlic cloves, peeled and left whole

100 g/4 oz dried haricot beans, pre-soaked

2 cloves

300 g/11 oz carrots

100 g/4 oz turnips, cut into large pieces

100 g/4 oz leeks, cut into large pieces

1 cabbage, cut into large chunks

1 kg/2¼ lb potatoes, cut into large chunks

200 g/7 oz pumpkin, cut into large chunks

300 g/11 oz toulouse sausage, cut into chunks

1 preserved duck leg (see Confit de canard, *page 263)*

In a large casserole, sweat the onions in the goose fat until soft. Add 3 l/5½ pt water, the bayonne ham, salt pork or beef, bouquet garni, garlic, haricot beans and the cloves.

Bring to the boil and simmer for 2 hours, skimming the surface as necessary. Add the carrots, turnips, leeks, cabbage, potato and pumpkin and simmer for a further 30 minutes. Put in the sausage and simmer for 20 minutes, then add the duck and cook for another 10 minutes. Make sure that the water just covers the vegetables during cooking; it must not drown them, or the soup will be too thin. Ladle off any excess liquid and reduce it if necessary, then return it to the soup.

Taste the soup before serving; it should not need extra salt, as the pork and ham are already salty.

Sunday was the only day on which Marcel did not have his usual siesta. As soon as the meal was over, he got on his *mobilette* again and went up to the village café where he would chat with his friends, drink glasses of wine and play cards until about 6 o'clock. My grandmother and I would walk up to my aunt's grocery shop, which was always very quiet on a Sunday afternoon, and she and Camille would spend the afternoon gossiping and talking. My aunt Marraine usually gave us something to bring home – some more sweets or tarts, and perhaps a bag of special food for the chicks which had just hatched. Whatever it was, when I was small, I was always very proud to be the one to carry it.

After spending most of the morning preparing the family lunch, Camille did not want to do any more cooking in the evening, so Sunday supper was always a big *casse-croûte* or snack meal. Marraine might have given us some salted sardines or yogurt, comparatively rare foods for us in those days and ones which Camille would probably never buy. We would arrive back about 7 o'clock, and I was always pleased that we did not set the big table formally with knives, forks and glasses, but just sat by the fire if it was cold, or, if it was warmer, outside in the evening sun in front of the farm.

We ate very simple things which I thought were absolutely delicious. Camille would cut slices of ham, pâté or sausage and we would have boiled eggs and salted sardines or cold *confit de canard*; every Sunday the food was different. My grandmother would just lay out all the various dishes together on the table, and I loved that informality. One Sunday I ate fourteen salted sardines one after the other – and they are quite large! Another time I ate twelve boiled eggs, plus, of course, all the other food as well. We would finish the meal with all sorts of *pâtisserie*, for Marraine always gave us any cakes that had not been sold that afternoon in the shop.

There was such a feeling of freedom and variety about these Sunday suppers, and it was that, I think, which gave me such a hearty appetite. From a gastronomic point of view, perhaps, the food would not rate very highly, but for me, at seven or eight years old, it was nothing less than a feast. I am sure that my love for Chinese food and the way it is presented dates from my delight in those Sunday suppers of my childhood. I still adore the way that the Chinese put every dish on the table at the same time.

Entering the house by the big double doors, with their massive locks and keys and iron bolts, you found yourself in a passage-way paved with hexagonal red tiles, with a door on your left leading into the kitchen. Opposite the door was the open fireplace, where logs burned all through the year, and which was deep enough at the sides to accommodate my great-grandmother's chair. The logs rested on a pair of tall andirons which, in their turn, could carry as many as three long roasting spits. An old cast-iron fireback, propped up against the back wall of the hearth, was embellished with a worn, soot-blackened relief of a sheaf of corn.

A black pot was suspended over the fire from a *crémaillère* (hook), while saucepans and the iron grill, with its long handle and four short legs, hung from nails on one side of the fireplace. Beneath them, standing on the hearth and always ready for use, was the *four de campagne*. This was a round iron cooking pot, with a handle on either side, and a deeply concave lid. It could be put on the fire, and hot embers were then piled into the hollow of its lid, so that inside it became like an oven, totally surrounded by heat.

On the wall above the fireplace were two shotguns, and below them a thick oak beam protruded to form a mantelpiece. This was always kept covered by a white cloth which hung down in front, its edge cut into neat, round scallop shapes, which Camille embroidered charmingly, giving each scallop a separate little flower and finishing the whole thing off with a brightly coloured border. All along the top of the mantelpiece she kept jars of salt, pepper, spices, sugar and other condiments, each jar or pot being graded in descending order according to its size; whenever possible, there were little vases of flowers as well.

To the left of the fireplace was a small wood-burning cast-iron cooking range with a flue pipe that went up the wall and then dived sharply into the main chimney breast. Near it, underneath the window, was the sink where all the washing up was done, though of course, there was no running water at the farm, and all the water we used had to be carried up to the kitchen from the well outside and heated on the fire in saucepans and pots.

Across the room, at right angles to the fireplace, stood the long kitchen table. From the beams which supported the open rafters of the ceiling hung an exciting profusion of smoked hams and sausages. In the corner near the door there was a cupboard; the top part contained all Camille's carefully labelled jars of jam and preserved fruit, and in the lower part was kept the little collection of old popular novels and thumbed copies of illustrated magazines which formed the library of the Oratoire. In the opposite corner stood the tall, fat-bellied long-case clock made by Monsieur Duprom, the Saint Puy clockmaker. I loved that clock and I would sit for minutes on end watching the round brass weight rock slowly from side to side behind its little window and listening to the muffled, comfortable explosions of its tick.

In February the work on the farm consisted mostly of preparation and mending. Marcel checked and repaired the various pieces of machinery which would be of such vital importance when harvest came in July. With a heavy metal container strapped to his back and a spray in his hand, he spent days walking up and down the lines of his vines spraying the trunks with insecticide, always moving and working, like all peasants, at exactly the same undisturbed pace; neither fast nor slow, but moderate, steady, dogged, and never once altered. In my kitchen at the restaurant I know I can set my own pace, working at a hundred miles an hour, if I want, or at ten. But whatever Marcel was doing, whether ploughing, sowing or spraying vines, he went always at about forty miles an hour, never a fraction more, never a fraction less.

Inside the house Camille would be mending, sewing and embroidering as well as looking after all the poultry and the smaller animals. At this time of year, her cooking would still be based on her winter repertory of *conserves* of fruit and vegetables and *confits* of pork, duck and goose. But for us children life at the Oratoire was an infinite variety of pleasures and enjoyments. In early spring, my grandparents got up at about six, then Marcel went out to work and came back for breakfast at 7 o'clock. Normally he was fanatically strict about meal times, and the kitchen clock had to be obeyed without question; but in the case of breakfast we had complete freedom to have it when we liked and on our own. There was hot *chocolat au lait* which we drank in large, thick bowls, never in cups, and there were big round loaves of country bread weighing 2 kilos, which we sliced, speared on the ends of our knives and toasted at the wood fire. We spread the toast lavishly with butter, jam and sometimes with chopped walnuts; these were especially good.

The great moment of the holiday came with *Mardi gras* itself, traditionally the last day of carnival before Lent. We celebrated the day in a convivial way with an important meal to which friends and relations were always invited. If it was a fine day, Camille would probably make a change from the thicker soups of winter, which could almost be a meal in themselves, and start by serving a *bouilli* which is a Gascon *pot-au-feu* containing veal, chicken and *confit de porc*. Camille always insisted on this precise combination of ingredients, and the *bouilli* was eaten in two stages. First the broth was served as a light, consommé-like soup with pearl barley, then the meat was eaten as a separate course. Camille would make the *bouilli* in the great iron pot, then cook the barley in a smaller saucepan resting on the wood fire. In principle a *bouilli* seems rather similar to a *garbure*, but the character and texture of the two dishes differ greatly.

Bouilli

GASCON BOILED MEATS WITH VEGETABLES—SERVES 8

1 boiling chicken, about 2.5 kg/5½ lb

1 kg/2¼ lb flank of beef

1 small knuckle of veal

300 g/11 oz carrots, halved

2 large onions, quartered

6 leeks, tied in a bundle

4 garlic cloves, peeled and left whole

15 peppercorns

1 bouquet garni

salt

500 g/1 lb 2 oz preserved pork spare rib (see Confit de canard, *page 263)*

100 g/4 oz pearl barley or tapioca

In a very large saucepan, bring 4.5 l/1 gal salted water to the boil. Put in the chicken, cover and cook slowly over low heat for 1 hour. Add the beef and veal, cover and simmer for another hour.

Put in all the vegetables, garlic, peppercorns and bouquet garni and add salt to taste. Simmer for another hour until the meat is so tender that you can pierce it easily with a darning needle, skimming the surface from time to time. When

the meat is ready, put in the *confit* of pork to warm through and add extra flavour to the soup. Pour about 2 l/3½ pt of the cooking broth into another saucepan and cook the barley or tapioca in it for about 20 minutes. Serve the broth and barley as a soup and the tender meat and vegetables as a second course.

After the *bouilli* would come *charcuterie*, sausages, ham and foie gras; and this in turn would be followed by a salad, perhaps a dandelion salad if the first green shoots had already started to appear.

Pissenlits au Lard avec Oeufs Mollets

DANDELION SALAD WITH BACON & POACHED EGGS—SERVES 4

500 g/1 lb 2 oz young dandelion leaves
4 eggs
4 teaspoons vinegar
100 g/4 oz streaky bacon
2 slices of white bread, diced
parsley, to garnish

Vinaigrette
50 ml/2 fl oz oil
4 teaspoons vinegar
1 small teaspoon french mustard
salt and freshly ground pepper

Clean the dandelion leaves and wash in several changes of water. Make sure there is no sand or earth left between the leaves. Dry the leaves and put them into a salad bowl. If necessary, dandelion can be replaced by curly endive or chicory.

Poach the eggs in water acidulated with the vinegar for about 3 minutes, until they are done to your taste, then put them into cold water to stop further cooking.

Fry the bacon until crisp. Take it out of the pan with a slotted spoon and fry the bread in the bacon fat until golden on all sides.

Prepare the vinaigrette by mixing all the ingredients, then pour over the dandelion leaves and toss well. Put the eggs, bacon and bread on top of the salad and garnish with parsley. Serve while still slightly warm.

The *confit de canard* was the highlight of the *Mardi gras* meal, but the recipe I give here is not the same as Camille's. She would have served it very simply and just on its own; I prefer to combine a *confit* with a *croustade*, which is the way I sometimes served it at La Tante Claire. A *croustade de confit* means that the *confit* is encased in the leafy paper-thin pastry of the Gers which is made from the special dough we call *pastis*. *Pastis* is more successful if made in large quantities; you will only need half the amount for this recipe, but you can keep the rest to make a *Croustade aux pommes* (page 145), or freeze it for another occasion. Afterwards, Camille would make us her deliciously light acacia flower fritters.

Croustade de Confit de Canard

PRESERVED DUCK LEGS IN FEATHERLIGHT PASTRY—SERVES 4

Pastis Pastry
1 kg/2¼ lb superfine plain flour, plus extra for dusting
4 eggs
a pinch of salt
2 tablespoons oil

Confit Filling
4 large onions, thinly sliced
75 g/3 oz duck fat
4 garlic cloves, chopped
4 preserved duck legs (see Confit de canard, *page 263)*
150 g/5 oz duck fat, melted

Start by making the *pastis* several hours or the day before you cook the dish. The given quantities will make enough pastry for 8 people, but you need a large amount of dough to pull it out to the required thinness. Freeze the surplus dough to use in another recipe. Making this pastry is hard work; to save time and effort, you can use bought filo.

Sift the flour into a large mixing bowl and make a well in the centre. Separate the eggs and beat the whites with the salt in an electric mixer until stiff. Still mixing, add the yolks and oil, then very gradually add 400 ml/14 fl oz lukewarm water and mix until smooth. Pour this mixture into the well in the flour and, using one hand, gradually draw in the flour with a circular movement and mix until you have a smooth dough. Lightly flour your hand and flip over the dough several times until it no longer sticks to the sides of the bowl.

Rub the work surface with a little oil, put the dough on the surface and beat it very hard along its length with a rolling pin for about 5 minutes, flipping over the dough 20 or 30 times as you beat, until it no longer sticks to the work surface and has become springy.

On a lightly-oiled surface, cut the dough into 4 pieces and roll each piece into a very smooth ball, making sure there are no air bubbles, or the dough will break when you stretch it. Oil each ball and wrap in oiled cling film. Freeze 2 for another use and leave the others to rest at room temperature for 3–6 hours or overnight.

While the *pastis* is resting, prepare the filling. In a frying pan, cook the onions in the duck fat until browned. Leave to cool. Take the duck meat off the bone and shred the meat with your fingers. Preheat the oven to 220°C/425°F/gas 7.

When the *pastis* has rested, spread an old sheet or tablecloth about 1.5 sq m/ 5 sq ft over the kitchen table. Sprinkle it very lightly with flour and put one ball of dough in the centre. Lightly oil your fingers, put them under the dough and, starting from the middle, carefully pull the dough evenly on all sides into a circular shape until it is so thin that you can read a newspaper through it and the sides hang over the edges of the table. Gently shake the edges of the *pastis* so that it undulates. Leave it to dry for 5–10 minutes, but no longer, or it will break. It should feel like smooth parchment. With a pastry brush, sprinkle on some of the melted fat like rain all over the stretched dough, or spray it on with a plant mister. Trim off the thickest part of the *pastis* from around the edge; you can re-use it, although it will not be as good. Prepare the second ball of dough in the same way to make the top of the *croustade*.

Cut out 3 circles of dough large enough to line the bottom of a 25 cm/10 in flan tin. Make 3 layers of *pastis* in the tin. Spread the onions and garlic over the pastry and top with the *confit* of duck.

Now make the top of the *croustade*. Take a large piece of stretched dough and spray or brush it with liquid duck fat. Crumple it gently without breaking it so that it looks like a crushed sheet of newspaper. Sit this on top of the pie like a hat or crown. It should look very decorative; you may need a little practice to achieve a really satisfactory result.

Cook the *croustade* in the preheated oven for about 15 minutes, until the top is a lovely golden brown. Serve with a red wine, cep or shallot sauce.

Beignets de Fleurs d'Acacia ou de Citrouille

ACACIA OR PUMPKIN FLOWER FRITTERS—SERVES ABOUT 6

12 acacia or pumpkin flowers
100 ml/4 fl oz rum
50 g/2 oz caster sugar, plus extra for serving
100 g/4 oz plain flour, sifted
3 eggs, separated
1 tablespoon oil
oil, for deep-frying

Macerate the flowers in the rum and sugar for 30 minutes.

Meanwhile, prepare the batter. Put the sifted flour into a bowl, make a well and put in the egg yolks and oil. Stir with a wooden spoon, gradually adding a little water to make a soft paste which will coat the back of the spoon. Beat the egg whites until stiff and fold them gently into the batter.

Drain the flowers and stir the macerating liquid into the batter. Heat the oil until sizzling, dip the flowers into the batter and fry in the hot oil until golden brown. Drain well and sprinkle with sugar.

As soon as the *Mardi gras* lunch was finished and Marcel had gone off to the café to meet his friends, it was a tradition for the children to rush away to dress up and put on disguises. We never thought of buying any special fancy dress, but made do with whatever we could find in the house. Looking back, I realize how much freedom we were given to hunt and rummage in cupboards and drawers, and we were delighted with what we found: old coats and hats, covers, blankets, ancient *sabots*, odds and ends from the stables, and so on. As a finishing touch we gave ourselves beards and moustaches which we applied with bits of charcoal from the fire. We might even go the whole hog and turn ourselves into Africans or Moors. We had never seen television; we had hardly even heard of Mickey Mouse or Donald Duck, so we copied characters from old legends and stories, and transformed ourselves into witches, devils, kings, queens, knights and princesses. We then processed round to all the nearby farms and houses in the village. We were invited into every house, and were given *crêpes*, *merveilles*, *queues de rat*, *gâteaux aux fers* and other such delicacies. Everyone knew we would be coming and either saved sweets and cakes from lunch or made us pancakes while we waited. I think I must have been about eight years old when I last dressed up and went round the village at *Mardi gras*.

Crêpes à l'Armagnac

ARMAGNAC-FLAVOURED PANCAKES—SERVES ABOUT 8

6 eggs
50 g/2 oz plain flour
50 g/2 oz sugar, plus extra to serve
1 tablespoon armagnac
1–2 tablespoons oil, for greasing the pan

Put the eggs, flour, sugar and the armagnac into a mixing bowl and mix thoroughly. Leave the batter to rest in a cool place for 2 hours; this will prevent it from sticking to the pan later.

Lightly oil a small frying pan, ladle in a little of the batter and cook for 1–2 minutes on each side, turning the pancake over with a palette knife, or tossing it. Immediately sprinkle a little more sugar over the warm pancake. Make more pancakes in this way until you have used all the batter.

Queues de Rat

'RATS' TAIL' FRITTERS—SERVES ABOUT 12

4 eggs
100 g/4 oz sugar, plus extra to serve
50 ml/2 fl oz oil
20 g/³⁄₄ oz fresh yeast
rum, orange flower water or vanilla, to taste
100 ml/4 fl oz double cream
500 g/1 lb 2 oz plain flour
oil, for deep-frying

In a bowl, mix together the eggs, sugar, oil, yeast, flavouring of your choice and the cream. Add the flour and mix until completely homogenous.

Take small pieces of dough, about 20 g/¾ oz each and roll them in the palm of your hand to make fattish 'rats' tails'.

Heat the oil in a deep-fat fryer until hot but not boiling, and cook the 'rats' tails' for 1–2 minutes until puffed up and golden. Drain on absorbent paper, roll them in sugar and serve hot.

Merveilles

'FANTASY' FRITTERS—SERVES ABOUT 8

250 g/9 oz plain flour

20 g/¾ oz sugar

a pinch of salt

2 eggs

50 ml/2 fl oz water

75 ml/3 fl oz milk

100 g/4 oz unsalted butter, chilled

oil, for deep-frying

icing or caster sugar, to serve

Put the flour, sugar, salt, eggs, water and milk in a bowl and mix to a very soft smooth dough. Roll it into a ball, wrap in cling film and refrigerate for 20 minutes.

Beat the cold butter with a rolling pin to flatten it into a 40 x 15 cm/16 x 6 in rectangle. Lightly flour the work surface and flatten the chilled dough into a rectangle of the same size. Lay the butter on the dough and fold into 3. Wrap in cling film and return to the fridge for 10 minutes. Roll and fold twice more, leaving the dough to rest for 10 minutes each time, then finally leave the dough to rest in the fridge for 30 minutes.

Roll out the dough to a thickness of 2 mm/¹⁄₁₀ in and cut it into any shapes you like – circles, squares or triangles. Fry in very hot oil until the *merveilles* are puffed up and golden, turning them over when they rise to the surface and the underside is golden. Drain on absorbent paper and roll in sugar before serving.

After *Mardi gras* came Ash Wednesday and the start of Lent. The six weeks of Lent were traditionally a time of *jours maigres* when the Church forbade the eating of meat, so during that time fish became the most important food on the table. Marcel deeply disliked the Church, which filled him with feelings of vague, undefined suspicion and crafty distrust. Fishing, on the other hand, he adored passionately, and when the fishing season opened at the time of the spring holidays, everybody felt and shared his excitement.

Marcel owned about ten fishing rods and an impressive collection of reels, lines, hooks, floats and all the other paraphernalia connected with the sport. Worms were his standard bait, but he also hung up an old dead hen on a tree at the back of the farm. This stank horribly and annoyed Camille intensely, but it nevertheless produced a magnificent crop of fat, wriggling maggots, irresistible to trout and carp. There were so many, in fact, that Marcel was able to sell off his surplus in 100-gram batches and built up quite a steady trade. Another favourite bait were the little grubs we called *papes*, which live in a sort of small shell. My grandfather would spend hours cracking them open and putting them into old jars.

Sunday morning, very early, was Marcel's regular hour for fishing. If time was short, he would just wander down to the nearby stream below the farm to try his luck. When he had more time and could go on his *mobilette*, he would make for the larger rivers farther away, such as the Gers, and for outlying ponds which were excellent for carp or tench. Marcel scorned to buy a wickerwork creel from a shop in Fleurance, and instead made himself a special wooden box which hung from his shoulder on a leather strap. Inside the box was one compartment for lines, hooks and bait, and another for the fish. We lined the box with freshly picked grass and laid the fish side by side on the grass in a long neat row as we caught them. Then we put another layer of grass on top of the fish as the bed for the next row, and so on until the box was full to the brim.

Marcel was the official *garde-pêche* (fishing warden) of the village, but, though the honour of his position never allowed him to fish in the closed season, it never crossed his mind to return an undersized fish to the water. When we were with my grandfather we never put anything back. Every fish we caught, whatever its size, went into the wooden box, and every fish we caught, we ate.

Tanches Braisées à la Tomate et Moutarde

BRAISED TENCH WITH TOMATO PURÉE & MUSTARD—SERVES 4

4 tench, about 150 g/5 oz each, cleaned and gutted

2 large shallots, finely chopped

20 g/¾ oz tomato purée

1 teaspoon mustard

10 tarragon leaves

200 ml/7 fl oz dry white wine

salt

1 egg yolk

75 ml/3 fl oz double cream

Preheat the oven to 190°C/375°F/gas 5. Put the shallots, tomato purée, mustard and tarragon into an ovenproof dish and pour over the white wine. Place the fish on top, add a pinch of salt, cover with greaseproof paper and cook in the preheated oven for 10–15 minutes, until tender.

Transfer the fish to a heated serving dish, leaving the cooking juices in the ovenproof dish. In a small bowl, mix together the egg yolk and cream. When they are well mixed, stir into the cooking juices to thicken them. Check the seasoning, pour the sauce over the fish and serve.

Marcel's fishing techniques were sometimes refreshingly unorthodox; he often made fish-traps out of old litre or 2-litre bottles with a hole knocked out of the ends of their inverted bottoms. The bait was put inside, the bottle was corked and submerged, the fish swam in, and only the very luckiest fish managed to swim out again. In spring and summer my grandfather would catch literally hundreds of gudgeon and minnows in this way. These made excellent *petite friture* and omelettes. I shall always remember my grandfather's return from a fishing trip; he would sit outside the front door methodically gutting and cleaning a whole pile of miscellaneous fish. Every now and then he would produce a fish's air-bladder which we would stamp on to make it explode with a satisfactory pop.

Omelette aux Goujons

GUDGEON OMELETTE—SERVES 4

200 g/7 oz gudgeons, cleaned and gutted

50 g/2 oz plain flour

100 ml/4 fl oz oil

12 eggs

salt and freshly ground pepper

Toss the gudgeons in flour. Heat 75 ml/3 fl oz oil in a frying pan, put in the fish and fry until crisp, crunchy and golden. Lift them out of the pan and lay them on kitchen paper to absorb the oil. Keep them warm while you prepare the omelette.

Break the eggs into a bowl, season with salt and pepper and beat lightly with a fork. Heat the remaining oil in another frying pan, pour in the eggs and stir gently with a wooden spatula until the omelette is almost set. Add the gudgeons and fold over the omelette.

Much as I delighted in going fishing with Marcel, there were few greater pleasures than spending whole April mornings and afternoons fishing by myself. Somewhere at the farm I discovered an old bicycle which had belonged to my mother when she was a young girl. This gave me the freedom to go wherever I wanted. Camille was overcome with anxiety each time I cycled past the village accident black-spot at the cross by the Lectoure road; indeed the fear that I might one day be *écrasé à la croix* was one of her permanent nightmares, I think. She had good reason to worry, for when I cycled to fetch the bread, I always pedalled hard up the hill, then flew back down it as fast as possible, only applying my brakes at the very last minute.

But when I went on a fishing expedition, I was far more careful and Camille need never have worried. It was a source of immense pride and responsibility to be seen with one of Marcel's fishing rods strapped to my bicycle. The other children of the village could not be seen with a rod and tackle because they had no fishing licence, but I was protected by Marcel's licence. At any rate, since he was *garde-pêche*, I knew that no one would ever question me.

I always used to fish in the river Gèle which runs along the valley to the south of the Oratoire, and my favourite places were the ponds of the two old mills of Saint Puy. Either I would take the ancient, unmade, tree-lined track which ran down the side of the farm and led to the ruined mill of Marin; or I would take the Auch road and turn right to the mill of Escapat. Both mills had belonged to the *seigneurs* of Saint Puy under the *ancien régime*, and had ground corn grown by generations of peasants who may well have included some of my own family's ancestors. On a ridge of land near the village, one can still see the stone tower of the windmill which belonged to Escapat. It was an Old Gascon practice to build a windmill near every watermill so that even if the river dried up in a drought, milling could still go on.

I liked Escapat best. It was such a pleasant, attractive spot for fishing that I went there often. The mill was not ruined, but it was empty and deserted; it had a good millpond surrounded by trees where I used to catch trout, tench, carp, roach and the occasional pike. The water poured over a wide weir; I loved its soothing roar, and spent hours there in complete happiness. The only thing which could destroy my feeling of contentment was if I had not caught enough fish. If I was dissatisfied with my catch at the end of a day, I would return home along the river and try to pick up a few trout by 'tickling' them, putting my hand under the stones to feel the fish and gradually squeezing them so tightly that I could lift them out of the water. But this was very difficult to do, and a great many fish got away. In the end, I made it a lot easier by holding in my hand an old piece of rubber tubing studded with drawing pins which gripped the fish like sharp teeth. Some people would disapprove, I suppose, but it was a very effective way of catching trout.

Spring was also the time when we enjoyed our first eels. In March and April these agile amphibious creatures come up the main rivers from the sea, and travelling through streams, springs, drains and muddy ditches, manage to infest the rivers of the Gers and waterways of the south-west. During the daytime, they live in holes that they dig in the mud of the river bank, and at night they swim out into the open water and feed. We used to catch them both by day and night.

By day, a traditional method was to build small makeshift dams across a stream to hold back the water, then to pull the eels out of their holes during the crucial quarter of an hour or so before the dam broke and the current flooded down again. Marcel, however, preferred to catch his eels by night, and he had a clever way of doing this. At dusk he used to throw bundles of vine branches into the river; during the night or towards dawn, the eels would discover the branches, swim in amongst them and stay there to rest after feeding. In the morning my grandfather would simply pull the bundles out of the river and extract all the clinging eels. Camille used to cook them with spring vegetables and red wine.

Anguilles au Vin Rouge

EELS IN RED WINE—SERVES 4

1 kg/2¼ lb eels, cleaned and gutted

1 l/1¾ pt strong red wine

100 ml/4 fl oz oil

100 g/4 oz carrots, thinly sliced

100 g/4 oz onions, thinly sliced

4 garlic cloves, peeled and crushed

50 g/2 oz plain flour

150 g/5 oz leeks, thinly sliced

1 celery stalk, thinly sliced

2 large tomatoes, peeled, deseeded and chopped

1 bouquet garni (a sprig of thyme, 3 bay leaves and a sprig of parsley)

15 peppercorns, crushed

salt

50 g/2 oz seasoned flour

50 ml/2 fl oz armagnac

100 g/4 oz bayonne ham, cut into julienne

70 g/2½ oz small button mushrooms

50 g/2 oz butter

1 tablespoon chopped chives, to serve

Cut the eels into chunks, pour over 850 ml/1½ pt wine and leave to marinate for 3 hours. Heat half the oil in a casserole and cook the vegetables in the following order: the carrots, then, when they start to caramelize, the onions and finally the garlic; cook until all the water from the vegetables has evaporated. Stir in the flour to make a dryish paste and cook gently for 5 minutes, then add the leeks, celery and tomatoes.

Drain the eels and pour the wine from the marinade into the casserole. Add the bouquet garni and bring to the boil, then boil fiercely to reduce the wine by one-third, skimming the surface several times. Add the crushed peppercorns and ¾ teaspoon salt, cover and cook gently for 1 hour.

Meanwhile, pat dry the eel pieces and toss in seasoned flour to coat them well. Heat the remaining oil in a flameproof casserole, put in the eels and seal on all sides. Pour off the excess oil from the pan, add the armagnac and flame it.

Strain the wine sauce through a fine sieve and pour it over the eels. Add the rest of the wine, bring to the boil and skim well. Put in the ham and mushrooms and cook for about 15 minutes, until just tender; check the seasoning, whisk the butter into the sauce, garnish with chives and serve with braised leeks.

In the 18th-century it was the custom for millers in this part of Gascony to drain down their millponds just before the start of Lent and invite their friends and relations to come and pick out enough fish to last them through the meatless season; the occasion was regarded as a *fête*, and the fish were taken home live and kept in makeshift tanks until they were needed. I have often thought about this custom. Quite apart from its religious implications, it seems to emphasize the great importance of freshwater fish in a place where sea fish is unavailable.

It is difficult to imagine today, in this age of supermarkets and frozen food, how much the opening of the fishing season meant to us. The Atlantic Ocean was only about a hundred miles away, but fresh sea fish never appeared on the table at the Oratoire. The cost of transport, even in the 1950s, made it too expensive for my grandparents, and indeed for most peasant families in central Gascony. The nearest we got to sea fish was the salt or smoked cod which Camille occasionally bought at Fleurance market so that we could enjoy a dish of her traditional *cassoulet de morue*.

I remember reading with interest about the soles with *sauce hollandaise*, the turbot and the *côtelettes de homard* that featured on the menus of the extravagant dinners given by the ducal family of Montesquiou-Fezensac at the castle of Marsan, not so very far from Saint Puy, during the fateful spring of 1870 just before the onset of the Franco-Prussian war. There the fish was brought directly from the coast by train, and the *maître d'hôtel* was a native of Paris. The difference between the 19th-century *haute cuisine* of the *château*, where the chef had the resources and power to select whatever ingredients he wanted, and the *cuisine du terroir* of the villages, which depended entirely on the availability of local produce, was very clear. At the Oratoire, for example, eating the first fresh trout or carp of the year always stood out as an important gastronomic occasion.

Truites au Lard

TROUT COOKED WITH BACON—SERVES 4

4 trout, about 350 g/12 oz each, cleaned, gutted and skinned

25 g/1 oz plain flour

16 rashers of streaky bacon

freshly ground pepper

50 ml/2 fl oz oil

150 g/5 oz butter

juice of 1 lemon

Lightly flour the trout and wrap each in 4 rashers of bacon. Season with pepper.

Heat the oil in a frying pan until very hot. Lower the heat slightly, put in the trout and add 50 g/2 oz butter. Cook the fish in the sizzling fat for 4–5 minutes on each side. Transfer them to a warmed serving dish and throw away the fat. Wipe out the pan with kitchen paper.

Put the remaining butter into the pan in which you cooked the trout and heat until bubbling. Add the lemon juice and pour the sauce over the fish.

Truites au Cresson

TROUT WITH WATERCRESS—SERVES 4

4 trout, about 350 g/12 oz each, cleaned and gutted

2 bunches of watercress

300 ml/½ pt dry white wine

100 ml/4 fl oz double cream

salt and freshly ground pepper

Preheat the oven to 200°C/400°F/gas 6. Wash the watercress and cut off the stalks. Lay in a flameproof gratin dish large enough to hold the 4 fish. Arrange the trout on top of the watercress and sprinkle on the white wine.

Cover the trout with greaseproof paper and set the dish over high heat until the wine comes to the boil. Transfer the dish to the preheated oven and cook for about 10 minutes, until tender.

Lift the trout into a heated serving dish. Set the gratin dish still containing the wine and watercress over high heat, pour in the cream and reduce by half. Check the seasoning, pour the watercress sauce over the trout and serve. If you prefer, purée the watercress and place the skinned trout on top.

Carpe à la Boulangère

CARP WITH POTATOES & HERBS—SERVES 4

1 carp, about 800 g/1¾ lb, or 2 smaller fish
400 g/14 oz potatoes, very thinly sliced
100 g/4 oz onions, very thinly sliced
salt and freshly ground pepper
3 bay leaves
1 sprig of thyme
50 g/2 oz butter, diced

Preheat the oven to 180°C/350°F/gas 4. Gut and scale the carp and rinse under cold water. Cut 3 deep slashes in each side of the fish and insert the bay leaves into the slashes on one side. Place the thyme into the cavity and set aside. Mix the potatoes and onions in a bowl. Season with salt and pepper. Transfer to a flameproof dish and pour over 100 ml/4 fl oz water. Cook in the preheated oven for 10 minutes.

Lay the carp on top of the potatoes, arrange the butter around it and cover with foil. Cook gently over low heat for 5 minutes, then place in the oven and cook for 20 minutes if the fish is large (a smaller fish will need less time). The potatoes must be tender and well cooked.

The rivers of the Gers *département* descend from the Pyrenees through gently curving valleys; they then either join the Garonne, like the Gers itself, or the Baïse or the Save, or else, like the Adour, make a great westward turn and flow directly into the Atlantic. Thus it is that the Adour is a salmon river. Although not many salmon are caught in it now, in the past they were plentiful at the right time of year.

When I was a child, my uncle Capuron used to bring us salmon; he owned a car and went on long trips to Bordeaux and the Pyrenees – in connection with his work as an insurance agent, he used to say, but I think he actually spent most of the time shooting and fishing. Salmon was a great spring luxury to us, something quite foreign to our own region; certainly Camille would never have dreamed of buying such an extravagant fish. But I remember how well she used to cook it with new vegetables and the *graisse d'oie* (goose fat) which she made herself at the farm.

Saumon de l'Adour Etuvé aux Légumes

ADOUR SALMON POACHED WITH VEGETABLES—SERVES 4

4 salmon steaks, 200 g/7 oz each, skinned

100 g/4 oz carrots, thinly sliced

100 g/4 oz mange-tout, topped and tailed

100 g/4 oz french beans, topped and tailed

100 g/4 oz broad beans, shelled

100 g/4 oz courgettes, thinly sliced

salt

100 g/4 oz butter

100 ml/4 fl oz dry white wine

Cook all the vegetables separately, one variety at a time, in a pan of salted water, using the same water each time. Take care not to overcook them; they should be tender but still crisp.

As each vegetable is cooked, put it in a flameproof casserole large enough to hold all the salmon steaks without touching. When all the vegetables are ready, lay the salmon steaks on top, season with salt and add 50 g/2 oz butter and the wine.

Cover the casserole, set over a low heat and simmer for 4 minutes. Turn over the salmon steaks and simmer for another 4 minutes.

Remove the salmon from the casserole. Stir the remaining butter into the vegetables, arrange them on a warmed serving dish and lay the salmon on top.

Saumon de l'Adour Confit à la Graisse d'Oie

ADOUR SALMON COOKED IN GOOSE FAT—SERVES 4

4 salmon fillets, about 150 g/5 oz each, skinned

250 g/9 oz goose fat

100 g/4 oz onions, sliced

2 red peppers, skinned and deseeded, cut into 2 cm/³⁄₄ in squares

1 garlic clove, crushed

6 large tomatoes, peeled, deseeded and diced

salt and freshly ground pepper

4 thin slices of bayonne or parma ham

coarse salt, to serve

Heat 25 g/1 oz goose fat in a frying pan, put in the onions and cook gently for 10 minutes, without letting them colour. Add the peppers and cook for 3 minutes, then add the garlic and tomatoes and cook for 5 minutes. Season to taste and keep hot.

In a deep saucepan, gently heat the remaining fat to 50°C/122°F (no hotter, or the salmon will dry out). Put in the salmon fillets (the fat should cover the fish completely) and cook for 7–10 minutes, depending on the thickness of the fillets. The salmon is ready when you can pierce it easily with a chef's fork. Place the salmon on a plate, cover with greaseproof paper and leave to rest in a warm place for 10 minutes.

Arrange the vegetable garnish in a serving dish and lay the salmon fillets on top. In a frying pan, fry the ham for 10 seconds on each side in a little hot goose fat, lay the slices over the fish and serve with a dish of coarse salt.

During the *Mardi gras* holiday, especially in years when Easter was late, one of the cows might calve in the stables underneath the farm. Every quarter of an hour or so, as the cow's time grew near, Marcel would get up from the table and go down to check it. When the birth was imminent he would go and fetch my uncle and couple of friends to help. Children were expressly forbidden to be present, but curiosity and excitement always got the better of us and, while Marcel was away, we would rush down to the stable and hide in a dark corner behind the door, where we could observe everything but where no one ever discovered us.

In the month of March, while we were back at school again, the earth was broken up around the roots of the vines; the ewe, which Marcel kept for breeding purposes, lambed, and young goats and rabbits were born. Chickens and pigeons began to lay regularly after the winter, and the first duck eggs appeared; this was a matter of great importance to my grandmother. Ducks lay far less frequently than hens and are bad mothers, yet much of the prosperity of the farm centred on Camille's ducks. She could sell them all year round and, of course, the fattened birds were particularly sought after at the end of December for Christmas and the New Year. They were prized for their foie gras, which was carefully nurtured through three weeks of attentive force-feeding.

I well remember watching Camille in the dark windowless larder, which we called the *chambre obscure*, picking up each duck's egg and holding it up to examine it by the light of an electric torch to see if it was fertilized or not. Those that were she kept on one of the long, cool shelves until the time came, probably in early May when the moon was rising, to put them under a hen to be hatched.

When we had a day off from school for *mi-carême*, and could come to the Oratoire, we ate more of the traditional *crêpes* and *beignets*, and hung up a folded pancake, the *crêpe au buffet*, on Camille's dresser in the dining room to bring luck to the farm. It stayed there all year, or at least until it was gradually nibbled away by mice.

Beignets

FRITTERS

50 g/2 oz butter
a pinch of salt
50 g/2 oz sugar, plus extra to serve
100 g/4 oz plain flour, sifted
4 eggs
2 l/3½ pt oil, for deep-frying

In a saucepan, bring to the boil 250 ml/9 fl oz water, then add the butter, salt and sugar. When the butter has melted, add the sifted flour and mix well, then cook, stirring continuously, until the mixture becomes firmer and no longer sticks to the sides of the pan. Take the pan off the heat and leave the mixture to cool.

Add the eggs one at a time to the cooled mixture, mixing each in thoroughly before adding the next.

Heat the oil in a deep frying pan until very hot, then carefully drop in spoonfuls of the mixture and cook until the *beignets* puff up and turn golden. Drain on absorbent paper, then roll the *beignets* in sugar and serve at once.

In April, when we arrived at Saint Puy for the Easter holidays, I always used to feel that spring was really there. All around the Oratoire the fruit trees were in blossom, wheat and barley had already grown quite high in places, the vines had budded, and I could plunge my hands into the warm, chirping mass of newly hatched chicks and ducklings. The countryside was still sharp with winter outlines, but they were softened by patches of green and by the colours of the orchards. In those days there were far fewer yellow rape fields than now, but the long, undulating lines of hills which rise up from the valleys of the Gèle and the Lauze, and gradually recede into the distance behind blue veils of haze until they merge completely with the sky, are the same now as they were when I was a boy. The daytime sun was warm and comforting, but in the evenings we were still glad to sit round the wood fire in the kitchen, gossiping or telling stories, while Marcel cut bunches of the square-shaped peas called *pois carrés* and shelled them so that we could eat them with a dash of salt, *à la croque-sel*.

Another change at the farm was the springtime transformation of Camille's kitchen garden, her well-kept, fenced-in domain down in the flat piece of land at the back of the house, which was suddenly alive with neat, green rows of new vegetables. From now on until the onset of winter it would provide my grandparents with an unfailing supply of broad beans, leeks, asparagus, onions, garlic, tomatoes, artichokes, peas, and all the other vegetables and salads they needed.

Among Camille's other spring dishes were her soups, which she made from her own vegetables and which replaced the thick meat soups of winter. Here are three simple recipes, made from cabbage shoots, new broad beans and peas.

Soupe aux Broutes

SPRING CABBAGE SOUP—SERVES 4

1 kg/2¼ lb young spring cabbage shoots or leaves

2 l/3½ pt chicken stock or boiling water

salt and freshly ground pepper

200 g/7 oz carrots, sliced

6 leeks, thickly sliced

5 garlic cloves, sliced

700 g/1½ lb potatoes, cut into chunks

1 bouquet garni

Cut out the central core and stems of the cabbage leaves and blanch the leaves in the stock or boiling water for 2 minutes, then lift out the cabbage with a slotted spoon and set aside.

Season the liquid with salt and pepper, put in all the remaining ingredients and cook for about 1 hour, until the potatoes begin to disintegrate. Adjust the seasoning, add the cabbage, pour into a soup tureen and serve.

Soupe aux Fèves

BROAD BEAN SOUP—SERVES 4

500 g/1 lb 2 oz broad beans, shelled and outer skins removed
2 l/3½ pt chicken stock or water
250 g/9 oz potatoes, very thinly sliced
5 leeks, thinly sliced
5 garlic cloves, thinly sliced
1 bouquet garni
salt and freshly ground pepper

Bring the stock or water to the boil. Add all the ingredients and cook for 45 minutes. Blend if desired and serve with a *Farci aux oeufs* (see next recipe).

Whenever Camille made a cabbage or broad bean soup, she would also make a special Gascon 'omelette' or patty to put into the soup. This added another flavour and transformed the soup into a more nourishing and substantial main dish in a pleasant meal.

Farci aux Oeufs

GARLIC & BREADCRUMB PATTY

4 eggs
75 g/3 oz breadcrumbs
2 garlic cloves, chopped
25 g/1 oz parsley, finely chopped
salt and freshly ground pepper
75 g/3 oz duck fat

Break the eggs into a bowl and beat lightly with a fork. Add the breadcrumbs, garlic and parsley and stir to make a thick paste. Season with salt and pepper.

Heat the duck fat in a frying pan, put in the patty mixture and fry for 3 minutes on each side, until cooked through. Slide it into the hot soup and serve.

Crème de Petits Pois

PEA SOUP—SERVES 4

500 g/1 lb 2 oz shelled fresh peas

600 ml/1 pt chicken stock

salt

100 ml/4 fl oz double cream

Bring the chicken stock to the boil, put in the peas and cook for 5 minutes. Add salt to taste, place in a blender and purée until smooth. Serve the soup hot or cold, pouring on the cream at the last moment.

Asparagus also featured in Camille's kitchen garden and she would serve it in a delicate omelette, made, of course, with fresh eggs from her own hens.

Omelette aux Asperges

ASPARAGUS OMELETTE—SERVES 4

12 asparagus spears, cut into thirds

75 g/3 oz butter

12 eggs

salt and freshly ground pepper

Cook the asparagus gently in a frying pan in 25 g/1 oz butter until tender.

Make 1 large or 4 small omelettes (see *Omelette aux goujons,* page 43), put in the asparagus, fold over the omelette and serve at once.

When Camille made a springtime *pot-au-feu*, she would, of course, use these new vegetables. Often, she would serve them on their own with a vinaigrette, and add a slice of foie gras. However, the recipe that follows is not quite Camille's. Her selection of vegetables was more restricted; she would have cooked them all together, and her presentation would have been far less sophisticated. At La Tante Claire I used a larger variety of vegetables; I cooked them separately in chicken stock, and I might add truffles, which of course are not found in the Gers and are therefore not used in the local cooking.

Ragoût de Légumes Nouveaux au Foie Gras

SPRING VEGETABLES WITH FOIE GRAS—SERVES 4

8 small new carrots with their tops

8 baby courgettes

8 small new turnips with their tops

8 small spring onions

100 g/4 oz french beans

100 g/4 oz mange-tout

8 asparagus spears

4 small artichokes

4 small beetroot with their tops

1 l/1¾ pt clear, salted chicken stock

12 small tomatoes, quartered

Vinaigrette

1 egg yolk

25 ml/1 fl oz wine vinegar

100 ml/4 fl oz vegetable or olive oil

salt and freshly ground pepper

2 tablespoons chopped parsley

2 tablespoons snipped chives

Garnish

75 g/3 oz Ballotine de foie gras *(recipe page 105)*

chervil leaves

truffle slices *(optional)*

First prepare the vegetables: peel the carrots, leaving on part of the tops; top and tail the courgettes; peel the turnips, leaving on some of the tops; cut off the onion roots and peel off the outer layer of skin; top and tail the french beans and mange-tout; peel the asparagus stalks; cut off the artichoke stems and bottoms; peel the beetroot, leaving on some of the tops.

Heat the lightly salted chicken stock in a saucepan and separately cook the carrots, courgettes, turnips, spring onions, french beans and mange-tout until just tender. As each vegetable is cooked, put it in a dish. Reserve the chicken stock (you will need it for the vinaigrette) and leave to cool completely.

In another saucepan, cook the asparagus, artichokes and beetroot separately in boiling salted water. Put them in the dish with the other vegetables, then add the tomatoes.

Now make the vinaigrette: in a blender combine the egg yolk, vinegar and 100 ml/4 fl oz of the cooled chicken stock in which you cooked the vegetables (the stock must be cold). Switch on the machine, gradually add the oil and blend for 30 seconds. The vinaigrette should not be too thick; if it is, add a few drops of cold water. Check the seasoning and stir in the parsley and chives.

Pour the vinaigrette over the vegetables and mix well. Arrange the vegetables attractively on 4 plates. With a sharp knife, cut the foie gras into thin slices and arrange them on and around the vegetables. Decorate with chervil leaves and, if you are rich, add some truffle slices as well.

The work on the farm in April was still largely one of steady preparation for summer and for the great events of the year: haymaking, harvesting and the *vendange* (grape harvest). The very last shoots would be trimmed off the vines and burnt, and the last check was made to see whether any supporting stakes still needed replacing. The stables were washed and swept and Marcel would clean, repair and wax the great wooden yokes which the cows wore when they worked in the fields. In the Gers, these yokes are not painted, as they are in the Basque country, but they are a deep, natural chestnut colour, the colour of wood which has rubbed for years against the necks of animals and acquired its own special patina.

Sitting outside the stables, for he spurned the kitchen as being a workplace fit only for women, my grandfather would spend entire afternoons weaving the net veils which the cows wore over their eyes to protect them from the flies, which might otherwise infect them and bring on blindness. I never quite understood how Marcel made these veils; he had a small oval wooden tool not unlike a weaver's shuttle, and he seemed to 'knit' them rather as a fisherman mends his nets. His style was quite special and unique. He would buy threads of many different colours and weave the veils in horizontal stripes of red, blue, green, white, black and so on, so that his cows could always be recognized from a great distance if you met them pulling a cart down a local road. While Marcel was occupied with all this, Camille might start to bottle some of the vegetables, such as the little gherkins and the new broad beans.

Cornichons au Vinaigre

PICKLED GHERKINS

700 g/1½ lb very small gherkins

10 black peppercorns

1 sprig of tarragon

500 ml/18 fl oz distilled vinegar (6% alcohol)

Wipe the gherkins with a clean cloth and place in a jar with the peppercorns and tarragon. Pour in the vinegar, seal the jar and leave for a month before eating the gherkins. If you like, you can add some garlic, chives or small shallots for extra flavour.

The first young rabbits had been born in March, and now, in April, they were about six weeks old and ready to eat. Camille might cook them with baby onions or prepare them with a delicious stuffing.

Lapin aux Oignons Nouveaux

RABBIT WITH BABY ONIONS—SERVES 4

1 rabbit, about 1.5 kg/3¼ lb, skinned and cleaned

100 g/4 oz goose fat

1 kg/2¼ lb small new onions, very thinly sliced

1 sprig of thyme

3 bay leaves

4 garlic cloves, peeled and left whole

salt and freshly ground pepper

Melt the goose fat in a large flameproof casserole, add the onions and sweat until transparent. Remove and set aside. Put in the whole rabbit, the thyme, bay leaves and garlic and season with salt and pepper. Cover and cook gently over low heat for 30 minutes, adding the onions after 15 minutes, until the rabbit is tender and the onions are brown and thick with the consistency of coarse marmalade.

Cut the rabbit into serving pieces, mix well with the onions and serve.

Lapin Farci aux Herbes

RABBIT STUFFED WITH HERBS—SERVES 4

1 rabbit, about 1.5 kg/3¼ lb, skinned and cleaned, with its liver, kidneys, heart and lungs

100 g/4 oz goose fat

1 handful of mixed fresh herbs (including parsley, chives and chervil), coarsely chopped

50 g/2 oz bayonne ham, chopped

2 garlic cloves, chopped

2 slices of white bread, made into breadcrumbs

2 egg yolks

salt and freshly ground pepper

100 g/4 oz small shallots

100 ml/4 fl oz dry white wine

20 g/¾ oz butter

Preheat the oven to 200°C/400°F/gas 6. Make the stuffing: heat half the goose fat in a frying pan, put in the rabbit liver, kidneys, heart and lungs and fry until browned. Chop them finely and place in a bowl. Add the herbs, ham, garlic, breadcrumbs and egg yolks and mix thoroughly.

Lay the rabbit on its back and fill with the stuffing. Season the rabbit with salt and pepper. Heat the remaining goose fat in a roasting pan, put in the rabbit and cook in the preheated oven for 30 minutes.

Add the whole shallots (plus extra garlic if desired) to the pan and roast for another 15 minutes. Transfer the rabbit to a serving dish and keep it warm while you make the sauce.

Pour off the fat from the pan, then pour the wine over the shallots, set over high heat and reduce by half. Add 100 ml/4 fl oz water, reduce by half, then whisk in the butter. Season to taste, pour the sauce over the rabbit and serve.

One of the best April memories I have of my grandmother is of travelling with her to the market at Fleurance. The market was held every Tuesday, and Camille went there to sell her rabbits, pigeons or ducks, or if she wanted to buy odds and ends for the house, like saucepans, nails, lengths of material, or items connected with her embroidery. She went most often to market in the spring; in summer it was generally too hot, and there was always far too much to do at the farm to lose a day away from Saint Puy. When I was small, Camille quite frequently went to market to sell her poultry, but, as the years went on and she gradually gave up the ducks, she had less and less to sell, and finally she went only to buy.

Whenever possible we travelled on a noisy, jolting local bus, which left Saint Puy at 6 o'clock in the morning and reached Fleurance at 7; we returned by the 3 o'clock bus which got us home at 4 in the afternoon. It was a day packed with all the excitements and uncertainties of trade. The bus had a great roof rack with metal rails and a ladder at the back for climbing up. In the morning the roof was crammed with crates and cages of poultry of every sort, among them Camille's ducks and rabbits. As we rattled into Fleurance we passed the town cemetery with its fine stone wall and its new gates. My grandmother thought this was the smartest cemetery in the whole of the *département* and never failed to remark with a sigh how sad she was that, being an inhabitant of Saint Puy, she would never have the right to be buried there.

The poultry market took place in a great, echoing warehouse which, during the rest of the week, was used as a sports stadium. On Tuesdays it was a cathedral dedicated to birds and to their buyers and sellers. Ducks, geese, guinea fowl, hens, pigeons, cocks, turkeys, all in their magnificent colours, squawked, fluttered and brooded while whistles blew and bargains were struck. Birds were carried away singly, beaks downwards, their wings beating, or were packed into boxes and removed by the dozen. If we did very well and my grandmother had sold everything by midday, we were able to have lunch at her favourite little restaurant near the church. Here, long rows of wooden tables with cast-iron legs accommodated a crowd of hungry market people; conviviality reigned with good soup and local wine and *confit de canard*; the floor was laid out with brown and yellow tiles, and at the end of the room stood a massive old dresser laden with glasses and loaves and lots of ornate little pots for salt, pepper and oil.

Before we set off for home, Camille would buy me a *pain à l'anis* from one of the stalls near the old market hall, not far from the fountains of the four seasons, each with a statue of its own goddess. The bread was round, like a crown, and the aniseeds scattered on top permeated it with a delicious taste and a wonderful smell, which lingered on in my mouth long after I had finished the last morsel. I do not think I have ever had *pain à l'anis* as good as that anywhere else.

I remember how much we enjoyed the first spring leeks, the first shallots and the first garlic and how good these fresh vegetables seemed after a winter of *confits* and *conserves*. We sometimes ate the garlic and spring onions raw *à la croque-sel*, but Camille also used them in other ways, especially when she cooked spring chickens. I think that garlic and onions have always been popular in south-west France. Certainly, the Romans in Gascony enjoyed them and I have read some wonderful descriptions of the Gascon penchant for these strong-flavoured foods written by the early 17th-century court physician, Joseph du Chesne. According to him, the French only ate leeks in the form of soup, while the Gascons took great delight in eating theirs raw, dipped in honey.

Our Gascon forefathers also ate their garlic raw, just as we did at the Oratoire. The peasants ate it to keep away the plague; apparently vermin also kept their distance from garlic eaters! I love the story of the infant Henri de Navarre: how on the night of 13th December, 1553, when the plague was raging in Béarn, the baby's grandfather, Henri d'Albret, struggled into his fur dressing gown and dashed down the cold stone stairs at Pau to rub a clove of garlic on the lips of his new-born grandson, the future Henri IV, to protect him from the ravages of the disease. Unfortunately, when the young Gascon prince arrived at court in Paris, he was said to exude such a stench of garlic that he could be smelt several yards away and his bride, Marguérite de Valois, refused to share his bed on at least one occasion because his breath was so unpleasant!

This salutary tale did not prevent us from enjoying our raw garlic at the Oratoire, but we also liked to eat it in the less potent form of *l'ail sous la cendre*. Marcel would put a whole head of garlic under the wood embers of the log fire and leave it to cook. Then, when it was tender, he would toast some bread, extract the cloves of garlic, and we would eat them on the toast. *Ce n'était pas gastronomique, mais c'était délicieux à manger.*

One wonderful dish of Camille's combined young spring chickens with fresh shallots. You really need an open wood fire for this dish; not too hot, or the chicken will burn. Obviously, you can cook the chicken under the grill if you prefer.

Poulet Grillé à la Vinaigrette d'Echalote

GRILLED SPRING CHICKEN WITH SHALLOTS & VINAIGRETTE—SERVES 4

1 spring chicken, about 1 kg/2¼ lb
25 g/1 oz goose fat
salt and freshly ground pepper
70 g/2½ oz shallots, chopped

Vinaigrette
100 ml/4 fl oz oil
2–3 tablespoons vinegar
2 teaspoons french mustard
salt and freshly ground pepper

Split the chicken down the backbone, open it out and flatten lightly with a mallet. Rub the goose fat over the skin side and season with salt and pepper.

Lay the chicken skin-side down on a traditional square iron grill set over the open wood fire and cook for 15 minutes. Turn over the chicken and cook for another 15 minutes.

Put the grilled chicken in a dish, skin-side down. Scatter the shallots over and around the chicken. Mix together all the vinaigrette ingredients and pour the vinaigrette over the chicken and shallots.

Cover with another dish of the same size and leave the chicken to rest in a warm place for 10 minutes; this will allow the shallots to cook slightly.

Onions also came into their own in this simple omelette, which Camille would often serve as a light lunch. You can make potato, cep or leek omelettes in exactly the same way.

Omelette aux Oignons Nouveaux

SPRING ONION OMELETTE—SERVES 4

100 g/4 oz butter
300 g/11 oz spring onions, finely chopped
12 eggs
salt and freshly ground pepper
salad, to serve

Melt half the butter in a frying pan, put in the onions and cook until soft. Take them out of the pan and keep warm.

Melt the remaining butter in the pan. Make a 12-egg omelette (see *Omelette aux goujons*, page 43), put in the onions, fold over the omelette and serve immediately with a salad.

When she made a *gratin* of leeks, Camille used roquefort cheese. This in fact comes from Aveyron, not from the Gers, which produces no cheeses of its own. Her own recipe was very simple – little more than leeks and cheese – but I use a béchamel in my own version.

Gratin de Poireaux au Roquefort

GRATIN OF LEEKS WITH ROQUEFORT

1 kg/2¼ lb small tender leeks
25 g/1 oz butter
20 g/¾ oz plain flour
300 ml/½ pt milk
100 g/4 oz roquefort cheese, crumbled
salt and freshly ground pepper

Cook the leeks in boiling salted water until tender. Lift them out of the water (reserve the water) and leave to drain in a warm place so that they do not get cold.

Melt the butter in a saucepan, stir in the flour and cook for 2 minutes to make a *roux*. Add the milk and 200 ml/7 fl oz cooking water from the leeks and cook for 10 minutes, stirring continuously. Add the roquefort and cook for a further 5 minutes, then check the seasoning.

Arrange the leeks in a gratin dish, pour over the sauce and brown the top under a hot grill.

By April, the lambs which had been born six weeks earlier while we were away at school were ready to eat. My grandfather slaughtered the lambs himself. One would be put on a table, lying on its back with its head hanging over the edge; someone would hold its legs and Marcel would cut its throat with one quick stroke of his knife. He would then empty it and skin it. It was never very nice to watch. With the bigger animals I felt quite differently; it is difficult to build up much of a relationship with a farm pig, for example, but we all used to play with the lambs and regarded them almost as pets. When a pig is killed, it yells, but a lamb cries like a child. It dies fairly quickly, although the nerves twitch for a moment or two afterwards. You need a very sharp knife to slaughter it efficiently.

It was only on special occasions, however, that my grandparents would actually think of cooking a leg of lamb. They did not consider it worth serving

unless there were seven or eight people to eat it. Normally there were always plenty of chickens of the right size to feed two, if Marcel and Camille were alone, or four or five if we were there as well, and nothing would be left over. But if Camille was entertaining friends or neighbours, this is how she would cook lamb.

Gasconnade de Gigot d'Agneau

GASCON LEG OF LAMB—SERVES 8

1 leg of lamb, about 2 kg/4½ lb

6 garlic cloves, cut into slivers

12 anchovy fillets, halved lengthways, soaked in water and drained

salt and freshly ground pepper

100 g/4 oz duck fat

100 g/4 oz carrots, chopped

100 g/4 oz onions, chopped

200 ml/7 fl oz dry white wine

a sprig of thyme

Preheat the oven to 200°C/400°F/gas 6. Use a sharp potato peeler or the point of a knife to push the garlic and anchovies into the lamb in several places. Put the meat in the roasting pan, season and spread the duck fat all over. Roast in the preheated oven for about 1½ hours turning the lamb over and basting every 10 minutes. Add the carrots and onions after 20 minutes.

Transfer the cooked lamb to another dish, cover with greaseproof paper and leave in a warm place for at least 20 minutes before carving. This allows the blood to spread through the meat and ensures that it is uniformly pink when it is served. Leave the vegetables in the pan.

Place the roasting pan over gentle heat on the hob and cook until the meat juices stick to the bottom of the pan. Skim off the fat which rises to the surface. Add the wine and thyme, reduce the liquid by one-fifth, then add 300 ml/½ pt water and reduce by one-third, stirring with a wooden spoon to scrape off the meat from the sides of the pan. Reduce again by one-third, then pass the sauce through a fine sieve, pour into a sauceboat and serve separately.

Camille did sometimes cook lamb when we were eating *en famille*; then it was served in a simpler form, like this *blanquette*, which is a soup-like stew.

Blanquette d'Agneau

LAMB STEW IN A WHITE SAUCE — SERVES 4

800 g/1¾ lb stewing lamb, cubed

12 small carrots, peeled

1 large onion, halved and stuck with 1 clove

1 bouquet garni

salt and freshly ground pepper

50 g/2 oz butter

50 g/2 oz plain flour

100 ml/4 fl oz double cream

2 egg yolks

a few drops of lemon juice

fried button mushrooms, to garnish

Put the lamb in a saucepan, add 1.5 l/2½ pt cold water and bring to the boil. Carefully skim the surface, then add the carrots, onion and bouquet garni and simmer for about 1 hour, until the lamb is tender. Remove the bouquet garni and season.

In another saucepan, melt the butter and stir in the flour with a wooden spoon. Cook gently for 3 minutes to make a white roux, taking care that it does not brown. Slowly add about 1 l/1¾ pt of the lamb cooking stock, stirring gently with a wire whisk until the sauce is smooth.

Drain the lamb and leave it in the saucepan in a warm place. Cook the sauce for another 15 minutes, skimming the surface very frequently. Pour it over the lamb and simmer over the heat for 5 minutes.

Make a liaison by mixing together the cream, egg yolks and lemon juice to taste. Stir into the sauce and cook until thickened, taking great care not to let the sauce boil, or it will curdle. Check the seasoning and serve garnished with button mushrooms.

Easter was the one festive meal at which we traditionally had lamb as the main dish, a Paschal lamb. As on *Mardi gras*, we would start with a *bouilli* which would be served in two parts; first the *bouillon*, then the meat, with gherkins, or pickled vegetables. Then would come foie gras, *charcuterie*, smoked ham, tomatoes, hard-boiled eggs, pâté and sausages; next would be the main dish,

Camille's *gigot pascal*, which was sometimes stuffed and roasted on a spit at the open fire and sometimes cooked in a light pastry crust. We always loved this version.

Gigot Pascal en Croûte

PASCHAL LAMB IN PASTRY—SERVES 8

3 kg/6 lb 10 oz leg of lamb, boned
½ quantity of Farce à tout faire *(recipe page 124)*
500 g/1 lb 2 oz puff pastry
egg wash (1 egg yolk, lightly beaten with 1 tablespoon milk)

Preheat the oven to 200°C/400°F/gas 6, roast the lamb for 45 minutes and leave to cool.

Lay the lamb out flat on the work surface and spread over the stuffing. Turn over the lamb and roll it up with the stuffing on the outside. Divide the pastry in 2, roll out to 2 sheets and lay the lamb in the middle of one piece. Brush the edges of the pastry with egg wash and cover with the second sheet. Carefully seal the edges. Place on a roasting tray, brush the pastry with egg wash and cut a hole in the top to let the steam escape. Bake for 45 minutes and leave to rest for 15 minutes before carving. If you like, you can make a gravy with the lamb bone and some carrots and onions.

There was no cheese course at the Oratoire because in those days the peasants of the Gers never ate it. We would go straight on to the desserts, of which there would be two or three: a *croustade aux pommes*, a local version of *crème brûlée*, and a *gâteaux aux fers*. These last were an Easter tradition and were cooked in the embers of an open fire in heavy, rectangular cast-iron waffle moulds with long, double handles like old-fashioned fire irons. The patterns of the moulds were often a source of family pride, and varied from simple rows of lozenges and dots to complex geometric fantasies which may well have originated with the Arab mathematicians of mediaeval Spain. One fine set of irons which I have seen belonged to the 18th-century bishop of Condom, Alexandre César d'Anterroche, and includes his coat of arms and his cardinal's hat and tassels in its design. Ideally, you need a log fire and a set of elaborate waffle moulds for this first recipe, but failing that a modern electric waffle iron would do.

Gâteaux aux Fers

TRADITIONAL EASTER WAFFLES—SERVES 4

250 g/9 oz plain flour

25 g/1 oz sugar

4 eggs

50 ml/2 fl oz oil, plus extra for greasing the waffle iron

vanilla essence, or flavouring of your choice

jam and cream, to serve

Put the flour and sugar in a bowl, then add the eggs and oil and mix well. Mix in a little water, a few drops at a time, taking care that the mixture does not curdle, until it is like a very thick pancake batter. Add the flavouring.

Heat a waffle iron and grease the grid. Pour in enough batter to cover the grid and close the iron. Place under hot embers to cook the waffle (or use an electric waffle iron, which is effective if unauthentic). Make more waffles in the same way and serve hot with jam and cream.

Crème Brûlée à la Gasconne

GASCON CRÈME BRÛLÉE—SERVES 4

6 egg yolks

250 g/9 oz sugar

25 g/1 oz plain flour

600 ml/1 pt milk

lemon verbena, vanilla or cinnamon, to flavour

Preheat the oven to 170ºC/325ºF/gas 3. Put the egg yolks and half the sugar in a bowl, add the flour and mix well. Bring the milk to the boil and pour it over the mixture. Stir in your chosen flavouring, pour the mixture into a saucepan and cook very gently, stirring continuously with a wooden spoon, until the custard is thick enough to coat the back of the spoon.

Pour the custard into an ovenproof dish or individual ramekins, place in a bain-marie and bake in the oven for about 20–30 minutes, until set. Leave to cool.

Put the remaining sugar in a saucepan and cook over a low heat until it caramelizes. Carefully pour the caramel over the custards, leave until cold and serve. The caramel will remain runny, as in a *crème caramel*.

Although Marcel kept about twelve cows at the Oratoire, my grandparents very rarely ate beef. This had to be bought from the Saint Puy butcher and was therefore an expensive luxury for Camille. The cows at the farm were kept to work in the fields, to produce milk and for breeding. If Marcel wanted to sell a cow because, say, it was getting old and he wished to buy a younger one or simply because he needed the money, he would sell it live to one of the local *maquignons*, the rough, hard-bargaining peasant cattle-dealers, who could always be recognized, I remember, by their black aprons. The *maquignons* would pay Marcel cash for the beast, then slaughter it and sell the meat to the larger butchers in the towns or to restaurants.

With calves the system was different. In April the animals, whose birth we had watched in secret from behind the stable door, were now about six or seven weeks old and right for eating. When Marcel had one ready, I would help him drive it up the road to the premises of the local butcher.

Monsieur Taste was a small, sturdy man, whom the farm people regarded as a foreigner because he came from a town and was not a peasant. His shop, above and behind which he lived, was in a small neat building on the corner opposite the *salle des fêtes*, and beside it a flight of stone steps ran down towards the Condom road. As a child, I always found Monsieur Taste a most impressive figure as he stood in his shop wearing a huge blue apron, surrounded by carcasses of animals and equipped with the largest collection of knives, choppers and sharpeners that I had ever seen. He was an excellent *charcutier*; his sausages had such a good reputation that people came all the way from Toulouse to Saint Puy to buy them.

We would drive the calf to the barn where Monsieur Taste did his slaughtering; it was not far from the shop, on the left hand side of the wide road which led up to the château. The village people always respectfully referred to the barn as '*l'abattoir*'; even for us children, though it was always something of an adventure to go there, it was not exactly a playground. Inside there was a sort of pen built with thick stone walls into which the calf was driven. Its head was fastened with ropes so that it could not move; Monsieur Taste climbed up to the top of the pen and stood astride the calf with one leg on each wall, then, taking in his hands a long-handled sledge-hammer with a thin, curved and very sharp spike protruding from its solid cast-iron head, he lifted it up with both arms as high above his head as he could. It was the stance of the executioner at the moment of a beheading. Down came

the hammer, and the animal fell immediately and heavily to the ground, its brain pierced by the long spike.

Calves were always slaughtered on a Friday, I remember, and on Saturday morning Monsieur Taste would call at the Oratoire with some veal taken from the animal. It was a traditional method of part payment not unlike the bartering system that existed in the old days between the peasants and the millers and bakers. The balance was paid in cash. It was Camille's custom to make a *fricassée de veau* each time a calf was killed, but she had other veal recipes in her repertoire which made use of all the offal. Nothing is wasted in peasant families!

Fricassée de Veau

VEAL TRIPE—SERVES 4

1 kg/2¼ lb veal tripe
salt and freshly ground pepper
100 g/4 oz duck fat
50 g/2 oz parsley, chopped

Cut the tripe into medium-sized pieces and season with salt and pepper.

Heat the duck fat in a large frying pan, put in the tripe and cook over high heat for about 20 minutes, until caramelized on the underside. Turn over the pieces and cook until the other side is also caramelized.

Add the parsley, cover the pan and simmer for 10 minutes before serving.

Rognons Blancs à l'Armagnac

CALVES' TESTICLES WITH ARMAGNAC—SERVES 4

4 large calves' testicles
50 g/2 oz duck fat
100 g/4 oz shallots, chopped
50 ml/2 fl oz armagnac
100 ml/4 fl oz dry white wine
salt and freshly ground pepper
20 g/¾ oz butter

Put the testicles in a saucepan of cold water and bring to the boil. Blanch the testicles for 2 minutes, then cool under running water. Cut into thick slices.

Heat the duck fat in a frying pan, put in the testicles and fry over not too high a heat for 3 minutes on one side. Turn them over and cook for another 3 minutes. Lift them out with a slotted spoon, transfer to a dish and keep warm.

Put the shallots in the frying pan still containing the fat and sweat gently until soft. Return the testicles to the pan, pour in the armagnac and flame. Add the wine, reduce by half, season with salt and pepper, then stir in the butter and serve.

Later in April, we might be eating our first wild snails. They were *petits gris*, the ubiquitous grey snails of south-west France, which Camille used to grill on the kitchen fire. When I was about twelve years old I enjoyed her snails almost more than anything else, and I think she enjoyed watching me eat them with such a hearty appetite. I would guzzle them by the dozen, and she said it was a sign of good health.

When Marcel came home from the fields on a rainy day, we could tell at once, from the look on his face, that he had collected some snails for us. It was a regular ritual for us children to rush up to him the minute he came into the house, pull off his beret and look inside it for the snails he had hidden there. His head was completely bald and sometimes we could see, running across it, slimy tracks which the bewildered creatures had made.

Even more exciting were the real snail hunts. These took place at nightfall, after it had rained; sometimes four or five of us took part, including my grandfather. We were all armed with electric torches (which had replaced the old acetylene lamps of earlier days), and carried potato sacks in which to bag our prey. We moved about the dark hedgerows like ponderous glow-worms, each with our roving, questing circle of electric light, as we filled our sacks with snails, capturing up to as many as two or three thousand in a single night. Since then the destruction of hedges and the use of chemical insecticides has led to the disappearance of large numbers of snails. Already by about 1960, we were finding far fewer than before.

Once the snails had been starved and purged, and Camille had washed them five or six times in a mixture of salt, vinegar and water, they were ready for grilling. The grill, a large square, old-fashioned grid-iron, with four legs and a long handle, was brought down from its nail at the back of the fireplace and placed over the hot embers of a fire of vine branches, the *sarments de vigne* that are stripped off the vines in late winter or early spring. Camille would put a pinch of salt on each snail so that the juice which oozed out as they cooked on the grill would become crusty and salty and tinged with the special aroma of the burning vine branches. We ate our snails skewered on the ends of pins; they were delicious, and I often think that this is by far the best way to cook them. How much better those wild snails tasted than today's commercially bred varieties! These may be larger and take less time to cook, but they can never have the same flavour.

Petits Gris Gros Sel

SNAILS GRILLED WITH COARSE SALT—SERVES 4

48 snails (or more if you wish)
700 g/1½ lb coarse salt
100 ml/4 fl oz vinegar

Remove the membrane which grows across the opening of the snail shells.

Put 150g/5 oz salt and 20 ml/¾ fl oz vinegar into 5 l/8¾ pt water and wash the snails in it for 5 minutes. Repeat the process 5 times, using a fresh solution each time.

Light a charcoal barbecue and leave until hot. Lay some chicken wire over the grilling rack to prevent the snails from falling through. Arrange the snails on the rack, with the opening of the shells facing upwards, away from the heat. Put a pinch of salt on each snail and cook for about 10 minutes, until the juices solidify.

Serve the snails in a dish and pick them out of the shells with pins.

The physician Joseph du Chesne says that in the 16th-century snails were already eaten a great deal in Gascony, as they probably had been since Roman times, and he gives contemporary Gascon recipes for cooking them, including boiling for six or seven hours in a *court bouillon* of salted water, butter and olive oil and serving with herbs and pepper, and frying them in oil or butter before serving with a sprinkling of orange juice. 'Delicious food for those who like it and are used to it' he remarks. Personally, I like my snails doused in a good quantity of red wine, as in the following recipe.

Petits Gris Farcis au Vin Rouge

STUFFED SNAILS IN RED WINE — SERVES 4

48 snails (or more if you wish)

700 g/1½ lb coarse salt

100 ml/4 fl oz vinegar

2 carrots, chopped

2 onions, chopped

10 garlic cloves, chopped

1 bouquet garni

salt and freshly ground pepper

50 g/2 oz goose fat

100 g/4 oz bayonne ham, finely chopped

50 g/2 oz parsley, finely chopped

250 g/9 oz sausage meat

1 tablespoon tomato purée

1.5 l/2½ pt red wine

50 g/2 oz fresh breadcrumbs

Wash the snails as in the previous recipe.

Fill a saucepan with 5 l/8¾ pt water, put in the snails, carrots, half the onion, half the garlic and the bouquet garni. Season with salt and pepper and cook for 2 hours, until you can easily skewer a snail out of its shell with a pin.

Meanwhile, prepare the sauce. In a saucepan, sweat the remaining onion in the goose fat until soft, then add the ham, the remaining garlic, parsley and sausage meat. Cook gently for 10 minutes, then add the tomato purée and cook for another 5 minutes.

Add the red wine, bring to a gentle boil, skim and add the snails. Check the seasoning. Cook gently for another 30 minutes, skimming the surface frequently. Sprinkle the breadcrumbs over the snails and cook for another 10 minutes. The sauce should be thickened and reduced so that it is no longer runny. As it becomes thicker, it will stick to the snails and fill the openings. Adjust the seasoning and serve the snails with the sauce.

A late Easter holiday might also be the time when Marcel found his first spring mushrooms. He was deeply proud to be the first to discover morels or *mousserons* in the neighbourhood. Whether he was fishing or shooting or walking at the head of a pair of cows and a cart along a country road, he was always on the lookout for mushrooms during the season. At the beginning of the last war, when Marcel was serving as an army muleteer near Strasbourg, he and another soldier who was also a countryman discovered large numbers of delicious ceps, which the rest of the unit, terrified of being poisoned, refused to eat. This was one of my grandfather's most cherished military anecdotes.

At the Oratoire the local postman provided good advance information about the whereabouts of mushrooms; he was a fellow sportsman and had an eye almost as keen as Marcel's. Over a glass of wine and a plate of *confit de canard*, he often let out crucial details overheard at another farm, or remembered that he had seen *mousserons* for the first time in some totally unexpected spot. Marcel's own favourite hunting ground was the rambling wood of La Plèche, to the north of Saint Puy, whither he would set off on his *mobilette* to bring back morels, *pleurottes* and tiny, greyish, pointed-topped *mousserons*; these he would show tantalizingly to his friends over an aperitif at the little arched café near the market hall, never once revealing where he had found them.

Mousserons en Persillade

WILD MUSHROOMS WITH PARSLEY

400 g/14 oz mousserons (Saint George's mushrooms) or oyster mushrooms
50 g/2 oz butter
salt and freshly ground pepper
6 garlic cloves, finely chopped
50 g/2 oz parsley, chopped

Remove and discard the *mousseron* stalks and wash the caps in several changes of cold water. (This is not necessary if you are using cultivated mushrooms.) Heat half the butter in a frying pan, put in the mushrooms and cook gently to evaporate the moisture. Drain the mushrooms, return them to the same pan and cook lightly once again in the remaining butter so that the flavour develops fully. Season, add the garlic and parsley and cook for another 3 minutes.

Omelette aux Mousserons

WILD MUSHROOM OMELETTE—SERVES 4

200 g/7 oz mousserons (Saint George's mushrooms) or oyster mushrooms
25 g/1 oz butter
salt and freshly ground pepper
3 garlic cloves, chopped
50 g/2 oz parsley, chopped
12 eggs
2 tablespoons oil

Clean and prepare the mushrooms as in the previous recipe. Fry them gently in the butter for 10 minutes, strain them and pour the butter back into the pan.

Return the mushrooms to the pan, season and add the garlic and parsley. Cook for another 3 minutes.

Make a 12-egg omelette (see *Omelette aux goujons*, page 43), put in the mushrooms, fold over the omelette and serve.

One of the most attractive buildings in Saint Puy is the 18th-century *pigeonnier*, or dovecote, which stands beside the old farm of La Colombe. It is built on a small hill, just outside the village on the Condom road, and consists of a thick, square stone tower with a pointed red-tiled roof ending in an elegant turret or *lanternon*. In the past, the pigeons which inhabited the upper part were an important source of food and also of *colombine*, a manure which was widely used until well into the 19th-century.

In the rest of France, by feudal custom, the right to breed pigeons and to build a dovecote was granted only to the nobility and to the clergy. In the south-west, however, the inhabitants obeyed the written law, based on that of Rome, and not the Frankish customary law of the north. Here, during the 16th-century, the *droit de colombier* was gradually extended to wealthy landowners and the richer peasantry, and in many cases ceased to be the sole prerogative of the aristocracy. As a result, a rich architectural heritage of *pigeonniers* such as the one at La Colombe was built all over Gascony, particularly during the 18th-century.

At the Oratoire there was no *pigeonnier*, but we were never without pigeons and we ate them often. In the space between the kitchen ceiling and the pitched roof of the farm, there extended the high space of the loft, and this was Marcel's

dovecote. Three small square openings, cut into the stone wall of the farm above the front door and the two flanking windows, allowed the birds to fly in and out as they wished or to sit on the ledges, murmuring and sunning themselves if the weather was fine.

Whenever I climbed up the barn ladder into the loft, I was struck for a moment with feelings of amazement: first at the massive complicated wooden skeleton of beams, uprights, diagonals and interlocking cross-pieces which stretched up above me to support the roof; then at the dusty, cobweb-covered pile of old German helmets, daggers, bayonets, belts, badges and other odds and ends which lay on the floor and made up Marcel's collection of wartime souvenirs. This collection was sacred. No one, not even the children on *Mardi gras*, dared to touch anything in it. No one knew how my grandfather had acquired it all, or how or when he had got it up into the loft. It was covered with dirt, and everything was rusting and rotting away to nothing. The eerie quality of these old weapons was heightened by the perpetual presence and activity of the scratching, fluttering, brooding pigeons in their rows of little nesting boxes that lined the tops of the walls underneath the eaves.

Pigeons are difficult birds; they are *des amoureux*, as we say, and if you lose the male bird of a pair, the female will never lay again; even at the best of times a pigeon never lays very many eggs. But Camille managed our pigeons at the Oratoire very well. In April, the young birds that had hatched out from the first eggs to be laid after the winter period were ready to eat. Here is how my grandmother would cook them with herbs from her garden.

Pigeonneaux au Thym et à l'Ail

YOUNG PIGEON WITH THYME & GARLIC—SERVES 4

4 young pigeons, cleaned
salt and freshly ground pepper
50 g/2 oz goose fat
4 sprigs of thyme
20 small garlic cloves, peeled
1 shallot, chopped
150 ml/5 fl oz dry white wine

Season the pigeons with salt and pepper. Heat the goose fat in a flameproof casserole, put in the pigeons and seal quickly on all sides. Turn them on to one breast, cover the casserole and cook gently for 15 minutes (10 minutes will be enough if the birds are exceptionally young and tender).

Turn the pigeons on to the other breast, add the thyme and garlic, cover the casserole again and cook for another 10–15 minutes. Turn the pigeons on to their backs, cover and cook for 5 more minutes.

Take the pigeons out of the casserole and put them on a dish, breast-side down. Cover with foil and leave to rest in a warm place for 10 minutes.

Meanwhile, make the sauce. Discard the fat from the casserole, put in the shallot and sweat until soft. Add the white wine, reduce by half, then add 100 ml/ 4 fl oz water and reduce by one-quarter. Check the seasoning.

To serve, turn the pigeons on to their backs and pour over the sauce. Top the birds with a sprig of thyme and arrange the garlic all round the edge.

Croustade de Pigeonneaux à la Gasconne

PIGEON IN TRADITIONAL GASCON PASTRY—SERVES 4

4 pigeons
400 g/14 oz onions, chopped
100 g/4 oz duck fat or oil, melted
1 quantity pastis (see Croustade de confit de canard, *page 35), or filo pastry*
a pinch of ground cinnamon
a pinch of saffron
a pinch of black pepper
1 tablespoon chopped parsley
cep sauce or Daube de cèpes *(recipe page 206), to serve*

Preheat the oven to 220°C/425°F/gas 7. Cut off the pigeon legs and breasts. Debone the legs and chop the meat. To make the stuffing, cook the onions in a little duck fat until soft. Mix with the chopped leg meat, spices and parsley.

Heat a little more duck fat in a frying pan and seal the pigeon breasts on both sides. Set aside.

Divide the pastry in half, if you are using pastis, and roll and stretch each piece as described on page 35–6. Cut out 3 circles a little larger than a 20 cm/ 8 in pie dish (the pastry must overlap the dish).

Grease the dish generously with duck fat, then lay a sheet of pastry in the bottom of the dish and smear it with duck fat. Repeat this operation twice to make 3 layers.

Place the stuffing and pigeon breasts in the dish and cover with 3 more layers of pastry and duck fat. Crumple the edges of the pastry to give a frilly effect and brush with a little more duck fat. Cook in the preheated oven for 20 minutes. Serve immediately with a cep sauce, or *Daube de cèpes*.

Towards the end of the Easter holidays, Camille would sometimes cook us a newly born sucking pig, which we regarded as a great delicacy. Marcel did not own a sow, so the sucking pig was always bought live from peasants at another farm and slaughtered at the Oratoire by Monsieur Montaud, the Saint Puy pig-killer. The animal was killed like the lambs; its throat was cut while it was held down on its back on a table, then Monsieur Montaud carried out the important processes of bleeding, boiling, scraping and cleaning. The shape of this small, plump, smooth creature was so amazingly complete, from its nose and ears right down to its twisted tail, that it seemed to offer us, all on its own, a self-contained feast that needed no additions. How right Joseph du Chesne was when he wrote: 'The flesh of young pigs which are not yet weaned has a delicious taste and is very nourishing. It is served roasted. It is the supreme delight of the Gascons.'

Porcelet Cuit à la Broche

SUCKING PIG COOKED ON A SPIT—SERVES 4

1 sucking pig with its liver, heart and lungs
600 g/1¼ lb boneless pork
400 g/14 oz pork fat
150 ml/5 fl oz dry white wine
4 egg yolks
2 onions, finely chopped
6 garlic cloves, chopped
200 g/7 oz fresh breadcrumbs
2 tablespoons chopped parsley
salt and freshly ground pepper
200 g/7 oz duck fat, melted

Prepare the stuffing by mincing together the liver, heart and lungs with the pork meat and fat. Add the wine, egg yolks, onions, garlic, breadcrumbs and parsley, season and mix thoroughly. Stuff the piglet with this mixture and sew up.

Put the piglet on a spit in front of the fire and roast for 4 hours, turning it constantly and basting with the duck fat to prevent the skin from cracking.

If you do not have an open fire, roast the piglet in the oven at 180°C/350°F/gas 4 for about 2 hours, basting frequently with duck fat. It can be eaten hot or cold.

Our spring holidays always ended on a Sunday night when my father came in his car to fetch us home to Tarbes and we knew that school was going to start again on Monday morning. It was a sad moment, but it was made better by Camille's characteristic way of saying goodbye. After insisting that we should all keep waving out of the back window of the car until we were well past the dangerous junction with the Lectoure road (a ritual which, to her mind, somehow ensured our complete safety) she would give us flowers and food to take back to Tarbes, and she would bring out a big glass jar of her *prunes à l'eau-de-vie*.

The *prunes* were reine claude greengages bottled in armagnac, and when we were very small, we were only allowed one each, as Camille considered the brandy to be too strong for children. As we grew older, we were allowed two, three, and finally four, the full ration for an adult. The moment was always good and we looked forward eagerly to it. We enjoyed the *prunes à l'eau-de-vie* so much that we almost forgot it was time to leave our beloved Oratoire.

Reine Claude à l'Armagnac

GREENGAGES IN ARMAGNAC

1 kg/2¼ lb very firm greengages (not too ripe)
1 l/1¾ pt armagnac
1 kg/2¼ lb sugar

You will need a large kilner jar or a glass jar with an airtight seal. Collect enough greengages to fill the jar but still be just covered by the armagnac. Leave a little piece of stalk on each greengage. Prick the fruit with a needle 5 or 6 times and place in the jar.

Sweeten the armagnac with the sugar and pour in enough just to cover the greengages. Seal the jar and stand it in a very deep bain-marie. Boil the water in the bain-marie for 1 minute, then leave to cool. Keep the jar sealed for one month before eating the greengages.

Grapes are also delicious preserved in this way.

Romance dans les Pyrences

pour mes parents

Summer

Summer meant haymaking, fruit-picking and harvesting, when the threshing machine clattered away in a cloud of dust and forty men sat down each day to eat harvest lunches of *poule au pot* and local wine and country bread. When it was over there was time at last for quiet fishing picnics beside the river, and the summer village *fête* with dancing, cycle races and a fair.

WHEN WE RETURNED to Saint Puy towards the end of June, at the start of the *grandes vacances*, we found the village surrounded in every direction by green leafy vines, thick maize and yellow cornfields. There were poppies everywhere, punctuating the wheat and barley with bright scarlet dots and growing in magnificent, fiery clumps at the corners of woods and fields. The grass banks at the side of the roads were full of wild orchids, bluets, wild sweet peas and hundreds of other tiny pink and white flowers. The hedges were hung with elder blossom, and below them, on all sides, you could see delicate, miniature forests of umbels. The whole landscape was ripe and full, and seemed to be waiting expectantly for the season of haymaking, harvest and fruit-picking.

These were the high spots of my grandparents' year and they gave the summer months of July and August their own particular character and purpose. June haymaking was a prelude to the long month of the wheat harvest, which affected all the farms of the village, and was as much a social event, involving the whole community as an agricultural one. The month of August, when the fruit was picked in the Oratoire orchards and melon fields, was also a busy one for Camille in the poultry yard. It was the hens' best laying time: the guinea fowl were in their plumpest condition; the ducks had to be driven out regularly to feed in the stubble fields; young cocks had to be caponized (castrated); and it was the time for making duck *terrines*, *galantines* of chicken and vegetable *conserves*, and for bottling fruit in *eau-de-vie*.

Flowers were always important at the farm, because my grandmother adored them. She had a natural gift for gardening, and was always trying out new plants and seeds whenever she could. Every summer, as the car turned the corner in the village and drove downhill towards the Oratoire, Camille's flowers were the first thing that struck us. The whole house was radiant with them. There was a window box on every sill; flowering plants grew in the piece of land between the farm and the side of the road; and, to the left of the door, in front of the kitchen window, climbing roses covered an arched, wrought-iron pergola, which curved up against the wall and made a little arbour within which my grandmother would sit on warm August evenings, preparing vegetables or fruit, or just doing her embroidery and talking to us.

This arbour was Camille's favourite place. Here, she would tell us stories about past happenings in the village, or about people and families she had known; her stories were full of odd characters, and were often more amazing even than the fairy tales of Charles Perrault or Hans Christian Andersen, of whom she had probably never heard. She would also try to teach us little things about cooking, knitting or embroidery, or about drying flowers such as honesty so that they could be used as a winter decoration, or preserving vegetables to enjoy after their season was over. Unlike Marcel, who was rooted in his habits, my grandmother was always open to new ideas; she loved to learn new skills, and, once she had learnt them, she always tried to teach them to us.

Haricots Verts Secs

DRIED FRENCH BEANS

french beans

small needle and 1 m/40 in lengths of cotton

salt

Top, tail and wash the beans. Using a small needle and 1 m/40 in lengths of cotton, thread the beans through the middle on to the cotton. Bring a pan of salted water to boil, put in some of the beans (not too many at once, or the cotton will tangle) and simmer for 5 minutes, then refresh. Cook all the beans in this way.

To dry the beans, hang them on the kitchen beams for several days until very dry. Slide the dried beans off the strings and put them in a cardboard box; they will keep indefinitely.

When you want to eat the beans, soak them in running water until they regain their original shape, then cook as usual.

Confiture de Noix Vertes

GREEN WALNUT JAM

1 kg/2¼ lb green walnuts (unripe nuts with no shells inside the husk)

1 kg/2¼ lb caster sugar

1 l/1¾ pt water

Collect the walnuts on 17th June, one week before the feast of Saint John. Pierce the skins with a needle and soak the walnuts for 9 days, changing the water every day.

Make a syrup with the sugar and water, add the walnuts and boil like jam until it reaches setting point. Pour into jars, cool and seal.

It was a sign of the adventurous, unconventional side of Camille's character that each room at the Oratoire was painted in a different colour, usually a soft pink, or a blue, or a green. In accordance with immemorial tradition, every other farm was painted plain white inside; but Camille loved colours, and she also loved changing them. She was absolutely thrilled, when, at the age of fifteen or sixteen, I sometimes offered to repaint the dining room or one of the bedrooms in a new colour. There were three bedrooms, and I remember painting all of them several times during the summer holidays.

My grandparents' room was next to the kitchen. It had a window looking out over the poultry yard and the well, and its only piece of furniture, apart from an old, dark wardrobe and a chest of drawers, was the great bed with its fine wrought-iron, semi-circular bedheads, smaller at the foot and larger at the head, which were divided up like leaves into intricate, flamboyant, outwardly radiating segments. The guest bedroom, in which my parents slept when they stayed at the farm, was in the other part of the house. Here the bed, the wardrobe, the dressing table, the chairs and the little tables were all made of honey-coloured imitation bamboo. They were a wedding present, I think, and I remember that when I first saw them, I though they were the prettiest furniture in the world.

There were no pictures on the walls, but Camille often used to frame her embroideries, which frequently showed scenes of animals or flowers, and hang them up. She also liked to crochet brightly decorated napkins, which she treated in a special way of her own. She first fitted them round the inside of a bowl, then soaked them in melted sugar. When the sugar dried, it hardened like starch, and the napkin retained the shape of the bowl and could stand up on its own. In summer she used them as fruit baskets. She also made swans and cocks in the same way, which were charming when she displayed them on the mantelpiece. We had never seen anything like them before, and thought they were wonderful.

Marcel hated change and was suspicious of anything new, so he never took any part in painting the kitchen or the bedrooms. His general appearance was immutable. He was never without his black beret, and he invariably wore a suit of *bleus de travail*, which consisted of blue overall trousers, a long blue shirt, and a blue jacket. To wear on Sundays, and for going to the café, he had another identical set of clothes, which was never used during the week and which Camille kept ready for him, clean, pressed and absolutely immaculate. For weddings and funerals he possessed a formal dark suit, made of heavy serge and only very rarely worn. It was in his blue overalls, and wearing wooden sabots lined with thick felt slippers, that he went out every day to work in the fields.

Marcel left the house at sunrise in summer and before dawn in winter, and worked until 7 o'clock when he came home for a breakfast of soup, bread, ham, eggs, sausage and red wine. At midday punctually, when the church clock struck and the fire station siren wailed and all work stopped instantly everywhere, he came back again for lunch, which consisted of more soup and bread, and often a chicken. Every day except Sunday, as soon as he had finished eating and Camille had taken his plate away, Marcel had his siesta. Without even leaving his chair, he slept for about thirty minutes, his arms folded on the table in front of him, and his bald head resting on top of them. Promptly at 2 he went back to work in the fields. Supper would be at about 7 o'clock, and by 9 o'clock he and Camille would be in bed and asleep.

My summer at Saint Puy normally started with the *grandes vacances*, but I do remember that one year I was there for the Armistice Day ceremonies on 8th May. The Saint Puy war memorial is a simple obelisk, shaded in the hot weather by a grove of chestnut trees; it stands in the centre of a little square about halfway between the market hall and the church. The grocery shop of my uncle and aunt, the Capurons, was at one corner of the square, and the *mairie* and the post office were diagonally opposite. Above the door of the *mairie*, between the two tall windows of the *salle des reunions* on the first floor, there protruded a stiff, metal *tricolore* flag, brightly painted, with RF (for *République Française*) added in large white letters.

This flag never shook proudly in a breeze, or sagged when the wind dropped; it was perpetually present, fully extended, rusty in places, but always giving a touch of gaiety to the square and to the ceremonial parade which took place there every 8th May.

The small group of *anciens combattants*, in their best dark suits and berets, wearing their medals and carrying real flags – the *tricolore* of France and the flag of Saint Puy embroidered with two crosses, a lion and a stag – came marching in to the sound of the drums and bugles of the fire brigade band. My uncle, the mayor, resplendent in his coloured sash, made a speech and then stepped forward to lay a large wreath at the foot of the war memorial.

The *anciens combattants* included my grandfather. Every year he duly took his place with the flags and the bugles beside the monument which bore, among the names of the fallen, that of his uncle, Marius Cadeillan. He himself was just old enough to have served for a short time at the very end of the first war, and he was in the army again between 1939 and 1940. He was stationed at Strasbourg, where his job was to look after mules. I do not think he was ever involved in any active fighting, and I very much wonder if he ever killed anybody. If so, he never mentioned it. Perhaps he did not want to upset us. Whenever he did talk about the war, it was always to tell us of the good times he had had, when he got an opportunity to go shooting wild boar or deer, or to fish, or to explore the warm, cosy Strasbourg bars; or, as I have mentioned, when he and a friend discovered a wood full of mushrooms.

While Marcel was away, it was Camille and her two daughters who looked after the farm and did much of the heavy work; yet when Marcel came home on leave he spent most of it, according to my grandmother, at the little café with his friends, and only seemed to call at the Oratoire to hang up his knapsack and jacket on arrival, to sleep, and to pick his things up again when the time came for him to go. Marcel had the luck not to be kept in Germany as a prisoner of war (my father was not so fortunate), and to be able to return to Saint Puy and to resume his life at the farm, where existence under the Occupation was fairly comfortable and the food good, if one compared country conditions to those in the towns. Only once, I believe, a party of German soldiers came to the farm; they camped there for a few days on the lower ground near the poultry yard, but they soon left, and did not cause any trouble.

The ceremony at the war memorial, and the laying of the wreath, was followed by the annual *banquet des anciens combattants*. This took place at midday in the *salle des fêtes*, above the fire station and opposite the shop of Monsieur Taste the butcher. Now the flags were reverently leant against the wall behind the mayor's chair, and the dark suits and medals mingled, all down the long table, with the lighter, more colourful clothes of the wives, children and friends. Wine was poured, soup was eaten, and conversation began to build up round wartime stories and memories as the *charcuterie* gave place to one of the special banquet dishes which would be followed in its turn by a roast, probably duck or lamb, then a dessert.

By tradition, there were certain things which were always eaten at banquets but never at home, partly because they were expensive items to buy, but also because they would seem genuinely out of place on the ordinary kitchen table of a local farm. Sweetbreads, for example, were a favourite banquet dish; another was hake, and the meal often ended with a dish of *oeufs à la neige*.

Ris de Veau à la Forestière

SWEETBREADS WITH MUSHROOMS—SERVES 4

4 veal sweetbreads, about 200 g/7 oz each, soaked in cold water for 2–3 hours
salt and freshly ground pepper
70 g/2½ oz duck fat
50 g/2 oz shallots, finely chopped
200 g/7 oz mushrooms (a selection of button and oyster mushrooms, chanterelles and morels if possible), cleaned and thinly sliced
20 g/¾ oz plain flour
150 ml/5 fl oz dry white wine

Blanch the sweetbreads in boiling water for 5 minutes, drain and carefully peel off the outside membrane without damaging the sweetbreads. Season with salt and pepper. In a large frying pan, heat the fat until sizzling, add the sweetbreads and seal on both sides. Add the shallots and cook for 1 minute, then put in the sliced mushrooms and cook for 5 minutes, stirring halfway through.

Stir in the flour and cook very gently for 3 minutes. Pour in the wine, season and cook over medium heat for 3 minutes, stirring continuously. Add 100 ml/ 4 fl oz water and cook for another 5 minutes. Check the seasoning and serve.

Darne de Colin aux Câpres, Safran et Tomates

HAKE WITH CAPERS, SAFFRON & TOMATOES—SERVES 4

4 hake steaks, about 2 cm/¾ in thick
2 shallots, finely chopped
250 ml/9 fl oz dry white wine
a pinch of saffron
salt
50 g/2 oz butter
50 g/2 oz capers
2 large tomatoes, skinned, deseeded and diced
1 teaspoon chopped parsley

RIGHT: OEUFS À LA NEIGE (P. 102)

Preheat oven to 190°C/375°F/gas 5. Put the fish in a flameproof dish with the shallots, white wine, 50 ml/2 fl oz water, saffron and salt to taste. Bring to simmering point, cover with foil and cook in the oven for 15 minutes.

Transfer the fish to a serving dish and keep hot. Reduce the cooking juices by half, then whisk in the butter. Check the seasoning and add the capers and tomatoes. Pour the sauce over the hake, sprinkle with chopped parsley and serve.

Oeufs à la Neige

POACHED EGG WHITES WITH VANILLA CUSTARD—SERVES 4

600 ml/1 pt milk
1 vanilla pod, split lengthways
6 eggs, separated
200 g/7 oz sugar

Bring the milk to the boil with the split vanilla pod. Whisk the egg yolks with half the sugar until pale. Gradually pour the boiling milk on to the egg mixture, whisking continuously.

Pour the custard into a saucepan and cook gently, stirring with a wooden spatula until you can run your finger through the custard on the spatula and leave a clean mark. Pass the custard through a sieve into a bowl and leave until almost cold, stirring from time to time.

Fill a medium saucepan with water and bring to the boil. Beat the egg whites with a pinch of salt until stiff, then fold in 50 g/2 oz sugar. With a large spoon, dig out 4 scoops of egg white and put them in the simmering water. Poach for 2 minutes, then turn them over and poach for 2 minutes on the other side. Lift out the egg whites and place on a tray.

Put the cooled custard in a serving dish and arrange the poached egg whites on top. Make a caramel with the remaining sugar by heating it gently in a thick-bottomed pan with 1 tablespoon water until deep golden brown, and drizzle it over the egg whites.

To us children, the ceremonies of Armistice Day did not really mean very much. We were all born after the end of the war, and we had never even known the Occupation. But to Marcel, and his friends who were of the same generation, it meant a great deal. Even if my grandfather had not done very much fighting, he knew others who had fought, or been killed, or who had been in the Resistance.

My own feelings about history and the past, especially about the past of Saint Puy, were aroused much more vividly when, one very hot day in August, my uncle Capuron took me up to the *salle des réunions* at the *mairie*, and showed me the parish archives. Built in the late 18th- or early 19th-century, the *mairie* must once have been the house of some village notable or a rich peasant who had retired from his farm and become a *bourgeois*. The *salon* on the first floor, which you enter through double doors after coming in from the sun and climbing up the cool, stone staircase with its elegant wrought-iron balustrade, is now used for council meetings, consultations of the cadastral map of the commune, and marriages.

Seen through the big windows, the square, with its trees and the war memorial and my uncle's shop, seemed to me suddenly smaller and more intimate. As I looked round at the marble bust of Marianne, the photograph of de Gaulle, the panelled walls and ceiling, and the large, framed map of Saint Puy, drawn during the reign of Louis Philippe, which hung above the fireplace, I little thought that one day my own marriage would take place in this room, and that my uncle would still be the officiating mayor.

The archives of Saint Puy are kept behind the oak doors of two large built-in cupboards. My uncle was particularly proud of the first great cadastral survey of the commune, which was produced in 1813 under the Napoleonic regime, and which shows in great detail and in several enormous volumes all the fields, farms, mills and houses, very much as they must have been in the years before the Revolution. The Oratoire was not yet built in 1813, but the map shows that many of the field boundaries were the same then as now, and that the old track at the edge of the farm, leading down to the mill of Marin, was in those days an important road.

A long line of thick volumes, bound in rough leather, contains the parish registers from the late 16th-century until the end of the 18th-. Kept by the village priest, they record monotonously all the births, deaths, baptisms and marriages which occurred in the parish. From 1675, however, the curé of Saint Puy was a certain Bertrand Dubarry, who, for some reason decided to break with the custom of his predecessors and enlivened the tedious catalogue of humble names with short diary entries about local weather conditions and their effect on the crops and cattle of the peasants.

As I gradually got used to Monsieur Dubarry's handwriting, I began to realize that the distant ancestors of Marcel and Camille were as dependent as my grandparents were on what the land in the immediate vicinity could produce; but of course, if things went wrong, the early peasants were far more vulnerable, and had no easy alternative sources of food. In August 1705 there was a terrible drought which destroyed all the fruit and began to threaten the animals. 'The great lack of water so necessary for the subsistence of man' became so alarming that Monsieur Dubarry, together with the consuls of Saint Puy in their black and scarlet robes, led a procession through the town and round the fields to pray for rain. On this occasion, to the priest's evident satisfaction, his prayers were heard, and, a week later rain fell. But not every disaster had such a happy ending. On at least three occasions, Saint Puy was hit by terrible hailstorms, which caused appalling floods and killed many animals and even people.

It is easy to understand the hopes and fears of the 17th- and 18th-century peasants. Even at the Oratoire, it was disastrous when the well dried up during a particularly hot summer; and, as a modern equivalent of the plague, I can remember the decimation of Camille's rabbits by myxomatosis in the 1950s, and how much anxiety and consternation this caused. But, of course, we were not a very religious family – Marcel, who doggedly distrusted the Church and hated the curé, would never have consented to take part in a procession. He never went to Mass, and only reluctantly attended marriages, funerals and first communions. Even then, he always used to stand at the church door, just on the threshold, and never really came inside.

I made my own first communion at Saint Puy in the summer of 1960, when I was twelve. My white robe, my *aube*, was hired from a shop in Fleurance; at the church I duly joined the other boys, all similarly clad, and the girls in their white dresses and crowns. I do not think that any of us really understood very much about the religious aspect of the occasion, even though the families attended the service. Marcel, I am sure, felt that the most significant part of it all was the big family lunch which took place at the Oratoire afterwards.

The lunch was a typical communion meal with traditional food, and everybody enjoyed it. The adults all ate and drank well, and told stories and laughed, while we children went away and amused ourselves in another corner of the room. A first communion was important for children because it was then that you received your first real, grown-up presents. I remember I was absolutely delighted to be given my first watch and my first camera.

The meal started with soup, a *bouilli*, which was followed by hams and terrines; it continued with a superb *ballotine* of foie gras and a leg of lamb, a special delicacy associated with *fêtes*; it then ended with an exciting *croquembouche*, without which no communion meal was ever complete. Ordered specially from the *pâtisserie* and carried in to cries of admiration and applause, it consisted of lots of little *profiteroles* built up into a tall tower, which was glazed with crisp caramel and crowned at the top with two tiny china figures of a boy and a girl dressed in their first communion clothes.

Ballotine de Foie Gras au Jurançon

BALLOTINE OF FOIE GRAS WITH SWEET JURANÇON WINE—
SERVES 8

1 kg/2¼ lb whole raw foie gras
salt and freshly ground pepper
3 l/5½ pt duck or chicken consommé
1 bottle sweet jurançon wine

Soak the foie gras in tepid water for 3 hours until slightly soft. Clean it and remove the green parts, nerves and veins. Lay it flat on the work surface, sprinkle with salt and plenty of coarsely ground pepper.

Wet a linen cloth, about 40 cm/16 in square, in cold water and lay it flat on the work surface. Put the foie gras on top, open side up, and roll it up in the cloth as tightly as possible into a sausage shape. Twist the 2 ends tightly to contract the foie gras and close up the opening. Tie the *ballotine* with string at 1 cm/½ in intervals, taking care not to tie it too tightly, or it will leave marks.

Heat the consommé in a saucepan large enough to hold the *ballotine*. Add the wine and heat to 80°C/176°F. Check the seasoning (it may already be perfect), put in the *ballotine* and cook for 25 minutes at a constant 80°C/176°F.

When the *ballotine* is cooked, stand the saucepan in iced water and leave until cold. At this stage, the foie gras will be so soft that it is almost liquid. Place the saucepan in the fridge and leave until the next day, so that the *ballotine* hardens up. Jellify some of the consommé with a little gelatine; the rest can be served as a soup.

The next day, carefully unwrap the *ballotine*, cut a few slices and arrange on a serving dish. Place some chopped jellied consommé around the edge. If the *ballotine* has lost its neat shape, roll it gently in the cloth to restore the shape before unwrapping it.

Gigot de Quatre Heures

LEG OF LAMB COOKED FOR 4 HOURS—SERVES 8

3 kg/6½ lb leg of lamb

50 g/2 oz duck fat

300 g/11 oz carrots, roughly chopped

500 g/1 lb 2 oz onions, roughly chopped

1 small bouquet garni

1 bottle dry white wine

100 g/4 oz garlic, peeled and wrapped in muslin

salt and freshly ground pepper

Preheat the oven to 170°C/325°F/gas 3. Heat the fat in a large flameproof casserole and seal the lamb until golden brown all over. Take out the lamb, put in the carrots and sweat gently for 5 minutes, then add the onions and sweat for another 5 minutes. Add the bouquet garni and put back the lamb. Pour over the wine and boil for 3 minutes. Add 2 l/3½ pt water and garlic and season.

Cover the casserole and cook in the oven for 4 hours. Check every hour that the cooking stock still comes halfway up the lamb; add more water if necessary. After 4 hours, the meat should be as soft as butter. Remove it from the casserole with great care and place on a serving dish.

Pass the stock through a conical sieve. Remove the garlic from the muslin bag, crush it to a paste and stir into the stock. Check the seasoning and pour on the sauce.

This lunch was eaten in the dining room, which was opposite the kitchen on the other side of the red-tiled passageway. The handsome old table and chairs were only used on special occasions, when there were important guests, or when, as now, there was a family feast to be celebrated. On either side of the fireplace, two built-in cupboards contained Camille's *eaux-de-vie* and liqueurs and aperitifs, and also her *conserves* of vegetables, chicken and fruit. Facing the window, there was a large dresser with six doors which housed my grandmother's collection of old china bowls and dishes, all of them decorated with pink and red flowers on a blue background. She also had a collection of black and white transfer plates, each one showing a different picture; I used to find these fascinating, and I loved looking at them and learning the verses imprinted on the china. One series was based on old popular French songs, and among them, I particularly remember La Madelon giving drinks to the soldiers. Another series illustrated the fables of La Fontaine: the fox and the grapes, the rat and the frog, the monkey and the leopard and several others.

The *grandes vacances* started in late June, and we often arrived in Saint Puy in time for the haymaking. I loved to see the big waggons piled high with light, sweet-smelling hay being drawn into the farm by cows, and to watch the hay being forked up into the loft above the stables. The stables were down at the back of the house on the ground floor, and were large enough to accommodate twelve cows, two horses and the ewe.

As on all farms in south-west France, the strong, docile, cream-coloured Gascony cows were of vital importance. They provided milk; they could be sold for their meat; and, above all, they did the heavy work on the farm, drawing carts, waggons, reaping machines and ploughs. Horses were less prized, and the pair which Marcel kept at the time I first knew the farm were mostly used to make the journey to other villages, when a cow-drawn cart would have been too slow. Later, after Marcel had acquired his *mobilette*, and when my father began to take my grandparents out in his car, he got rid of the horses.

Next to the stables was a big open barn, with thick wooden trusses, tie-beams and a tiled roof, and here Marcel kept all the bigger machinery and the carts. The haycutter, the rake and the reaper and binder were all of prime importance for the summer while the plough, the harrow, the roller and the sowing machine waited to come into their own in autumn and winter. Each cart had its own peculiar character and purpose. There was the water cart, a round tank on wheels, which was used exclusively for watering the animals; it was never filled from the well, but always from one of the ponds, where Marcel used to scoop up the water with an old German helmet tied on to the end of a long pole. There was the manure cart, long, low, narrow and high-sided. There were three or four really big waggons, which required two pairs of cows to pull them; these were used at haymaking and harvest.

There were also *tombereaux*, ordinary working carts, and smaller carts still, with benches in them, for carrying people. I well remember riding in these carts, with my legs dangling out at the back, enjoying the slow, rolling motion of the cow, while Marcel walked along the road at the animal's head, leading it. All these old carts were painted a light blue, the traditional colour in that part of France, and they all had iron-rimmed wheels. Later on, my uncle had them fitted with rubber tyres; but all my early memories of Saint Puy have, in the background, the unmistakeable, scraping, grinding, crushing sound of iron wheels lumbering over country roads.

Haymaking was only a prelude to what was really the most important event in the whole year, the July wheat harvest. At Saint Puy this lasted for about a month. Three or four neighbouring farms would organize themselves into a group, so that all their combined workforces would visit each farm in turn, to cut, thresh, and store the wheat, only moving on to the next when the harvest at the previous farm was finished.

For a farmer and his family this involved a great deal of preparation. Marcel, for example, had to hire the threshing machine, and to check, oil and repair the reaper and binder. Its great cutting blade, which must have been a good six feet long, had to be sharpened, and I always helped to do this. Marcel held the blade and did the skilled work of sharpening, and it was my task to turn the grindstone. The job seemed endless. The blade had a serrated edge and was very difficult to sharpen. From time to time, when we paused to pour fresh water into the trough of the grindstone, I could change the position of my arms, but it was very tedious, and very rough on the hands.

Blade-sharpening was the only thing on the farm which I hated doing, but it was vitally important. It was essential that from dawn on the first day of harvest everything worked as faultlessly as possible. You did all you could, but the hub of a cartwheel or the axle of a reaper could always break unexpectedly, and valuable harvest time was lost while the village blacksmith came out to repair it. Sometimes, when the knotting mechanism had jammed or the threshing machine had broken down, I remember they used to work all through the night by the light of acetylene lamps and torches to get it repaired for the next morning.

The total numbers of men working at the Oratoire during the harvest week, or *dépiquage*, as it was called, was between thirty and forty. They consisted of all the male members of the families of the other farmers, together with all the day-labourers who worked for them. Every day, at midday, everyone had to be fed; and in the evening, though the farmers generally went home, the labourers always stayed to eat a supper which they traditionally regarded as being part of their wages. This meant an enormous amount of work for Camille, but she was helped by the wives, daughters and sisters of the other farmers, and, when the harvest at the Oratoire was over, she would join them to work in the kitchen of whichever farm was next on the list.

Tarte au Jambon et à l'Ail

3 heads of garlic

50 g/2 oz duck fat

75 g/3 oz bayonne ham, thinly sliced

1 tablespoon chopped parsley

200 ml/7 fl oz milk

2 egg yolks

2 slices of white bread, crumbled

freshly ground pepper

250 g/9 oz Pâte à tarte *(see next recipe)*

Preheat the oven to 200ºC/400ºF/gas 6. Cut three 10 cm/4 in squares of foil. Place a head of garlic and one-quarter of the fat in the middle of each square and wrap tightly in the foil. Place in a roasting pan and bake in the preheated oven for 20–25 minutes, until soft.

Heat the rest of the fat in a frying pan and quickly fry the ham for about 10 seconds on each side, adding the parsley at the last moment.

To make the custard mixture, mix together the milk, egg yolks and breadcrumbs and season with a little pepper. Place in the fridge until needed.

Roll out the pastry into a circle to fit a 20 cm/8 in flan dish and line the dish with the pastry. Bake blind in the preheated oven for 10 minutes.

Meanwhile, unwrap and peel the garlic. Place it in the part-baked flan case together with the ham. Pour in the custard mixture and bake in the hot oven for 25 minutes. Serve hot.

Pâte à Tarte

SAVOURY FLAN PASTRY

250 g/9 oz plain flour, sifted

200 g/7 oz butter, softened

a pinch of salt

50 ml/2 fl oz water

2 egg yolks

Put the flour on the work surface and make a well in the centre. Put in all the other ingredients and mix with your fingertips at first, then with your fist to make a smooth dough. Roll the dough into a ball, wrap in cling film and leave to rest in the fridge for 30 minutes before using.

Gâteau de Riz aux Abricots

MOULDED RICE PUDDING WITH APRICOT COULIS—SERVES 4

100 g/4 oz long grain rice

750 ml/1¼ pt boiling milk

25 g/1 oz butter

a handful of raisins

a pinch of salt

75 g/3 oz sugar

4 egg yolks

Caramel

70 g/2½ oz sugar

100 ml/4 fl oz water

Apricot coulis

400 g/14 oz ripe apricots, quartered and stoned

100 g/4 oz caster sugar

1 teaspoon lemon juice

Preheat the oven to 190°C/375°F/gas 5. Boil 600 ml/1 pt water and blanch the rice for 2 minutes. Drain immediately and place in an ovenproof dish. Pour 500 ml/18 fl oz boiling milk on to the rice, add the butter, raisins, salt and 40 g/1½ oz sugar, mix well and bake in the preheated oven for 30 minutes.

Meanwhile, cook the sugar with the water until caramelized, pour into a 1.1 l/2 pt mould and rotate the mould to coat the inside with caramel.

In a bowl, mix the rest of the boiling milk with the egg yolks and the remaining sugar. Mix into the cooked rice, then pour into the caramelized mould. Stand the mould in a bain-marie and cook in the oven for another 30 minutes. Leave to cool, then chill until set.

Make the coulis: put the apricots in a saucepan with 150 ml/5 fl oz water, the sugar and lemon juice. Cover, bring to the boil, then reduce the heat and simmer for 5 minutes until the apricots are soft. Leave to cool, then purée and rub through a fine sieve. Unmould the pudding and pour the coulis around.

The day before harvest started, we had to kill all the chickens and ducks we would need during the week, and this meant slaughtering about thirty birds. It was quite a job, which needed at least two people to do it. The birds were bled to death, with one person holding the body, while the other held the head and made a quick cut in the outstretched neck. All the blood was carefully collected in a large dish, and Camille used to make a very good *sanquette* which we ate that night at supper. The chickens were dipped into a cauldron of boiling water, and were then plucked and gutted. When they were ready, they were wrapped in clean white cloths, put into baskets and lowered down the well to just above the water line to be kept cool and fresh until they were needed.

Sanquette de Poulet

COOKED CHICKEN BLOOD—SERVES 4

1 shallot, finely chopped

1 teaspoon chopped parsley

4 chickens, ready for killing

20 g/¾ oz duck fat

salt and freshly ground pepper

Put the shallot and parsley in a deep dish. When you kill the chickens, let the blood drip into the dish and leave it to coagulate.

Heat the fat in a frying pan until sizzling and put in the congealed blood, shallots and parsley. Cook for 30 seconds, turn over and cook for another 30 seconds. The *sanquette* should be slightly crispy on the outside and soft and pink in the centre. Season and eat hot.

The preparations for the *dépiquage* took about three or four days. In addition to getting the poultry ready and preparing all the vegetables, there was the crockery to think about. Plates and glasses which had been kept all year in the dining room cupboard had to be taken out and washed. Tables and trestles and benches had to be cleaned and scrubbed. The bottles of aperitif had to be checked and new ones bought if necessary; the wine had to be organized, and the menus arranged.

Camille relied heavily on her home-made hams and sausages to feed all the workers. All her *charcuterie* was excellent, but I was particularly fond of her chicken liver pâté and an unusual 'ham' which she prepared from a leg of lamb about a month before the harvest.

Gâteau de Foies de Volaille aux Câpres

CHICKEN LIVER PÂTÉ WITH CAPERS—SERVES 4

150 g/5 oz chicken livers

2 egg yolks

250 ml/9 fl oz milk

1 garlic clove, chopped

salt and freshly ground pepper

a pinch of nutmeg

20 g/¾ oz fresh breadcrumbs

1 tablespoon butter, softened, for greasing

Sauce

2 shallots, chopped

2 tablespoons butter

100 ml/4 fl oz dry white wine

200 ml/7 fl oz double cream

1–2 tablespoons capers, rinsed and drained

1 tablespoon chopped chives

Preheat the oven to 170°C/325°F/gas 3. Put the livers, egg yolks, milk, garlic and seasonings in a food processor or blender and purée for 1 minute until smooth and liquid. Pass through a sieve, then stir in the breadcrumbs. Butter four ramekins and fill with the liver mixture.

Place the ramekins in a roasting pan, half-fill with very hot water and bake in the oven for 20 minutes, until set.

To make the sauce, sweat the shallots in the butter until soft. Pour in the wine and reduce it almost completely over high heat. Pour in the cream, add the capers and cook gently until the sauce coats the back of a spoon. Unmould the gâteaux on to serving plates and pour the sauce around. Sprinkle with chives and serve hot.

Jambon de Mouton

LAMB CURED LIKE HAM

3 kg/6½ lb leg of lamb
20 g/¾ oz saltpetre (optional)
600 g/1¼ lb coarse sea salt
100 g/4 oz cane sugar
150 g/5 oz black peppercorns, coarsely ground
enough wood ashes to fill a wooden wine crate

Trim the lamb of any fat and press firmly to squeeze out the blood.

Mix together the saltpetre if you are using it, salt, sugar and pepper. Take a cloth large enough to enclose the leg of lamb and sprinkle the mixture evenly over the cloth. Put the lamb in the middle of the cloth and fold over the four corners so that the salt mixture covers the leg completely.

Put half the wood ashes in a wooden box (a wine crate is ideal) and put in the lamb. Cover with the rest of the ashes and press down firmly.

Leave in a cold, dry place for 30 days, then take out the lamb and wipe it thoroughly. Wrap in a cotton bag and hang from the ceiling to cut off slices as and when you wish.

For the first day or two, the main harvesting work took place in the fields. A pair of cows, their heads shaded against the sun by Marcel's brightly coloured veils, and with long driving reins attached to their ears, drew the rumbling reaper and binder round and round the cornfields. The cows walked with a cumbrous, rolling motion, quite unlike the piston-like plunge of horses, and behind them the revolving wooden sails of the reaper pushed the golden sea of wheat against the blade I had laboriously helped to sharpen.

The cut corn was carried upwards to the binding mechanism, to be tied and knotted into sheaves which were dropped out at intervals on the opposite side of the machine. Six or seven men followed the reaper to gather the sheaves and stand them together in stooks. When I helped to do this, I was always waiting for the exciting moment when a hare would run out of the corn with all its young and we would make a mental note of their hiding place in the next field or wood. Everyone knew then where to find a hare when the shooting season opened in September.

RIGHT: CAILLES SUR LA CENDRE (P. 118)

Sometimes, also, quails would suddenly come fluttering out of the corn and start to run across the stubble. They had eaten so much corn and were so fat that they could not fly. We chased them on foot, and in a few moments, caught them with our hands quite easily. It was the time when they were at their plumpest and tastiest, and we would take them back to the farm for Camille to cook for our supper, sometimes roasting them and sometimes cooking them in little paper parcels which we called *sarcophages* (coffins).

Cailles Sur La Cendre

QUAILS COOKED OVER THE EMBERS—SERVES 4

4 quails, drawn
2 sheets of greaseproof paper
50 g/2 oz duck fat
salt and freshly ground pepper
50 ml/2 fl oz armagnac

Fold the sheets of greaseproof paper to make a double thickness and brush with duck fat. Cut each in half to give you 4 squares large enough to enclose a quail.

Season the quails, put a few drops of armagnac inside each one and wrap in the greaseproof paper, folding over the edges to seal.

Prepare a good log fire, where the flames have died down and the wood glows red. Place the quails on a grill over the embers and cook until the underside of the paper becomes brown, then turn over the parcels and cook the other side in the same way.

The total cooking time will be about 6 minutes. Serve the quails in their paper parcels and eat them with your fingers.

The next stage in the harvest was the arrival of the threshing machine and the steam engine on the flat lower ground at the back of the Oratoire. The steam engine is one of my earlier memories, as its place was later taken by my uncle Capuron's Massey-Ferguson tractor, but it stays in my mind as a vivid link with the old farming methods. Its long, iron belly was bound round with brightly polished brass bands, its wheels and the curved spokes of the two large flywheels were painted red, and its tall funnel and roaring furnace gave out a feeling of heat, strength and power.

The threshing machine, on the other hand, was made of wood; it was painted light pink and was bigger than the steam engine. It was a vast, clumsily built box with cupboards in it, and with belted wheels which stuck out at all sorts of unexpected places. It was rather like an outsize stage-coach from an early American western. The engine fire was lit at about 5 o'clock in the morning; two hours later, the safety valve would be hissing with steam, there would be a strong smell of hot iron, the engineer would push a lever, the piston and the governor would start, the long leather driving-belt connecting the engine to the threshing machine would shudder and shake into life. Over the next four or five days, cartload after cartload of sheaves was brought to the side of the machine to be rolled, shaken and blown, until sack after sack of grain was filled and carried away, and a river of straw was loosed from the ceaselessly clattering wooden tongues at the back. The noise and the dust and the labour never once slackened.

Under the hot Gascon sun, the machine seemed insatiable, both for wheat and for men. It needed about thirteen or fourteen pairs of arms to work it and feed it. In addition, there were about five men who did nothing but heave the heavy sacks of grain on to their backs and carry them up the ladder to the loft. There must have been several hundred of these sacks every harvest, and the work of the *porteurs* was incredibly hard. Once in the loft, the sacks were emptied, then taken down again to be refilled. Gradually the golden mountain of wheat grew higher and higher, and as it did so, we played and rolled in it, and threw ourselves at it, letting it pour over our faces and bury us. We pretended it was the sea we had never seen.

At midday sharp, all the harvesters came back to the Oratoire for lunch. The trestle tables and benches were arranged on the open ground near the wine press, and the tables were covered with clean, white sheets. At each place there was a napkin, a glass and a pile of four or five earthenware plates, one for each course. Only the men sat down to eat. The women, all wearing wide-brimmed hats to protect themselves from the sun, were on their feet the whole time, cooking and pouring and carrying. Some of the harvesters just wore their berets, but most of them had immense straw hats, very yellow and glazed, with often a handkerchief or a large cabbage leaf tucked in at the back to hang down and protect the back of the neck. As soon as everyone had sat down, aperitifs, which included some that Camille had made herself such as a *vin d'orange* or cherry *guignolet*, besides the more usual Byrrh, Dubonnet and Saint Raphael, were poured, and these were followed by wine.

Vin d'Orange

1 l/1¾ pt white wine

zests of 2 large oranges

250 g/9 oz sugar

100 ml/4 fl oz armagnac

Mix everything together in a large pot, cover and leave to infuse for 12 days before drinking.

All down the middle of the table were bottles of red and white wine and large, round loaves of bread. After the first glasses of wine came the cutting of bread and the hubbub of talk. The topmost plate in front of each man was always a deep one for the soup, and as each harvester finished his soup, he always made what we call a *chabrot*, by mixing some red wine with the last spoonful of broth left at the bottom of his bowl, then lifting it up to his lips to drink. The next plate was for the *charcuterie*, the next for the chicken, the next for the *rôti*, and the last for the dessert. Whenever a bottle on the table was finished, it was immediately filled up from one of the big wine barrels propped up on nearby trestles.

The *dépiquage* menus were always much the same, though there might be slight variations during the course of the week. Every meal included a *poule au pot*, the *bouillon* of which often provided the soup. As a change we might sometimes have a bean or vegetable soup, but there was always a chicken. Tradition on this point was inflexible. The men were never tired of eating *poule au pot*, which was often served with Gascon dumplings called *miques*. It was the custom, and they would never have wanted to change it. There was some variety in the terrines, pâtés and sausages, and the roast might change from duck to turkey on certain days; the salads might vary too, with tomatoes, gherkins or cucumbers. But it was, after all, a basic meal for working harvesters, not lunch at a restaurant.

Poule au Pot

STUFFED CHICKEN IN THE POT WITH STUFFED CABBAGE &
POACHED BRIOCHE—SERVES 8

1 boiling chicken

Stuffing
100 g/4 oz damp breadcrumbs
100 g/4 oz bayonne ham, chopped
2 eggs
a pinch of cinnamon
100 g/4 oz chicken livers, fried in fat and chopped
2 garlic cloves, chopped
25 g/1 oz shallots, chopped
salt and freshly ground pepper

Stock
5 l/8¾ pt cold water
3 onions
6 carrots
4 leeks
2 celery stalks
2 cloves
1 bouquet garni
15 peppercorns
6 garlic cloves, peeled and left whole
2 kg/4½ lb veal bones, chopped

Mix together all the stuffing ingredients and stuff the chicken. Sew up the neck
and body openings with a needle and thread. Put the chicken in a very large
pot with the cold water and bring to the boil. Simmer for 10 minutes, skimming
the surface carefully, then add all the vegetables, seasonings and the veal
bones. Simmer, uncovered, for 2½ hours.

Brioche
20 g/¾ oz fresh yeast
100 ml/4 fl oz lukewarm water

700 g/1½ lb plain flour

100 g/4 oz duck fat

3 eggs

a pinch of salt and sugar

Dilute the yeast in the water, then add all the other ingredients and mix well to make a smooth dough. Shape into a ball, cover with a cloth and leave to rise for 1 hour. An hour before eating the chicken, put the brioche into the pot with the chicken, cover and cook for 30 minutes, then turn it over and cook for another 30 minutes. Remove the brioche from the pot with a slotted spoon and serve it instead of bread.

Stuffed Cabbage

1 savoy cabbage

500 g/1 lb 2 oz Farce à tout faire *(see next recipe)*

Blanch the 8 largest cabbage leaves in boiling water. Lay a clean muslin cloth on the table and arrange the cabbage leaves overlapping like a rosette. Put the stuffing in the middle and wrap it in the leaves like a ball. Enclose it all in the muslin, tie the top and cook with the chicken for 1 hour.

Boudins Verts (Green Sausages)

50 g/2 oz plain flour

4 eggs

150 ml/5 fl oz milk

1 onion, finely chopped

20 g/¾ oz duck fat

25 g/1 oz bayonne ham, diced

2 garlic cloves, chopped

1 tablespoon chopped parsley

100 g/4 oz spinach, cooked and chopped

1 teaspoon chopped tarragon

1 tablespoon chopped chives

salt and freshly ground pepper

75 cm/30 in sausage casing

Mix together the flour, eggs and milk and leave to rest for 15 minutes.

Meanwhile, sweat the chopped onion in the duck fat for 5 minutes. Mix together the ham, garlic, parsley, spinach, tarragon and chives. Add the cooked onion and mix into the milk mixture. Season to taste. Put the mixture into the sausage casing and tie at 15 cm/6 in intervals to make about 5 sausages. Heat a saucepan of water to 90°C/194°F, put in the *boudins* and poach for 15 minutes.

Milhas (cornmeal porridge)
750 ml/1¼ pt milk
100 g/4 oz cornmeal
15 g/½ oz duck fat
salt and freshly ground pepper

Bring the milk to the boil in a saucepan, then sprinkle in the cornmeal like rain and stir with a wooden spoon. Add the duck fat, season to taste and cook over a low heat for 5 minutes. Pour the broth into a tureen. Serve the chicken on a large dish with all the garnishes on top and beside it, and leave the broth on the table at the same time, so that everyone can help themselves.

Farce à Tout Faire

ALL-PURPOSE STUFFING

600 g/1¼ lb pork fat
600 g/1¼ lb lean pork
100 g/4 oz chicken livers
1 garlic clove, peeled and left whole
1 tablespoon chopped parsley
75 g/3 oz fresh white breadcrumbs
salt and freshly ground pepper
100 ml/4 fl oz dry white wine
25 ml/1 fl oz armagnac

Mince the meats, garlic and parsley in a mincer. Place in a food processor and process at a low speed until smooth. Add the breadcrumbs, season to taste and process for 3 minutes. Pour in the wine and armagnac and process for another 5 minutes, until the stuffing is very smooth.

Mique à la Royale

DUMPLING WITH KIDNEYS & MOREL SAUCE—SERVES 4

20 g/¾ oz yeast

75 ml/3 fl oz warm water (30°C/86°F)

500 g/1 lb 2 oz plain flour

3 eggs

100 g/4 oz butter, softened

a pinch of sugar

a pinch of salt

3 l/5½ pt chicken or beef stock (home-made or made from a cube)

2 veal kidneys

50 ml/2 fl oz oil

Sauce

20 morels

3 shallots, chopped

50 g/2 oz butter

100 ml/4 fl oz madeira

100 ml/4 fl oz port

200 ml/7 fl oz cream

To make the *mique*, mix the yeast with the lukewarm water, then add the flour, eggs, 50 g/2 oz of the butter, sugar and salt. Knead thoroughly and leave the *mique* to rise in a warm place.

Heat the stock. Wrap the *mique* in a piece of cheesecloth sprinkled with flour and poach in the hot broth for 30 minutes, turning it over after 15 minutes.

Cut the kidneys into medium slices and fry lightly in the oil for 2 minutes on each side. Transfer to a warmed dish and keep warm while you make the sauce.

Put the morels in a saucepan with the chopped shallots and butter and sweat until soft. Add half the madeira and port and reduce completely. Add the remaining madeira and port and reduce by half. Add the cream and reduce by half. Pour the sauce over the kidneys.

Cut the *mique* into 1 cm/½ in slices and fry in the remaining 50 g/2 oz butter until light golden on both sides. Pour the kidneys and sauce over the *mique* and serve.

There were usually about five or six women from other farms who came to help Camille. Even in the kitchen there was no escape from the July heat; the shutters were held half-closed by their long hooks, but the excluded sunlight was replaced by the heat of the log fire, which was built up to boil the big iron soup cauldron, and to roast the eight or nine chickens and ducks which slowly turned on two or three separate banks of spits. In addition to the main fire, the iron cooking range was also called into action, and this added to the general heat.

All the food was carried down on trays to the tables outside, and all the dirty plates had to be carried up again. By the end of the meal, there was an apparent infinity of dishes, plates, glasses and cutlery to be washed up, and, of course, there was no running hot water or washing-up liquid. When the washing-up water became too greasy, it was never thrown away, I remember; the scraps left on the plates were tipped into it and it was kept on one side to be fed to the pigs. Nothing on the farm was ever wasted.

In the evening, when the din of the threshing machine mercifully stopped, and the never-ending clouds of dust began at last to settle, the peasant farmers went home and only the labourers stayed for the evening supper which was served about 7 o'clock. The men left at about 9 o'clock, but the women worked on for about another two or three hours before they could go to bed. All the linen had to be washed, dried and ironed every night, because otherwise there would simply not be enough sheets and napkins for the next day, and at that time nobody in Saint Puy had ever seen or heard of a paper napkin.

For Camille, and the women who had been helping her, the end of the harvest at the Oratoire only meant that the whole business would start again the following morning at another farm. For us children, however, the silence and the calm seemed always rather sad. The harvesters worked hard, but there was a gaiety and a happiness about them which I shall always remember, and after they had gone, the farm seemed very empty. They all talked in patois, never in French, but they had a wonderful fund of stories and jokes and memories; they laughed a lot, and were great singers of songs. They drank a good deal of wine, of course; the bottles were being filled up all the time during the midday meal, but I do not think it was just the wine which made them happy. Their gaiety went deeper than that, and now that the old harvests have gone, the gaiety and the songs have gone as well.

Some of the wheat piled up in the loft was used to make the bread which my grandparents would eat during the ensuing year. Marcel would deliver about a dozen sacks of wheat to Monsieur Trille, the Saint Puy baker, and receive in return a quantity of tickets, each one valid for a loaf of a certain weight. During the year all Camille's bread would be 'bought' with one of these tickets. The baker milled the flour and baked the bread, but kept a proportion of the wheat for his own profit. No money changed hands; it was a very ancient system of bartering.

The bakery was near the fire station; it had a little balcony and a window with a curved top over the door. Monsieur Trille wore blue trousers, a little skull-cap and a vest which just covered his chest; he was hot, half-naked and pale. His shop, too, was hot with the heat of the oven in the back room, but it was filled with the good smell of bread, croissants and cakes.

I have always been fascinated by bread; you cannot make it well if you have no instinct for it. To make bread, you have first to love it. The greatest joy in bread-making comes when you are able to tell, just by the feel and the look of the dough, that the magic moment has arrived when the degree of fermentation is absolutely right; you can never learn this from a book.

Bread, together with soup, was the basic food of the peasants. They ate it with everything. Crunching the crust of a good bread always excites your appetite, and even a good sauce is better if you eat it with a bit of bread. In Gascony we have quite a number of different local breads: the *pain épis*, shaped to look like an ear of wheat, the *méture*, cooked in cabbage leaves, the *fougasse*, which serves to test the heat of a wood-fired oven and several others given here.

Pain Gascon

GASCON BREAD

20 g/¾ oz yeast
600 ml/1 pt warm water (30°C/86°F)
1 kg/2¼ lb strong white flour, plus extra for dusting
20 g/¾ oz salt

Mix the yeast into the water, add the flour and mix well by hand for 10 minutes. Leave to rest for 20 minutes, then work the dough again for another 10 minutes. Add the salt and knead for a final 5 minutes. Leave to rise in a warm place for 1 hour. Cut the dough into 5. Roll the pieces into balls, place on a lightly floured baking tray, cover with a light cloth and leave to rise again for 2½ hours.

Preheat the oven to 250°C/500°F/gas 10. Sprinkle the bread with flour, slash the top with a razor blade and bake in the hot oven for 30 minutes. Sprinkle a little water into the oven to make some steam when you put in the bread and 3 minutes before the end of baking.

Pain Tordu du Gers

'CORKSCREW' LOAF

40 g/1½ oz fresh yeast
1 l/1¾ pt warm water (30°C/86°F)
1.15 kg/2½ lb strong white flour, plus extra for dusting
400 g/14 oz rye flour
35 g/1¼ oz salt

In a large bowl, dissolve the yeast in the lukewarm water, add the 2 flours and mix well for 5 minutes. Add the salt and mix for 2 more minutes. Cover with a cloth and leave to rise in a warm place (24°C/75°F) for 45 minutes.

Cut the dough lengthways into 4 and roll each piece into a 40 cm/16 in length. Sprinkle a little flour over the top and twist the ends of the loaves twice, like a corkscrew. Place on a floured baking tray and leave to rise in a warm place for 30 minutes.

Preheat the oven to 230°C/450°F/gas 8. Place a small dish of water in the bottom of the oven to produce some steam. Bake the loaf in the hot oven for 40 minutes, or until it sounds hollow when you tap the bottom with your knuckles. Leave to cool on a wire rack.

Pain a l'huile

OIL BREAD

25 g/1 oz fresh yeast
600 ml/1 pt warm water (30°C/86°F)
100 ml/4 fl oz oil
1 kg/2¼ lb strong white flour, plus extra for dusting
25 g/1 oz salt

Dissolve the yeast in the water, then add the oil and flour and mix for 5 minutes. Add the salt and mix for 5 minutes. Add the salt and mix for 2 more minutes. Leave to rest in a warm place (24°C/75°F) for 40 minutes.

Cut the dough into 350 g/12 oz pieces and roll into *baguette* shapes. Place on a floured baking tray, cover with a light cloth and leave to rise for 30 minutes.

Preheat the oven to 230ºC/450ºF/gas 8. Put a dish of water in the bottom of the oven to create some steam, or throw a little water into the oven. Bake the bread for 25 minutes. To make walnut bread, add 200 g/7 oz walnuts to the dough.

Pain Baguette

FRENCH BREAD STICKS

40 g/1½ oz fresh yeast
850 ml/1½ pt warm water (30ºC/86ºF)
1.5 kg/3¼ lb strong flour, plus extra for dusting
25 g/1 oz salt

Combine the yeast and water in the bowl of an electric mixer. Add the flour and mix for 4 minutes. Add the salt and mix for 1 more minute, then cover the dough and leave to rest for 1 hour.

Divide the dough into 250 g/9 oz portions and roll into long *baguettes*. Place on a floured baking tray, cover with a light cloth and leave to rest for 1 hour. Preheat the oven to 230ºC/450ºF/gas 8. Turn the bread over, sprinkle a little flour op top and slash it in 3 places with a razor blade.

Bake for 30 minutes. Sprinkle a little water into the oven to make some steam when you put in the bread and 5 minutes before the end of baking.

With the harvest safely in by the end of July, August was a month when the work in the fields became easier, although for Camille, who was in charge of the poultry, it was a busy time. The poultry yard, the *basse cour*, was at one end of the farm, below the bedroom window and near the well. Built against the house wall were cages for the ducks which had been specially selected for fattening; next to these were the rows of rabbit hutches which housed about two hundred long-eared, black-eyed rabbits. At the very head of the population of the *basse cour*, surrounded by all their hens, ranked the three or four fine cocks, which my grandmother always selected very carefully, never hesitating to slaughter any cockerel which was not quite up to standard. I remember one cock in particular who was superb, and could crow like a trumpeter; but he was so fierce that it was almost impossible to get near him.

The guinea fowl were not much better; they were wild, exotic birds who screeched all day, and would fly up into the branches of the trees when you tried to catch them. They were at their best in August, and, because Camille fed them on grain and maize, they were almost as good to eat as pheasant. They were usually sold to the dealers so we did not often eat them at the farm. When we did, we regarded them as a great luxury, reserved for important family occasions and *jours de fête*; then Camille would prepare them with oranges or garlic and serve them on savoury croutons.

Fricassée de Pintade à l'Ail

FRICASSÉE OF GUINEA FOWL WITH GARLIC—SERVES 4

1.2 kg/2¾ lb guinea fowl
salt and freshly ground pepper
75 g/3 oz duck fat
15 garlic cloves, unpeeled
1 sprig of thyme
4 chicken livers
25 g/1 oz shallots, finely chopped
4 slices of toasted french bread
100 ml/4 fl oz dry white wine
20 g/¾ oz butter

Preheat the oven to 200ºC/400ºF/gas 6. Cut the guinea fowl into 8 pieces and season with salt and pepper. Heat the duck fat in a flameproof casserole, put in the guinea fowl and seal all over. Add the garlic and thyme and cook in the preheated oven for 25–30 minutes, until the juices run clear when you prick the guinea fowl with a fork.

Transfer the cooked guinea fowl to a dish and keep in a warm place. Peel the cooked garlic and set aside. Chop the chicken livers and mix with the chopped shallots; season to taste. Spread this mixture on to the toasted bread and cook in the oven for about 8 minutes until the liver is cooked.

Pour off the fat from the roasting pan, add the wine and reduce by nine-tenths over high heat. Add 100 ml/4 fl oz water and reduce again by two-thirds, then beat in the butter. Check the seasoning.

Put the croûtons on a dish, arrange the guinea fowl on top with the garlic around it, and pour over the sauce.

There were also usually four or five turkeys and a dozen grey tall-necked, orange-beaked geese, which, as soon as they saw my grandmother coming, would advance on her in a tight group like a little army of robots, moving mechanically over the ground and uttering their strange, menacing, guttural cries as they approached. It was the time when the hens were laying the most eggs; these now had to be collected at least twice a day.

Chicken was plentiful in the summer months, providing the principal dish at the *dépiquage* and making for delicious Sunday lunches; among Camille's other midsummer occupations was the making and bottling of *conserves* of chicken which would be kept in the store cupboard and eaten during the winter.

There were about a hundred ducks on the farm, and it was my job, after the harvest, to drive them out to feed in the stubble fields, and to make certain that none of them got lost. It was a difficult thing to do, because ducks are not as obedient as geese, and they rush all over the field in every direction, just as they please. I was armed with a long stick, with which I had to try to keep them together. It meant a lot of running about, but I was always very proud of the fact that I never lost a bird, though I was never as quick at counting them as my grandmother was.

The spring ducklings were now fully grown, and Camille had to select the ones she would fatten and force-feed in the late autumn, so that they and their livers would be in fine condition for Christmas. The others were ready for eating. Though we did not often eat duck, we did occasionally have it for lunch on Sundays in summer, when it made a pleasant change from the habitual chicken, especially when Camille cooked it with olives or fruit. The summer was also the time when she made her duck *terrines*.

Terrine de Canard

TERRINE OF DUCK—SERVES 4

400 g/14 oz boneless duck leg meat
400 g/14 oz hand and belly of pork
150 g/5 oz chicken livers
25 ml/1 fl oz armagnac
25 ml/1 fl oz madeira

50 ml/2 fl oz dry white wine

salt and freshly ground pepper

180 g/6 oz pig's caul

250 g/9 oz tinned foie gras mousse, cut into 4

Preheat the oven to 180°C/350°F/gas 4. Finely mince together the duck, pork and livers. Add all the alcohol, season and mix well.

Line a terrine with the caul, leaving an overhang. Put in half the duck and pork mixture and top with the foie gras. Spread over the remaining mixture and fold over the caul to wrap it. Place the terrine in a bain-marie and cook in the preheated oven for 1½ hours. The terrine will shrink during the cooking. Leave to cool in the mould before turning it out.

Canard aux Olives

ROAST DUCK WITH OLIVES—SERVES 4

1 duck, about 2–2.5 kg/4½–5½ lb

50 g/2 oz duck fat

salt and freshly ground pepper

200 g/7 oz black and green olives, stoned and blanched

100 ml/4 fl oz dry white wine

Preheat the oven to 230°C/450°F/gas 8. Season the duck inside and out, smear with fat and roast in the hot oven for 30 minutes. Drain off the fat and add the olives to the roasting pan. Roast for another 15 minutes.

Transfer the duck and olives to a serving dish. Pour the wine into the roasting pan, reduce by two-thirds and pour it over the duck.

Canard aux Pêches

ROAST DUCK WITH PEACHES—SERVES 4

1 duck, about 2–2.5 kg/4½–5½ lb

salt and freshly ground pepper

2 large peaches

300 ml/½ pt dry white wine

50 g/2 oz sugar

2 tablespoons armagnac

50 ml/2 fl oz wine vinegar

Preheat the oven to 230°C/450°F/gas 8. Season the duck inside and out and roast in the hot oven for about 55 minutes. Peel, stone and halve the peaches. Heat the wine and sugar, put in the peaches and poach until tender. Set aside.

When the duck is cooked, transfer it to a serving dish and pour the armagnac into the cavity. Cover the duck with foil and keep warm.

Pour off the fat in the roasting pan, then pour in the vinegar and reduce completely, taking care that it does not burn. Add the wine in which you poached the peaches and reduce by half. Check the seasoning. Slice the peaches and arrange them around the duck. Pour over the sauce and serve.

Canard au Sang

DUCK WITH BLOOD SAUCE—SERVES 4

1 mature duck cut into 8 pieces, blood reserved if possible

salt and freshly ground pepper

2–3 tablespoons plain flour

100 g/4 oz duck fat

500 g/1 lb 2 oz onions, sliced

50 g/2 oz garlic cloves, crushed

1 bouquet garni

75 g/3 oz smoked bacon, diced

1.2 l/2 pt red wine

blood from the duck, or 100 g/4 oz duck or chicken livers

Preheat the oven to 200°C/400°F/gas 6. Season the duck pieces and roll them in the flour. Heat the duck fat in a large frying pan and fry the duck until golden on both sides. Use a slotted spoon to transfer the duck to a casserole.

Fry the onions in the same fat until golden, then add the crushed garlic, bouquet garni and bacon and pour in the wine. Bring to the boil and pour the contents of the frying pan into the casserole, so that the wine covers the duck. Cook in the oven for about 1 hour, until the duck is tender (check by inserting a large fork into the flesh; it should meet with no resistance).

Skim the fat off the surface of the sauce with a large spoon, remove the bouquet garni, then pour one-quarter of the sauce into a blender and switch on. Gradually drip in the blood or add the poultry livers and purée until very smooth. Pass the sauce through a sieve into the casserole, check the seasoning and heat until everything is very hot but not boiling.

Poultry were killed in different traditional ways. Guinea fowl were always hanged; pigeons were drowned; and chickens, ducks, geese and turkeys had their throats cut. And in August, Camille gelded some of the young cockerels so that they could eventually be sold as fat Christmas capons. It was an operation she performed with considerable dexterity. She held the bird firmly between her knees, plucked a few feathers away, made a quick incision with a razor blade, pulled out the testicles and sewed up the wound with a needle and thread, before finally cutting the wattles away from the bird's neck. The capons were a bit under the weather for a while; they had, after all, undergone quite a serious operation. But they usually recovered and Camille looked after them carefully and fed them well, until in the end they weighed about six or seven pounds each. They could take no more interest in the hens, and so the only thing left for them to think about was food.

I remember another more mysterious operation which my grandmother used to carry out on the young ducks at this time of year – she used to make a little slit in their tongues and extract something that looked very like a small worm. Perhaps that is what it was. It is not an operation I have seen done anywhere else, nor have I ever heard anyone mention it. Camille used to put a bit of salt on the wound after it was over and none of the ducks ever seemed any the worse for it.

August was also the main month for fruit picking. At the Oratoire we had peaches, apricots, almonds, quinces, plums, medlars, apples, strawberries and raspberries. Among the vines there were always a few rows of muscat dessert grapes, and Camille hung bunches from the beams in the passageway so that they could turn into the sweet, dried currants we would eat in December and January. Marcel also grew quite an important crop of melons, and I also remember the big, delicious, yellow eating apples which Camille used to keep in crates in the *chambre obscure*, the dark larder next to the dining room. The first ceps were also picked and hung to dry in the kitchen fireplace.

Everyone took part in the picking, and most of the fruit was sold to my uncle's shop. The rest went to the dealers who called regularly at the farm with a lorry, and who also bought Camille's eggs and poultry besides the vegetables and fruit. It saved her from going to Fleurance market, if she was busy, though she got less money this way.

We usually sold all the perfect melons, and so kept only the damaged ones for ourselves, those which were so ripe they had split open. But, though they looked rather messy, these were the fruit which had the best and sweetest taste of all. Sometimes we would just eat the melons *à la croque-sel* (peeled, cut into squares and sprinkled with a touch of salt) or Camille might make a melon tart. Strawberries she marinated in the sparkling white monluc wine which was made at Saint Puy, and sometimes she would build up a fantastic *confiture de célibataire* with lots of coloured layers, each layer being made from a different fruit.

Fraises au Vin de Monluc et au Poivre

STRAWBERRIES IN SPARKLING WINE WITH PEPPER

1 kg/2¼ lb strawberries

150 g/5 oz caster sugar

1 l/1¾ pt sparkling white wine

coarsely ground black pepper

Put the strawberries in a bowl and sprinkle over the sugar. Leave to macerate for at least 30 minutes. Just before serving, pour over the wine and grind on black pepper to taste, making sure that it is not too finely ground.

Tarte au Melon

MELON FLAN—SERVES 4

250 g/9 oz Pâte à tarte sucrée *(see next recipe)*

1 large charentais melon

200 g/7 oz sugar

5 eggs

25 g/1 oz arrowroot

250 ml/9 fl oz milk

Preheat the oven to 220°C/425°F/gas 7. Line a 25 cm/10 in flan dish with the pastry and bake blind for 15 minutes.

Peel and slice the melon. Make a syrup with 75 g/3 oz sugar and 2 tablespoons water and poach the melon slices for 1 minute. Drain and pat dry. Set aside.

Prepare the filling by mixing together the eggs, arrowroot and 75 g/3 oz sugar. Beat well, then mix in the milk.

Pour the filling into the pastry case and lay the melon on top. Bake for 25 minutes, then sprinkle the top of the flan with the remaining sugar and glaze under a hot grill for about 8 minutes, or until the sugar has caramelized. Leave to cool in the dish and serve cold.

Pâte à Tarte Sucrée

SWEET FLAN PASTRY

250 g/9 oz plain flour, sifted

100 g/4 oz butter, softened

100 g/4 oz icing sugar

a pinch of salt

1 whole egg

2 egg yolks

Put the flour on the work surface and make a well in the centre. Put in all the other ingredients and begin by mixing gently with your fingertips, gradually drawing in the flour. When all the ingredients are mixed, work the dough harder with the heel of your hand. Roll the dough into a ball, wrap in a cloth and leave to rest in the fridge for 1 hour before using.

Soupe de Fruits au Vin Rouge

SUMMER FRUITS IN RED WINE

1 l/1¾ pt red wine

½ cinnamon stick

10 black peppercorns

150 g/5 oz sugar

4 small ripe peaches, skinned

100 g/4 oz cherries, stoned

100 g/4 oz raspberries

100 g/4 oz strawberries

Put the wine, cinnamon, peppercorns and sugar in a saucepan, boil for 3 minutes, then take the pan off the heat and add the peaches and cherries. Cover the pan and leave to cool.

When the liquid is cold, remove the cinnamon, add the raspberries and strawberries, leave to marinate for 2 hours, then serve.

August was also the time for harvesting the haricots, and for laying them out in their pods in the *chambre obscure* to become dry enough to thresh in the autumn. It was the time, too, for bottling fruit in armagnac and for making aperitifs, and also *conserves* of vegetables. This is an art which is rather forgotten today, when there are so many freezers and frozen foods; but in those days we looked on preserved vegetables as being an important part of our winter diet.

The sun of a Gascon summer is pitilessly hot, and August was also a month of pleasures and festivities, well earned after everybody's gruelling labour at harvest time. Marcel now had time to go out with his gun and his ferrets; we could enjoy idyllic fishing picnics in the cool shade by the side of the river; and there was the summer festival of the Assumption on 15th August. If my uncle and aunt or my parents came to lunch at the farm on this festival day, Camille might cook a shoulder of lamb *à la boulangère*, which she regarded as being another ideal dish for a *fête*, when there were more people than usual to eat it.

Epaule d'Agneau à la Boulangère

SHOULDER OF LAMB WITH POTATOES—SERVES 6

1 shoulder of lamb, about 1.8 kg/4 lb

salt and freshly ground pepper

6 garlic cloves, slivered

150 g/5 oz duck fat

2 large onions, sliced

700 g/1½ lb potatoes, thinly sliced

2 teaspoons fresh thyme, or ½ teaspoon dried

Preheat the oven to 200ºC/400ºF/gas 6. Season the lamb, inserting slivers of garlic into the meat. Heat 100 g/4 oz duck fat in a roasting pan, put in the lamb and roast in the preheated oven for 40 minutes, basting frequently.

Fry the onions in the remaining duck fat until golden brown. Remove the lamb and make a layer of potatoes in the roasting pan. Spread the onions on top, then make another layer of potatoes and add 100 ml/4 fl oz water. Sprinkle the thyme over the potatoes. Put the lamb on top and roast for another 30–35 minutes, until the potatoes are cooked, basting the meat and potatoes from time to time. Season to taste and serve.

On 21st August, Marcel and I celebrated our birthdays, both of which, as I have mentioned, fell on the same day. This was yet another *fête*, and again the Capurons and other friends would join us for a long lunch eaten in the dining room, and Camille would kill and stuff one of the turkeys. For dessert she would make a flaky Gascon *croustade* of apples, which she cooked in the *four de campagne* all covered over with glowing embers from the wood fire, using, in fact, the technique described in the old cookery books of the 17th- and 18th-centuries as *feu dessus, feu dessous*, 'heat above and heat below'. The making of the *pastis* pastry for the *croustade* is quite complicated, and you may prefer to use bought filo pastry, which is quite acceptable.

Croustade aux Pommes Caramélisées

A FLAKY CROUSTADE OF CARAMELIZED APPLES—SERVES 4

2 balls of Pastis *(see* Croustade de confit de canard, *page 35)*

6 eating apples, peeled, cored and sliced

100 g/4 oz lard or clarified butter, melted

200 g/7 oz sugar

50 ml/2 fl oz armagnac

Leave the *pastis* to rest at room temperature for 3–6 hours, until soft but not sticky. In a saucepan, melt 50 g/2 oz lard or butter and cook the apples very lightly with 75 g/3 oz sugar and the armagnac. Drain and leave to cool.

Preheat the oven to 220°C/425°F/gas 7. Stretch one *pastis* ball as described on page 35–6 and leave it to dry a little. Then, with a pastry brush or plant mister, sprinkle some of the melted fat like rain all over the stretched pastry. Dust with 40 g/1½ oz sugar and trim off the thick part of the pastry from the edge.

Butter a 25 cm/10 in flan tin and dust with 20 g/¾ oz sugar. Cut three circles out of the pastry, keeping the finest for the top layer. Put one in the flan tin, place on another and top with the third pastry circle. Arrange the apples on top.

Clean any pieces of pastry and sugar off the tablecloth, then put on the second ball of pastry and stretch it in the same way as the first. Cut it into 15 cm/6 in triangles and crinkle them up to form small mounds, like crumpled chiffon scarves. Pile these little mounds on the apples, sprinkle with more butter and the remaining sugar and bake for about 20 minutes, until the top is golden and

the sugar has caramelized. Serve warm. This *croustade* is also delicious made with pears, cooked quinces or prunes, as one sharing dish or individual portions.

Everybody enjoyed Marcel's birthday. He was always good-natured and kind to us children, and I think, on the whole, we behaved well with him. When we were very small, if we woke in the night, it was always Marcel who heard us crying and came along to see what the matter was and get us off to sleep again.

At first, I remember, he tried to keep our exuberance in check by acquiring a *martinet*, a little whip with leather thongs. It seems he must have used it once, because we decided we did not like it, and one day, when there was no one at home, we cut the thongs off with a pair of scissors, and put the whip back in the cupboard. Next time Marcel tried to apply it, he was so taken aback by the ingenuity of our revenge that he never had the heart to buy another one. Instead, in moments of exceptional fury, he took to wrenching his beret off his head, and, with one dramatic sweeping movement of his arm, would bring it down with a thwack across the bottom of any child who had not scampered away from him fast enough. But I must say that we were never really afraid of him.

Marcel was a great swearer, however. I do not think he meant any harm by it, but he could go on swearing all day if he felt it was necessary. He always swore in patois, never in French; but it upset Camille nevertheless and pained her terribly. His repertory of oaths was wide, imaginative, and blasphemous.

The worst examples arose when Camille had asked him to do something rather troublesome, like feeding the ducks or fetching the cows, just when he was about to leave for the café or go fishing. Then a cow would not go into the stable, or a duck into its cage, or the pig would escape from the sty, and Marcel would curse and curse away until the volleys of oaths became so torrential that Camille had to open the bedroom window, and call down to him to be quiet. 'Just listen to him!' she would exclaim to us, 'Just listen to the fool! He's still swearing!' But a moment later there would be silence, and my grandmother would breathe a sigh of relief. Camille, of course, did all her work quietly and industriously, and never left the farm until she had finished everything she had to do; but Marcel would do whatever he was asked as quickly and roughly as possible, just to be able to get away.

It was in the heat of August that we really learnt to value and appreciate water. It was devastating for us when the well dried up one year, and we had to depend on bought bottled water. During another summer, however, when water was not so short, Marcel bought a very primitive tin shower-bath at Fleurance and set it up at the back of the farm, near the poultry yard and Camille's garden. You hauled a perforated container up to the top of a pole then pulled a string for it to shower water over you like a garden watering-can. To the amazement of the ducks we were all delighted, and played about with it, shrieking with laughter and completely naked, though we did know that if we used up all the water we would have to go and heave the next lot up from the bottom of the well.

The refreshing splash of water was what attracted us, I think, when Marcel, Camille and myself set off on bicycles on a hot Sunday morning for a fishing picnic. Marcel gave up his customary hot roast chicken on these occasions, and agreed to have a cold one instead. So Camille filled up baskets with *charcuterie*, foie gras, salads and fruit, and we spent the whole day beside the river, fishing, eating and sleeping under the trees, while we kept our wine cool by trailing the bottle in the water at the end of a piece of string.

We never cooked the fish by the riverside, as some fishermen do. Instead it was always something we looked forward to, when we had cycled home at about 6 o'clock, and had fed the animals and the poultry; then Camille would cook our catch at the kitchen fire. It was one of the best moments at Saint Puy; as we ate our fresh pike, perch or barbel, it seemed that the day's outing had still not come to an end, and was being prolonged magically into the deepening summer dusk.

Brochet au Vinaigre et au Poivre

PIKE STEAKS WITH WINE VINEGAR & CRUSHED PEPPERCORNS—SERVES 4

4 pike steaks

20 g/¾ oz peppercorns, crushed

50 g/2 oz plain flour

75 g/3 oz duck fat

1 shallot, chopped

50 ml/2 fl oz white wine vinegar

salt

boiled new potatoes, to serve

1 tablespoon chopped parsley

Sprinkle the peppercorns over both sides of the pike steaks. Roll the steaks in the flour. Heat the fat in a frying pan, put in the pike steaks and fry for 4 minutes on each side. Transfer to a serving dish and keep warm.

Tip out the fat from the pan, put in the shallot and sweat gently until soft. Pour in the vinegar and reduce completely. Add 100 ml/4 fl oz water and reduce by four-fifths. Season to taste and pour over the fish. Serve with boiled new potatoes tossed in chopped parsley.

Summer was also the season when I went off with Marcel to catch crayfish. The day before we would have purchased our bait, which was usually an old sheep's head, preferably rotten and maggoty, from Monsieur Taste, and we would have checked our dipping net. This net hung from a round wire frame connected to the end of a long pole by three or four strings, so that it was suspended like one of the trays of an old-fashioned pair of scales. We put the sheep's head into the net and lowered it into the river, using a forked stick as a pivot. Immediately crowds of crayfish would come swarming round the bait. The art was to pull the net up very quickly and vertically. If it drifted at all from side to side, all the crayfish swam out and escaped.

Marcel was an expert at crayfish catching, and sometimes we would come back with two potato sacks absolutely full of them. He loved to empty them out on to the kitchen floor, so that he could watch them squirming and clawing all over the room. Of course, this annoyed Camille, but Marcel took such pleasure in it all that he could never resist doing it. But eventually he was forgiven, and then my grandmother set about preparing us a positive banquet of crayfish. Sometimes she would flambé them with armagnac, or she might cook them with *pacherenc*, one of the local dry white wines of Gascony.

Ecrevisses au Pacherenc

CRAYFISH IN WHITE WINE

60 crayfish, gutted and washed

100 g/4 oz carrots, thinly sliced and fluted

100 g/4 oz onions, thinly sliced and fluted

100 g/4 oz leeks, sliced

1 bouquet garni

3 garlic cloves, peeled and left whole

1 bottle of dry white wine

250 ml/9 fl oz water

pinch of cayenne pepper
salt and freshly ground pepper
mayonnaise, to serve (optional)

Put everything except the crayfish into a large saucepan, bring to the boil and cook for 20 minutes. Add the crayfish and simmer for 8 minutes, tossing them from time to time. Leave to cool in the stock, then serve them plain, with the stock as a sauce, or with mayonnaise.

Ferreting was another of Marcel's August pleasures. He always kept two ferrets at the Oratoire, in a cage near the stable, and he loved to go off with his gun and the ferrets in a bag slung over his shoulder. After spending a whole afternoon in the woods near the village, he would come back with thirty or forty rabbits packed into old potato sacks. These, too, he loved to empty out on to the kitchen floor, to the fury of Camille; it was the story of the crayfish all over again.

Fricassée de Lapin aux Artichauts

FRICASSÉE OF RABBIT WITH ARTICHOKES—SERVES 4

1 rabbit, cut into serving pieces
1 bottle of dry white wine
100 g/4 oz carrots, sliced
100 g/4 oz onions, sliced
3 garlic cloves, chopped
1 bouquet garni
100 g/4 oz duck fat
20 button onions, peeled
50 g/2 oz bayonne ham, diced
25 g/1 oz plain flour
4 large globe artichokes, trimmed to leave only the bottoms, washed and cut into 6
salt and freshly ground pepper

In a bowl, combine the wine, carrots, sliced onions, garlic and *bouquet garni*. Put in the rabbit pieces and leave to marinate for 12 hours.

Drain the marinated rabbit and pat dry. Heat the duck fat in a large shallow saucepan, put in the rabbit pieces and seal on all sides. Add the button onions and ham, and cook over medium heat for 5 minutes, then sprinkle on the flour

and cook for another few seconds. Strain on the wine from the marinade, add the artichokes, season, cover and cook for about 30 minutes, until the rabbit and artichokes are tender. Sprinkle with chopped parsely to garnish.

When Marcel was away ferreting, I often used to spend long late-summer afternoons fishing for frogs in the ponds near the farm. I used a fishing rod and line, and, at the end of it, a trident hook, which I baited with bits of brightly coloured cloth or rag, or almost anything which was either red or yellow. Frogs are incredibly silly creatures, and I can even remember catching them by just putting a flower petal on to my hook. They bite at once, and you can go on pulling them out of the water until you have enough to make a really good meal. We used to take them off the hook, grab hold of their legs, knock their heads on a stone to kill them, make a small cut in the skin near the neck, pull the skin away, cut off the legs we were going to eat, and throw the rest into the grass.

At this time of year, too, Marcel would be looking for the first *champignons de peuplier*, wild oyster mushrooms which grow in roadside hedges and round old tree stumps. If he had picked some up on the way home from ferreting, and I came back at the same time with frogs, Camille would cook them all together to make a delicious dish of mushrooms and frogs' legs.

Cuisses de Grenouilles aux Champignons

FROGS' LEGS WITH OYSTER MUSHROOMS—SERVES 4

200 g/7 oz oyster mushrooms

150 g/5 oz duck fat

salt and freshly ground pepper

12 or more frogs' legs

50 g/2 oz plain flour

4 garlic cloves, crushed

1 tablespoon chopped parsley

Put the mushrooms in a saucepan with a drop of water, cover and cook for 5 minutes to make them render their water. Drain the mushrooms, place in a frying pan with 50 g/2 oz duck fat, season and cook over gentle heat until they begin to caramelize. Keep in a warm place.

Season the frogs' legs, roll them in the flour and tap off the excess. Heat the remaining fat in a frying pan until sizzling, then cook the frogs' legs for about 7 minutes, depending on their size, or until golden. Add the garlic and parsley and cook for 1 more minute. To serve, place the mushrooms in a dish and arrange the frogs' legs on top.

At Saint Puy the end of the summer was always marked by the village *fête*. This was held during the final weekend in August and was spread out over three whole days, from Friday evening to Monday. It included a fair and bicycle races besides the usual music and dancing. The main street and the market hall, where the dancing took place, were hung with coloured lights and flags, and the whole atmosphere was one of gaiety and excitement.

Before the Revolution, this *fête* was always held on 8th September, the Feast of the Nativity of Our Lady, who is the patron saint of Saint Puy and whose blue-robed statue, guarded by the four-winged beasts of the Apocalypse, stands near the church tower. In the past, on the day of the feast, the streets were decorated with garlands and arches of fresh flowers.

Wearing their best uniforms, the musicians of the fire brigade band marched through the town to the sound of trumpets, cymbals and drums; they halted in the little square to perform fanfares and to play medleys of popular tunes. A funfair was erected at the big crossroads near the Condom road, complete with a large roundabout, several shooting galleries and stalls which sold souvenirs and toys and things to eat.

There was none of the unpleasant smell of bad frying which pervades any modern fairground; there were no chips or hamburgers, nor, as yet, any *merguez* sausages. Instead, the food stalls sold mostly sweets and confectionery such as nougat, *pommes d'amour*, barley sugar, *beignets*, pancakes and waffles. The *bal* at Saint Puy brought a lot of trade to the café under the arches and to the village shops, but it also brought cars, crowds and noise, and many people complained vociferously about it.

Dancing started at 5 o'clock every evening; it stopped for an hour at about 7, and then continued until 2 in the morning, and there was also dancing on Sunday afternoon. The dance band at Saint Puy was considered to be one of the best in the area. Their traditional accordion was supported by a trumpet, percussion and a saxophone; indeed, the band was one of the principal attractions of the *fête*.

The other main attraction was the series of cross-country bicycle races which took place on the Monday afternoon. The starting and finishing point was a white line drawn across the road near the *salles des fêtes*. The cyclists followed a course which took them downhill, by the Auch road, until they had crossed the Gèle; then they turned right along the flat until they reached the mill of Escapat, when they turned right again, re-crossed the river, and started the difficult uphill climb back towards Saint Puy. The cyclists were a very attractive sight, all in their different colours, and the races were well-known and very popular, drawing spectators and participants from all over the *département*.

There were prizes for the first three riders to cross the finishing line; but there were also runner-up prizes for the first cyclist to pass certain intermediate points along the course. These extra prizes, or *primes*, as they were called, were announced by a commentator who followed each race in a car with a loudspeaker, and they added enormously to the excitement of the event. Gift prizes were usually provided by the local shopkeepers, and were all splendidly arrayed on a table near the finishing line. Monsieur Taste, for example, might give a leg of lamb; the cycle shop a spare wheel or a lamp; the electrician a radio; while the fire brigade might give a cash prize.

In the evening there were more cycle races, but these were of a different nature, involving one or two well-known professionals, and they took place in the *vélodrome*, the oval-shaped racetrack at the western end of the village. Saint Puy was very proud of its *vélodrome*; you had to pay to get through the canvas screen and to sit on the grass banks to watch the ambitious amateurs whizzing round the track in their efforts to compete with the hardened professionals, who were hired annually by the commune to give an extra touch of excitement to the last night of the *fête*. It was another sort of cycling altogether, but, though it was fun to watch, it never gave me as much enjoyment as the cross-country races in the afternoon.

Marcel always made the most of the *fête*, and spent much of the time sitting in the shade at one of the café tables with some of his friends, watching the dancing. Camille, of course, liked it less; and, if she did come to the village during the festivities, she would always go and sit with my aunt at the shop, and pass the afternoon talking to her. For me it was great fun and I enjoyed it hugely, but at the same time I always felt a little sad because I knew that the end of the holidays was near and that, in a few days, my father would arrive in his car to take us back to Tarbes.

Mamie Camille
ma grand mère

Autumn

After the October grape-picking, mists crept up the valley and we sat by the kitchen fire in the evenings, stripping maize cobs and telling stories. Marcel ploughed and sowed, and Camille made conserves and jams. There were now hares and pheasants to eat, and delicious little ortolans which Marcel trapped, fattened and cooked in the embers of the wood fire.

THE EARLY AUTUMN weather at Saint Puy was always magnificent. I can never remember it being anything else. There was a splendid, majestic plenitude about the sunlight which burned all day, and then seemed to switch itself off abruptly in the early evening, when all at once the air became very cold, and dusk fell quickly. The sun had a special warmth which you never felt in summer and which never came again in winter. It was a time when the landscape of the valleys, edged along the tops of the hills by clumps and fringes of golden, autumnal woods, still repeated a summer pattern of green and yellow; though now the green was of the leafy vines almost ready for the *vendange*, and the yellow came from a blending of stubble fields with the russet, earthy colour of land that had been freshly ploughed. In the warmth, everything was amazingly peaceful and quiet. The noise and disturbance of harvest was over, the *fête* had been celebrated, and the tourists and holiday-makers with their chatter and their cars had disappeared. The land was at rest; even the first shots of the shooting season sounded slow and lazy, nobody hurried in the streets, and everywhere you could smell the scent of ripe fruit.

Autumn activity at the Oratoire started with the *regain*, the second cutting of the hay, which was gathered in during the first weeks of September. This was followed by ploughing and sowing, and by fruit-picking, which had started in the summer, and would go on until late October. Haricot pods, which had been drying in the dark larder for the last two months, were now spread out on the ground and threshed with flails; once they were broken up, they were winnowed to produce the dried white beans which are such an important ingredient in the cooking of south-west France.

In September, too, the shooting season opened, and Marcel would be out with his gun as often as possible to bring home the first partridges and hares. Early October was the time of the *vendange*, when the grapes were picked and pressed, and the first stages of wine-making took place. Once that was over, and the *bal des vendangeurs* had been danced and enjoyed, and the bands of grape-pickers had left the village to return to their own homes, the maize harvest began. Cartloads of corn cobs were pulled back to the farm by cows, and the cobs were stored in cages in the barn to await stripping.

At the beginning of the month, the little birds called *ortolans* passed over Gascony on their way to spend the winter in Africa. Marcel would be much occupied in preparing and setting traps for them, and in seeing to the fattening, drowning and cooking of those he managed to catch. He would also be bringing back his first pheasants. Farm work in November included the first careful ploughing of the earth round the trunks of the vines, and the first trimming away of the old branches. At home, sitting round the fire in the evening, we would start to strip the maize cobs, detaching the orange-yellow corn from the stems.

Autumn was a busy season for Camille in the kitchen: apart from the extra meals she had to provide for the *vendangeurs*, there was the game to be cooked, which might include venison and wild boar. Then there were the conserves she made from the autumn vegetables growing in her kitchen garden, which would provide welcome additional dishes to winter meals, and also all the year's jam to be made from the various fruits as they were picked.

In September, then, when it was time for the *regain*, Marcel would once again harness the cows to the haycutter and bring in this second harvest. It was a sort of farewell to summer, and was followed by ploughing. In those days before intensive farming, Marcel never grew wheat two years running on the same ground. He used to alternate corn with maize, or let the land lie fallow between crops. Fields were smaller then and hedges more numerous, but ploughing was still very hard work.

The ploughshare was made of metal, but the shafts and handles of the plough were made of wood. It was not very heavy but you had to keep pushing down very hard to make the ploughshare bite deeply into the earth. As he ploughed, Marcel also had to manage the long driving reins, which were attached to the ears of the cows. It was easier when someone walked in front of the animals, to lead them from the front at the same time as they were being driven from the back; this used to be one of my jobs. I walked along with a pointed stick over my shoulder like a goad. Behind me, I felt the breath of the cows and heard my grandfather's doleful cries of command, always uttered in patois, and the outbursts of jovial swearing which interrupted them from time to time. The first ploughing broke up the straw stubble and mixed it in with the earth; then came the other stages of manuring, harrowing, second ploughing and sowing. Marcel had a heavy roller which crushed the larger clods, then he would reduce them still more by harrowing them.

It all involved a great deal of labour and time, and the contrast between my grandfather's methods and those of modern agricultural technology is truly amazing. Most of the sowing was done by a very simple machine, a sort of tank on wheels with a perforated base through which the seed fell, but often there were parts of a field where the cows could not manoeuvre or where the machine had proved inefficient and here Marcel was obliged to sow by hand. With a deep bag of seed suspended across his body, he would stride across the ploughed land at a regular, monotonous peasant's pace, while the rapid, mechanical jerks of his arms, and the fixed expression in his eyes as he stared unwaveringly into the infinite, gave him the appearance of a strange and slightly lonely clockwork toy.

There was quite a variety of fruit trees at the Oratoire and the fruit-picking continued all through the early part of the autumn.

There were the small peaches called pêches de vigne, because in the past they were planted in the vineyards to mark the different rows of vines, or to fill up the bare spaces where vines had not prospered. Camille used to cook these with white wine as a dessert. Apples, another autumn fruit, she put into tarts and into her wonderful flaky *croustades*. At this time of year we would have a *croustade* of fruit nearly every Sunday.

Flan de Pêches de Vigne au Vin Doux

4 vineyard peaches

250 ml/9 fl oz sweet white wine

75 g/3 oz caster sugar

3 whole eggs

4 egg yolks

20 g/¾ oz slivered almonds

Preheat the oven to 180°C/350°F/gas 4. Peel the peaches by dipping them briefly into boiling water and rubbing off the skin with your nail. Halve and stone the peeled peaches and place in cold water.

Make the custard mixture by mixing together the wine, sugar, eggs and yolks. Lay the peaches in a flan dish, cut-side down, and pour over the custard mixture. The peaches should look like islands in a sea of wine.

Place the dish in a bain-marie and cook in the preheated oven for 25 minutes, then scatter the almonds over the surface and cook for a final 5 minutes. Leave to cool and serve cold.

Figs, pears, plums, quinces and medlars were all plentiful at this time, so September and October were Camille's great jam-making months. I remember her standing by the fire, carefully watching the big bubbling copper pot as the sugary smell of boiling quinces, plums or blackberries filled the whole kitchen, or sitting studiously at the long table, writing out the labels for the large jars of jam she was about to arrange on the shelves of the kitchen cupboard. Besides all the ordinary fruit jams, my grandmother also used to make an unusual, very good jam from the unripe tomatoes in her kitchen garden.

Gelée de Coings

QUINCE JELLY

quinces

caster sugar

Wash the quinces well in cold water, then drain. Do not peel them, but cut into 6. Cut out the pips and wrap them in a muslin bag. Put the quinces and pips in a saucepan, cover with cold water and cook until tender. Strain the juice through muslin and measure it. Add 800 g/1¾ lb sugar to each 1 l/1¾ pt juice, pour into a preserving pan, add the bag of pips and boil until the temperature reaches 103º–105ºC/217º–221ºF and round bubbles form on the surface of the syrup.

Pour the hot jelly into sterilized jam jars, leave to cool, then cover the jelly with waxed paper and seal the jars.

Confiture aux Prunes

PLUM JAM

1 kg/2¼ lb very sweet plums, halved and stoned

150 g/5 oz caster sugar

1 vanilla pod or a few slices of lemon (optional)

Sprinkle the plums with the sugar and leave to macerate overnight. Next day, put the plums in a saucepan with the vanilla or lemon, if you like, and cook over low heat for about 3 hours, until the temperature reaches 103º–105ºC/217º–221ºF and round bubbles form on the surface of the syrup. The jam should still be slightly runny.

Pour the jam into sterilized jars while it is still hot. Leave to cool, then cover the jam with waxed paper and seal the jars.

Gelée de Mures

BLACKBERRY JELLY

blackberries

caster sugar

Put the blackberries in a pan and cover with water. Cook until the berries are soft, then strain through muslin. Measure the juice and add 800 g/1¾ lb sugar for every 1 l/1¾ pt juice. Boil the juice and sugar until the temperature reaches 103°–105°C/217°–221°F and round bubbles form on the surface of the syrup.

Pour the syrup into sterilized jars while it is still hot. Leave to cool, then cover the jelly with waxed paper and seal the jars.

Confiture de Tomates Vertes

GREEN TOMATO JAM

3 kg/6½ lb green tomatoes

2 kg/4½ lb caster sugar

1 lemon

Wash and dry the tomatoes. Slice them finely, cover with sugar and leave to macerate for 24 hours. Finely slice the lemon and remove the pips. Place the tomatoes and sugar in a preserving pan, add the lemon and cook until the jam is jellified and amber-coloured. Pour into sterilized jars while still hot, cool and seal.

Another autumn activity in which I often took part was the threshing of the haricot beans. When the haricots were picked in summer, a certain quantity was always put aside for drying. The pods were first dried for a short while in the sun, then they were laid out on shelves in the dark larder behind the dining room, where the drying process continued. Camille was always very careful to see that the pods never touched each other, so that they would not be damaged.

In September we spread out a canvas sheet on the flat ground at the back of the Oratoire. Then we scattered the haricot pods over it, and threshed them with old-fashioned wooden flails. This broke open the pods and released the

RIGHT: SOUPE DE HARICOTS BLANCS (P. 166)

beans, but they still had to be winnowed. In the old days, instead of putting down a canvas sheet, a dust-free threshing area was made by spreading out fresh cow dung and leaving it to dry hard in the sun. I never saw this, but Marcel could remember it being done when he was a boy.

The winnower stood in the barn; it was equipped with rollers and a fan, which you turned with a big wheel like a grindstone. My grandfather was very proud of this machine, but it was really just an up-to-date version of a machine invented in the 18th century, called a tarare (supposedly the peasants' corruption of the Latin word ventilare, 'to ventilate'; a name it acquired from the efficacy of its fan which blew away the chaff).

Brought to France from the New World early in the 16th-century, the haricot, especially in its dried form, became an important traditional ingredient in the cooking of the south-west. In the autumn Camille regularly made conserves of haricots; among her many other haricot dishes, I especially used to enjoy her combinations of beans, sausages and tomatoes, which was almost a sort of cassoulet.

Soupe de Haricots Blancs

WHITE BEAN SOUP—SERVES 8

500 g/1 lb 2 oz dried haricot beans

100 g/4 oz carrots, diced

150 g/5 oz onions, diced

1 bouquet garni

3 garlic cloves, peeled and left whole

500 g/1 lb 2 oz pumpkin, diced

300 g/11 oz potatoes, diced

salt and freshly ground pepper

2 preserved duck legs, halved (see Confit de canard, *page 263)*

Soak the beans overnight. Drain and place in a cooking pot with 3 l/5½ pt cold water, bring to the boil and skim. Add the carrots, onions, bouquet garni and garlic, bring back to the boil, then lower the heat so that the soup is just simmering and cook for about 2 hours. Add the diced pumpkin and potatoes, season well and cook for another 20 minutes. Finally add the duck and cook for a further 10 minutes before serving.

Saucisses aux Haricots et Tomates

TOULOUSE SAUSAGES WITH WHITE BEANS & TOMATOES—SERVES 4

500 g/1 lb 2 oz dried haricot beans

100 g/4 oz duck fat

4 large toulouse sausages

1 large onion, sliced

100 g/4 oz bayonne ham skin or bacon

1 bouquet garni

4 garlic cloves, peeled and left whole

salt and freshly ground pepper

2 large carrots, halved lengthways

400 g/14 oz tomatoes, peeled and deseeded

Soak the beans overnight in cold water. Drain and cook in boiling unsalted water for 30 minutes, then drain. In a large heavy saucepan, melt the fat and quickly fry the sausages until browned all over. Take them out of the pan, put in the onion and cook for 5 minutes until golden. Add the ham skin or bacon, the beans, bouquet garni, garlic and seasoning and pour in enough cold water to cover the beans.

Cook slowly, uncovered, for 2½–3 hours, skimming off the scum which rises to the surface whenever necessary. Add the carrots and tomatoes after 1½ hours and the sausages after another 30 minutes. The dish is ready when the water is just underneath the beans and has become thick like a sauce.

The cassoulet, though always associated with haricots and with the south-west, is not really a traditional dish of the Gers. It is an essential item in the cooking of nearby Languedoc, and is closely connected with such places as Toulouse and Castelnaudary. The only true cassoulet which I can remember Camille making was a *cassoulet de morue* (salt cod). I have already explained how important salt fish was for us, since most fresh sea fish was too expensive for my grandparents to buy.

The first recipe I give for *cassoulet de morue* is exactly as Camille cooked it; the second is a more elaborate version, which I served at La Tante Claire. It includes scallops, mussels and smoked salmon, which, of course, Camille would never have used.

Cassoulet de Morue

TRADITIONAL SALT COD CASSOULET—SERVES 6–8

400 g/14 oz dried haricot beans

400 g/14 oz fillets of salt cod

1 onion, sliced

1 small bouquet garni

75 g/3 oz bayonne ham or bacon, sliced

3 garlic cloves, chopped

1 tablespoon chopped parsley

Soak the beans overnight in cold water. Soak the salt cod overnight under cold running water. Drain the beans, cover with fresh water and add all the other ingredients except the cod and ham. Bring to the boil and simmer for about 30 minutes.

Lay the salt cod on top of the beans, cover the casserole and simmer for about 30 minutes more, until the fish and beans are well cooked and tender. Grill or fry the ham until crispy. Add to the casserole and serve at once.

Cassoulet de Morue à la Tante Claire

SALT COD CASSOULET À LA TANTE CLAIRE—SERVES 4

250 g/9 oz dried haricot beans

300 g/11 oz fillets of salt cod

1 kg/2¼ lb mussels, scrubbed and debearded

200 ml/7 fl oz dry white wine

4 shallots, finely chopped

1 tablespoon chopped parsley

1 large onion, sliced

2 large carrots, sliced

4 garlic cloves, chopped

1 bouquet garni

4 scallops, cleaned

20 g/¾ oz butter

100 g/4 oz smoked salmon or smoked eel, sliced

Soak the beans overnight in cold water. Soak the salt cod overnight under cold running water.

Put the mussels in a saucepan with the wine, shallots and parsley. Cover and cook over high heat, shaking the pan occasionally, until all the shells have opened. Remove the top shells, leaving the mussels in the half shells. Strain the cooking stock into another saucepan and keep it and the mussels warm.

Drain the beans, place in a flameproof casserole, cover with cold water and bring slowly to the boil. Drain, cover with fresh water and add the mussel stock, sliced onion, carrots, garlic and bouquet garni. Bring to the boil, then simmer for about 30 minutes until the beans are tender. Lay the salt cod on top of the beans, cover and simmer gently until the fish is soft and flaky. Remove the bouquet garni.

Fry the scallops in the butter for 1 minute on each side, then add them to the beans and fish. Add the mussels, lay the smoked salmon or eel on top and serve.

The opening of the shooting season in September made it a specially important month for Marcel. My grandfather kept three fine twelve-bore shotguns at the Oratoire, though one of them really belonged to my uncle Capuron, and was always ready for his use if he happened to call by and wanted to go off shooting at once with Marcel. Two of the guns, as I said, were hung up in the kitchen on the chimney breast above the fireplace; the third, which was my grandfather's favourite, was kept in the bedroom, propped against the wall near the bed, where it was instantly handy in case of unwanted intruders.

Marcel always had two dogs at the Oratoire, one for guarding the house and for bringing in the cows and the other as a gun dog. The guard dog, *lou flic*, as he is called in the south-west, was an Alsatian named Rex; he had the privilege of being allowed to sleep inside the house in the kitchen. The gun dog, a sort of retriever, was never allowed in the house, and was always kept tied up in the barn, where he slept on straw, or in a kennel. Both dogs were well fed, and were given exactly the same food, but I always felt it was unfair that the gun dog had a harder time of it than the other.

Once the shooting season had started, Marcel never left the house without a gun slung over his shoulder and the dog at his heels. When he drove the cows out to the fields or went to work in the vines or the wood, he always took his gun, so he was able to go shooting virtually every day. He was an excellent shot, and it was rare for him to come back empty-handed. Towards the end of his life, however, his eyesight began to fail and he was less successful.

Marcel made all his own cartridges. There was a shop at Fleurance where he bought cases, gunpowder, wadding and shot; he also had a gauge for measuring out powder, and a little machine with a handle, which rammed the contents of a cartridge and turned down the ends. The cartridge cases were different colours, according to the size of shot. When Marcel went shooting, he carried them in a belt round his waist, with the larger shot on the left and the smaller on the right.

Marcel always preferred to go shooting alone, though sometimes he went with my father and uncle and a few friends. In the evening, if there was no more work on the farm, he could never resist taking one last walk 'behind the hill', as he used to say. He usually came back half an hour later with another hare. September was the first month for hares; the younger animals were roasted on the spit and Camille served them with beetroot or a gratin of fresh beans, but the older ones were usually cooked in a civet or *à la royale*.

Levraut Rôti à la Moutarde et aux Betteraves

ROAST HARE WITH MUSTARD & BEETROOT—SERVES 4

1 young hare, skinned and drawn

salt

100 g/4 oz duck fat

150 g/5 oz carrots, chopped

100 g/4 oz onions, chopped

1 sprig of thyme

2 bay leaves

10 peppercorns, crushed

25 ml/1 fl oz armagnac

250 ml/9 fl oz dry white wine

200 ml/7 fl oz double cream

25 g/1 oz dijon mustard

200 g/7 oz beetroot, cooked, peeled and thickly sliced, to serve

Preheat the oven to 200ºC/400ºF/gas 6. Sprinkle the hare with salt and tie the hind legs together with string. Heat the fat in a roasting pan, put in the hare and seal on all sides. Add the carrots, onions, thyme, bay leaves and peppercorns. Sweat the vegetables for 3 minutes, stirring occasionally, then place the roasting pan in the oven and cook for 20 minutes, basting the hare with the fat every 5 minutes or so.

Pour off the fat and flame the hare with the armagnac. Transfer the hare to a serving dish and keep warm. Pour the wine into the roasting pan and reduce by one-third. Add the cream and boil gently until the sauce is thick enough to coat the back of a spoon. Add the mustard and mix well. Pass the sauce through a conical sieve and check the seasoning.

Cut the hare into portions or serve it whole. Pour over the sauce and arrange thick slices of beetroot around the edge.

Lièvre à la Royale

STUFFED HARE IN WHITE WINE—SERVES 4

1 hare, skinned and drawn
blood, heart, lungs and liver from the hare
150 g/5 oz raw foie gras
75 g/3 oz pork fat
50 g/2 oz shallots, chopped
1 garlic clove, peeled and left whole
2 tablespoons chopped parsley
75 g/3 oz breadcrumbs, soaked
salt and freshly ground pepper
100 g/4 oz duck fat
200 g/7 oz carrots, diced
150 g/5 oz onions, sliced
2 l/3½ pt dry white wine
1 bouquet garni
50 ml/2 fl oz armagnac

First prepare the stuffing. Mince together the heart, lungs, liver, foie gras, pork fat, shallots, garlic and parsley. Add the breadcrumbs, salt, pepper and blood and mix well. Stuff the hare with the mixture, sew up the skin and truss the hare, tying the hind legs tightly against the body.

Heat the duck fat in a large casserole and sweat the carrots and onions for 15 minutes. Place the hare on top and pour over the wine. Bring to the boil, then lower the heat. Add the bouquet garni, season, cover the casserole and braise the hare for 2½–3 hours, turning it halfway through cooking.

Transfer the cooked hare to a serving dish. Strain the cooking wine, check the seasoning, add the armagnac and serve.

RIGHT: GRATIN D'HARICOTS VERTS (P. 174)

Gratin d'Haricots Verts

FRENCH BEANS IN CREAM

300 g/11 oz french beans

50 g/2 oz butter

75 g/3 oz onions, finely chopped

50 g/2 oz bayonne ham, thinly sliced

1 garlic clove, crushed

1 tablespoon parsley, chopped

150 ml/5 fl oz double cream

salt and freshly ground pepper

Top and tail the beans and cook in boiling salted water until tender. Drain. In a saucepan, melt the butter, add the onions and cook gently for 5 minutes. Add the ham, garlic and parsley and cook for 3 minutes. Add the cream and beans and boil for 3 minutes. Check the seasoning, put the beans in a serving dish and serve.

It should be quite clear by now that my grandfather was a born hunter. When it came to birds, animals and fish, he shot, caught or killed anything in sight if it had the misfortune to be in season. As far as the wild life of Saint Puy was concerned, his mere presence was synonymous with universal havoc and carnage. And then one day, an extraordinary thing happened. A fine and very plump turtle-dove appeared from nowhere and settled on the branches of one of the trees near the Oratoire. Normally, Marcel would have shot it immediately, but on this occasion, instead of killing it, he fell in love with it and absolutely refused to harm it. Odd as it may sound, he just fell hopelessly and totally in love with this bird; he began to think that it only cooed when he was there and that it was silent when he went away; that it watched for his coming home and was depressed when he left to drive the cows into the fields, and so on.

When I came to the farm for the autumn holidays, nobody told me about my grandfather's obsession; of course, as soon as I spotted the dove in the tree my only thought was to kill it and get Camille to cook it. One morning I picked up a stone and threw it at the bird. I had no real hope of hitting it, but, to my amazement, I did – and furthermore killed it. Very pleased with myself, and bursting with pride at my brilliant marksmanship, I picked up the dove and rushed with it into the kitchen, where I was told the whole story by my horrified grandmother. Nevertheless she cooked it and served it for lunch.

We said nothing to Marcel about what had happened, but I think he knew. He just said sadly that he was not hungry that day and refused to eat anything but soup and bread. After all, the bird had been Marcel's very own turtle-dove; it had sung for him alone; it had been sacred, and my grandmother and I ate it in silence. If it had settled on a tree near anyone else's farm, Marcel, of course, would have shot it without hesitation, but my grandfather had a romantic side to his nature, and somehow that dove had just managed to touch it.

The turtle-dove was not the only bird at the Oratoire which managed to enjoy (if briefly) a charmed and protected life. Whenever we left the farm at the end of a holiday Marcel and Camille always gave us a present to take to my parents, which was usually either some flowers or something good to eat. One time they gave us a live chicken, but when we got back to Tarbes, my father refused to kill it. He hated killing anything and usually made my mother do it, but this time not even she could bring herself to slaughter it, so the chicken stayed alive and became a household pet. We kept it in the house and the garden for five or six months, and we all came to adore it. My sister Martine, who thought that all chickens laid chocolate eggs like the toy hens which are given to French children at Easter, used to feed it with chocolate sweets to improve its egg production.

175 AUTUMN

In the end the chicken grew into a large white hen; it was impossible to keep it any more in the Tarbes house, so we took it back to my grandparents. At the Oratoire, history repeated itself. We had by now given the hen a name, Amoureuse. She was so used to being with people that she walked straight up to Camille to be caressed and clucked with pleasure when my grandmother stroked her neck. Both she and Marcel were so taken with the hen that even they had not the heart to kill it. And so Amoureuse ended her days as the Oratoire pet; I am quite certain that she was the only hen at that farm ever to die of old age.

My grandparents also had a tame sparrow. Fixed to the end wall of the house, facing downhill in the direction of Fleurance, there was a large metal sign advertising Dubonnet. One day the sign became so rusty that it fell down, and behind it Marcel found a sparrow's nest with a baby bird in it. We kept this young bird and Camille fed it on milk and breadcrumbs, which it ate from the end of a match. In time it became another pet and lived at the Oratoire for about ten years, flying quite freely in and out of the house. It hopped about the table while we ate, picking up all the crumbs and scraps, but if you annoyed it, the sparrow would peck your finger and spread out its wings in anger, like a tiny eagle.

By the end of September, we were all ready for another *fête*, and this was provided by the feast of Saint Michael celebrated on 29th September. To mark the occasion, Camille cooked us a traditional Michaelmas goose (as it would be called in England). For centuries the migratory goose, which disappeared during the winter, was considered to be a bird of the sun, and was symbolically eaten at the time of the autumn equinox – though, curiously enough, in south-west France, which produces many geese, the custom is not often followed. Where Camille learnt of it, I do not know, but she always liked to observe it and on the day would usually make a goose alicot, a stew whose name comes from the words *ailes cuites*, cooked wings or possibly from *ale y cot* (patois for wing and neck). In Camille's menu it would of course be preceded by soup, and was sometimes followed by a gratin of courgettes, and then by one of her fruit tarts for dessert.

Alicot d'Oie aux Légumes d'Hiver

GOOSE GIBLETS WITH ROOT VEGETABLES—SERVES 4

1.5 kg/3¼ lb goose giblets and offal: necks, wings, gizzards, feet, hearts and livers

100 g/4 oz duck fat

200 g/7 oz bacon, diced

300 g/11 oz onions, diced

300 ml/½ pt dry white wine

1 small bouquet garni

5 garlic cloves, crushed

salt and freshly ground pepper

100 g/4 oz carrots, diced

75 g/3 oz leeks, diced

100 g/4 oz potatoes, diced

50 g/2 oz turnips, diced

50 g/2 oz savoy cabbage, diced

100 g/4 oz pumpkin, diced

Heat the fat in a flameproof casserole and fry the bacon until golden. Remove the bacon, put in the goose giblets and offal and seal all over. Add the onions and cook gently for 10 minutes.

Pour in the wine and enough water just to cover the goose. Add the bacon, bouquet garni, garlic and seasoning, cook gently for 15 minutes, then add the carrots and leeks. After 5 minutes, add the potatoes, then 5 minutes later, add the turnips. Cook for 10 minutes, then add the cabbage and pumpkin and cook until tender. The liquid must always cover the vegetables while they are cooking, so add more water if necessary. Check the seasoning and serve.

Gratin de Courgettes

GRATIN OF COURGETTES

50 g/2 oz butter

1 kg/2¼ lb courgettes, sliced

2 garlic cloves, crushed

1 tablespoon chopped parsley

150 ml/5 fl oz double cream

4 egg yolks

salt and freshly ground pepper

50 g/2 oz gruyère, grated

Preheat the oven to 180°C/350°F/gas 4. Heat the butter in a saucepan and cook the courgettes until mushy, adding the garlic and parsley 1 minute before you stop cooking. Mash the courgettes, then place in a piece of muslin and squeeze out as much water as possible to leave a solid purée. Put the purée into a bowl and stir in the cream and eggs. Season to taste and pour into a gratin dish. Sprinkle over the cheese and bake in the oven for about 20 minutes, until golden.

Tarte aux Pommes et à la Crème de Lait

CREAMY APPLE TART—SERVES 4

250 g/9 oz Pâte à tarte sucrée (recipe page 142)

flour, for dusting

4 large reinette or cox apples

100 g/4 oz butter

200 g/7 oz caster sugar

250 ml/9 fl oz double cream

4 egg yolks

ground cinnamon to taste

Preheat the oven to 200°C/400°F/gas 6. On a lightly floured surface, roll out the pastry and use it to line a 25 cm/10 in flan dish. Bake blind for 15 minutes.

Peel and core the apples and cut each into 8 segments. Heat the butter in a large saucepan and add the apples and 75 g/3 oz sugar. When the apples are half cooked, take them out, leave the pan on the heat and let the sugar caramelize.

Arrange the apples in the flan case and pour over the caramel. Mix together the cream, egg yolks, the remaining sugar and cinnamon to taste. Pour this mixture over the apples and bake the tart for 35 minutes.

The cream my grandmother used for the tart was the thick, rather solid cream which rose to the top of the milk after it had been boiled to prevent it from turning sour too quickly (there was no refrigerator at the Oratoire, of course). We children used to spread this clotted cream on our toast at breakfast, then add butter, jam and walnuts, topped with a sprinkling of sugar.

It was Camille who usually milked the cows, sitting on a strange, one-legged stool. Some of the milk was sold; this was left outside the farm in 50-litre churns to be picked up during the day. The rest was kept in smaller churns in the chambre obscure, so there was never any shortage of milk and cream at the Oratoire.

I have already mentioned that Marcel was the official *garde-pêche* for the commune of Saint Puy; he was also its official gamekeeper, the *garde-chasse*. He had to make certain that anyone who went shooting had a valid game licence and no-one shot any game out of season. This job must have come very naturally to someone like Marcel. He knew everyone in the village and they all knew him, and shooting was in his blood. Sometimes he might meet a stranger with a gun and dog, when he would ask to see his licence, but I never heard of any unpleasantness, and I do not think he ever arrested or reported anyone to the gendarmes.

One of Marcel's duties as *garde-chasse* was to suppress foxes. Whenever a peasant had had his hens killed by a fox, he would inform Marcel, who knew the location of most of the earths; then my grandfather would go out and shoot the fox. Leaving one hole open, he would block all the others with rags soaked in liquid gas, and wait with his gun for the foxes to emerge from the only exit left to them. Afterwards he would cut off the brush or the tongue or an ear, and take it to the mairie, where he was paid a reward for each fox he killed. The young foxes were beautiful animals, and I used to feel it was a great pity that we had to kill them, but it was the law of the countryside.

At other times, a wild boar would get into a field of maize and charge through it, doing a good deal of damage. A boar is a heavy animal, and you could always tell where it had gone from the wide path it made in the crop. Marcel, with four or five other men, would follow it down one of its tracks and shoot it. I remember being at Saint Puy one September weekend when a wild boar had recently been shot and the animal was hanging up outside Monsieur Taste's shop. I do not know where it was killed, but we had some of the meat at the Oratoire, and Camille cooked it on the open fire in one of her deep iron casseroles.

Estouffade de Sanglier

CASSEROLE OF WILD BOAR—SERVES 4

800 g/1¾ lb escalopes of wild boar, from the leg, cut into 5 cm/2 in pieces
150 g/5 oz duck fat
700 g/1½ lb onions, sliced
3 garlic cloves, chopped
50 g/2 oz plain flour
1 bouquet garni
1 bottle dry white wine
salt and freshly ground pepper
mashed potato and sautéed carrots, to serve

Preheat the oven to 200°C/400°F/gas 6. In a large saucepan, heat 100 g/4 oz fat until sizzling. Put in the onions and cook until golden, stir in the garlic and set aside.

Roll the escalopes in the flour and tap off the excess. Heat the remaining fat in a frying pan, put in the escalopes and seal quickly on both sides. Spoon some of the onions into a flameproof casserole, then put in a layer of meat, add the bouquet garni and make more layers of onions and meat, finishing with one of onions.

Pour in the wine, season and slowly bring to the boil on the hob. When the wine is boiling, cover the casserole and cook in the preheated oven for 3 hours. Check that the meat is tender and adjust the seasoning. Serve the wild boar straight from the casserole with mashed potato and carrots sautéed in butter.

Although we were normally back at school in Tarbes by mid-September, I do remember spending one weekend at the Oratoire in early October, when I was about nine or ten, during the *vendange*, or grape-picking. I also have a much earlier memory of being present at the same event when I must have been about six years old, and before I had started to go to school. I had never seen the *vendange* before, but I felt I knew all about it from the scene depicted on the long-case clock made by Monsieur Duprom in the Oratoire kitchen.

I never saw Monsieur Duprom, who made the clock, for he died before I ever came to Saint Puy. Old photographs show him to have been a stout, bearded figure in a black peaked leather cap, which gave him a somewhat nautical appearance, rather like the captain of an ocean-going liner. He had, in addition, the reputation of being a great bon vivant, a gargantuan eater of pancakes and a man who greatly enjoyed wine, so it is fitting, perhaps, that the finely embossed brass plate round the clock's dial should show a busy *vendange* in which grapes are being picked and wine-making is beginning. The clock and its picture always attracted me, and I always wished that I could be at the Oratoire for the grape-harvest.

The labour, energy and endurance of the crowds of workers, the open-air meals eaten at long trestle tables, and the atmosphere of good humour and gaiety made the *vendange* seem very much like the wheat harvest, but there were certain important differences. For one thing, the workers were not local people. Most of them were Spaniards, who crossed the Pyrenees every autumn to work in the vineyards; the rest came from all over France.

It was during the *vendange* at the Oratoire, shortly after the war, that my father and mother first met each other. Albert Koffmann, who was born in France but whose family originally came from Odessa, was at that time a furrier in Paris; like so many others, he travelled down to Saint Puy for the grape harvest and worked temporarily for my grandfather as a *vendangeur*. Instead of just staying for a week or two, however, he married Marcel's elder daughter, Germaine, and settled permanently in the south-west.

For my mother, I think, the marriage was, more than anything else, a welcome means of escape from the daily life at the farm, where she had not always been very happy. She adored her father, but did not get on at all well with her mother, rather in the same way that Camille herself, in the past, had not got on with her mother-in-law, my great-grandmother.

The *vendange* was much less important than the harvest. Wheat was a vital source of income, whereas only just enough wine was made to provide for home consumption over the coming year, and for distilling into *eau-de-vie*; none was sold. Though some of the wine was white, most was red – an ordinary *gros rouge*, which was not very strong; you could aways drink a litre or two without being too seriously affected.

In fact my grandparents were very ignorant about wine. Every day, Marcel drank the wine that came from his own vines; for an important occasion or a *fête*, Camille would go to my aunt's shop and buy a bottle of a more expensive wine whose name was familiar to her. Even that would be nothing particularly special – just a vin d'Alsace, Côtes du Rhone or Beaujolais. They had no critical sense, no knowledge or experience by which to judge whether they were buying a good wine or a bad one, or even to worry much about where it came from.

The *vendangeurs* were organized into groups, according to the work they did. There were the *coupeurs*, who cut the grapes from the vines, and who were paid the most because all day they had to work stooping down. There were the *porteurs*, who carried the baskets of cut grapes on their backs to the carts, and the carters who managed the cows. Then there were the men who worked the wooden wine-press which stood in one of the big rooms on the ground floor of the farm, and who pumped the juice up into the nearby *foudres*. My very earliest memories were of men treading the grapes with their feet, but by the time of my second *vendange* this old method had been superseded by a press with a screw and a large lever.

The great *foudres*, in which the wine was left to ferment, were made of concrete and had specially vitrified interiors. They were built in a corner of the room, and were almost as high as the ceiling. One thing I remember about them is that their builder had embellished their front sections with fantastic sculptures of tree trunks, all realistically moulded or modelled in concrete, and afterwards painted. The meticulous detailing of the bark and the lopped-off branches was a wonderful example of naive, popular art.

A few months later, when the wine had fermented sufficiently, it was put into barrels called *barriques*, and from these it was bottled. One of the pleasures of the *vendange* was to drink the new grape juice about three days after it had been pressed, when it had only just started to ferment. This was called *bourrit* in patois; it was white, sweet, cloudy and quite strong, and we would sit round the kitchen fire in the evenings, drinking *bourrit* and eating walnuts and new bread.

There were plenty of fresh grapes, of course, so another favourite food we used to eat near the fire on October evenings was *pain aillé aux grappes de raisins*. You took a *quignon* of bread, rubbed it with garlic, mixed the white crumb with some oil or duck fat, put it back in the crust, salted it with sea salt and ate it with a bunch of grapes. It was delicious.

October and November were also the months when the nuts were gathered from the walnut trees which grew round the farm; these my grandmother used to make into a very good sweet, walnut tart.

Tarte aux Noix

WALNUT FLAN—SERVES 4

225 g/8 oz Pâte à tarte sucrée *(recipe page 142)*

flour, for dusting

300 g/11 oz shelled walnuts, broken into pieces

150 g/5 oz sugar

120 g/4½ oz butter, softened

150 g/5 oz honey

5 egg yolks

100 ml/4 fl oz double cream

50 ml/2 fl oz rum

2 teaspoons icing sugar

Preheat the oven to 190°C/375°F/gas 5. Roll out the pastry on a floured surface and use it to line a 22 cm/9 in flan dish.

Gently mix together the walnuts, sugar, butter, honey, egg yolks, cream and rum. Pour the mixture into the flan case and bake in the preheated oven for 40 minutes. Leave to cool, then sprinkle with icing sugar and serve.

Now that the harvest and the *vendange* were both over, Camille had more time to spend on cooking. When my grandparents were alone, especially when they were old, they mostly ate soup, usually a *soupe au pain trempé* or one made from leeks or vegetables, into which Camille put some *confit* of pork or duck so that the soup did contain some meat, besides having a good flavour. She never used the best bits of meat, probably just a gizzard, feet or neck, with a piece of bayonne ham.

When we were visiting the farm, Camille tried to give us meat or game twice a day, even though she and Marcel would never have eaten as well as that in the ordinary course of events. In autumn when one of the Oratoire calves was slaughtered by Monsieur Taste, she would try and find some new way of cooking the veal which the butcher brought us on the Saturday morning. Or, she often used to kill one or two of the older cockerels and cook them with red wine, perhaps even buying a bottle of madiran for the purpose.

Alouettes Sans Têtes

'HEADLESS LARKS': STUFFED VEAL ESCALOPES—SERVES 4

4 veal escalopes, beaten very thin

100 g/4 oz minced pork

100 g/4 oz minced veal

100 g/4 oz minced pork fat

2 garlic cloves, chopped

2 shallots, chopped

50 g/2 oz white breadcrumbs, soaked in milk

salt and freshly ground pepper

sautéed vegetables, to serve

Sauce

50 g/2 oz duck fat

2 onions, thinly sliced

20 g/¾ oz plain flour

100 ml/4 fl oz madeira

Mix together the minced pork, veal, fat, garlic, shallots, breadcrumbs and seasoning. Spread this stuffing over the escalopes and fold up to make parcels. Tie with string. Preheat the oven to 180°C/350°F/gas 4.

In a shallow pan, heat the duck fat, put in the escalopes and seal until golden on both sides. Take the escalopes out of the pan, put in the onions and cook until golden. Add the flour and cook for 3 minutes, stirring all the time with a wooden spoon. Pour in the madeira, boil for 1 minute, then add 200 ml/7 fl oz water and boil for 5 minutes. Check the seasoning and return the escalopes to the pan. Cover and cook in the oven for 30 minutes. Serve hot with sautéed vegetables.

Coq au Madiran

COCKEREL IN MADIRAN WINE—SERVES 6

1 cockerel or roasting chicken, cut into 6 pieces

100 g/4 oz plain flour

100 g/4 oz duck fat

100 g/4 oz bacon, diced

1 l/1¾ pt red madiran wine

4 garlic cloves, crushed

1 bouquet garni

100 g/4 oz mushrooms

75 g/3 oz button onions

salt and freshly ground pepper

1 chicken liver

25 ml/1 fl oz armagnac

Season the cockerel pieces and roll in flour. Heat the fat in a large flameproof casserole and seal the cockerel on all sides, then add the bacon and fry for 5 minutes. Pour off the fat and add the wine to the casserole. Bring to the boil and skim the surface, then add the garlic and bouquet garni. Cover and cook gently for about 2 hours, depending on the age and tenderness of the cockerel.

Twenty-five minutes before the end of cooking, add the mushrooms and onions and adjust the seasoning. Purée the liver and mix it with the armagnac, then stir it into the sauce, taking care not to let it boil any more. Serve at once.

Though Saint Puy is situated geographically in the Ténarèze, one of the three main armagnac-producing areas of Gascony, there was no distillery in the village, so no armagnac was made commercially. Each farmer, however, used to employ the services of the local *bouilleur*, who travelled round the countryside in the late autumn, his mobile still drawn slowly along by a pair of cows. With this cumbrous, complicated alambic, he would stop outside each farm for a day. The wine was brought out to him and he would distill it into clear white *eau-de-vie*. The still, hot and hissing, consisted basically of two great copper containers. One was large and fat; in it the wine boiled above the wood-burning furnace. The other was smaller; here the steam which had condensed inside the long, worm-like serpentine pipe, cooled itself and became *eau-de-vie*.

At that time, the legal ration of home-distilled armagnac was twenty litres a year for each man on each farm, none at all being allowed for the women. Marcel found this regulation rather tough, as he was the only man at the Oratoire, but the *bouilleur* was usually willing to help matters by doing a little clandestine distilling on his behalf. So as not to attract the attention of the gendarmes, this was always done at night, in a quiet and unobserved corner of the Saint Puy cemetery. In the morning, the *bouilleur* and his still would have disappeared, but knowing visitors to their family tombs would find there, as expected, the correct, agreed number of bottles of *eau-de-vie* tucked beneath the incised inscriptions of their names. The *bouilleur* was a lank, lugubrious man, but his sense of graveyard humour was impeccable.

Camille used *eau-de-vie* for making her aperitifs and for bottling fruit. At the time of the *vendange*, she used to bottle grapes in *eau-de-vie*, and I remember how much we looked forward to her prunes in rum. The prunes were always the famous Agen prunes, which she bought at Fleurance, and which she preferred even to her own dried plums from the Oratoire.

Pruneaux d'Agen au Rhum

AGEN PRUNES IN RUM

1 kg/2¼ lb Agen prunes

4 tea bags

250 g/9 oz sugar

200 ml/7 fl oz rum

Pour 500 ml/18 fl oz boiling water on to the tea bags, put in the prunes, cover with a lid and leave overnight. Next morning, remove the tea bags, add the sugar and rum, mix gently with a spoon and put the prunes and liquid into jars. They will keep in the larder for 3 months.

Although, as I have already said, she was able to identify different blends of armagnac and to detect their places of origin just by dabbing some on the back of her hand and sniffing it, Camille never drank spirits, and always disapproved deeply of Marcel's natural inclination to enjoy a glass of *eau-de-vie* whenever an occasion presented itself. This brings me to Marie-Jeanne. Marie-Jeanne lived in the village and went from house to house working as a freelance cleaner and washerwoman. She was unmarried – a short big woman, very strong and robust, with fine black eyes and a slight moustache. She was always gay and laughing, and had an inexhaustible fund of dubious jokes and stories and amusing gossip; she was also always ready to enjoy a drink. She was about the same age as Marcel, and they got on wonderfully well.

Marie-Jeanne came once a week to the Oratoire, where there was always a lot of washing to be done, because, in addition to our own linen, there was all that of my uncle and aunt who were far too busy in the shop to do any laundry. The night before Marie-Jeanne came, my grandmother would put all the washing to soak; in the morning, Marie-Jeanne would boil it all in the big copper which stood in a separate building near the well. She had lunch at the farm, when she ate and drank with a hearty appetite, and in the afternoon she loaded all the wet, boiled linen into an enormous wheelbarrow, which she pushed up the hill to the Saint Puy lavoir, which was near the vélodrome and quite a long way away. There was only enough water at the Oratoire to do the boiling.

At the lavoir, Marie-Jeanne had to do all the rinsing, re-washing and beating. She did this with an old-fashioned washerwoman's paddle and a plank, kneeling in one of the special wooden kneeling-boxes which you can still see sometimes in French village lavoirs. Then she would have to bring all the clean but still wet linen back to the Oratoire in her barrow, and spread it out to dry. It was a long and hard day's work, since the hill up to the village was quite steep, and the wet linen was very heavy, to say nothing of the weight of the barrow.

The morning, however, was made easier for Marie-Jeanne by the presence of Marcel near the boiling copper, and by the armagnac they were able to consume. Marcel must have thought that Marie-Jeanne had been sent to him from heaven. They drank glass after glass together and accompanied their drinking with a good deal of laughter, stories and general hilarious ribaldry.

If the great event at the Oratoire during the first part of October was the *vendange*, the principal event of the second part of the month was the maize harvest. The ripe cobs of corn were picked by hand from the plants, whose flowing leaves had long since lost their green summer splendour and were now only a dry, autumnal yellow. They were carried in basketfuls to the carts in which they were taken to the farm, where they were stacked in cages in the big barn to await the time when they could be peeled and stripped.

Though it was another of the novelties brought to Europe from the New World by the 16th-century Spaniards, maize was not widely cultivated in

Gascony until the early part of the 18th-century. It replaced millet and rye, which had been the standard mediaeval cereals, and the French first called it *gros millet*, under which name Monsieur Dubarry describes it being grown at Saint Puy in 1708. Millers and bakers mixed maize flour with millet flour in ever greater proportions until, in the 19th-century, maize flour was completely supplanted by flour made from wheat.

Although Camille used wheat flour to make us delicious *milhas* or *millasons*, the very names of these desserts hark back historically to the time when, like *armottes* and the dumplings called *miques*, they would have been made from maize. Maize bread, called *méture*, was revived in south-west France during the Occupation, and my grandmother still made her maize soup. We children used to grill maize cobs over fires we made in the fields in the open air. But normally maize was regarded as being solely an animal food, although Camille used to cook it even before feeding it to the poultry, because she thought it fattened them better this way. She would just bring it to the boil in a big cauldron with some pepper and a little duck fat.

Marcel had another more practical use for maize; he sowed it alternately in the same row with haricots blancs. The maize would grow first and provide a good support for the climbing haricots which sprouted later, so there was no need to put in sticks for the beans.

Miques de Maïs

CORNMEAL CAKES

a pinch of salt

25 g/1 oz duck fat, plus extra for frying

250 g/9 oz cornmeal

Boil 750 ml/1¼ pt water with the salt and fat, then sprinkle in the cornmeal like rain and simmer over low heat for 30 minutes, until the mixture no longer sticks to the pan, stirring continuously with a wooden spoon.

Pour the mixture into a rectangular dish or spread it over a tray. Leave until cold, then cut into 3–5 cm/1¼–2 in squares or small batons and fry in duck fat until golden on both sides.

You can eat the miques as they are, or sprinkle with sugar and flambée with armagnac. They can also be made with fine semolina, when they are called *armottes*.

Biscuits de Maïs

CORNMEAL BISCUITS

2 eggs

450 g/1 lb caster sugar

100 g/4 oz butter, softened, plus extra for greasing

grated zest of 1 lemon

a pinch of salt

200 g/7 oz cornmeal

100 g/4 oz plain flour

Preheat the oven to 200°C/400°F/gas 6. Mix the eggs and sugar until creamy. Add the butter, lemon zest, salt and flours and stir very well. Shape into walnut-sized balls and place, spaced well apart, on a greased baking sheet. Bake in the hot oven for 15 minutes, until golden.

Early October was also the time when large flocks of grey, yellow-breasted ortolans flew over Gascony on their way south to Africa. These tiny, bunting-like birds have always been regarded as one of the great gastronomic delicacies of south-west France, and Marcel was one of their most ardent pursuers. He owned about a hundred *matoles*, as the wire traps which are used to catch them are called. He would bait these with wheat and maize and set them in the fields where he knew the ortolans regularly came to feed. The birds pecked eagerly at the bait until at last they hopped on to the lever which closed the trap and imprisoned them. As they fluttered round the rows of *matoles*, my grandfather would lure more and more victims down from the sky by cleverly imitating their shrill, monotonous cries.

The ortolans were taken back to the Oratoire, where Marcel would shut them up in dark cages and feed them intensively on maize for about a week, until they were so plump they could hardly walk. When they were big enough, he drowned them by immersing their heads in a glass of *eau-de-vie*, a traditional method of slaughter which allowed no blood or fat to escape, and which also impregnated the birds with a strong flavour of armagnac. Plucked, but not gutted, the ortolans were wrapped up in little paper packets and cooked in the embers of the fire.

It was best to eat the ortolans as soon as they were ready, putting the entire bird into your mouth at a single thrust; they were quite delicious. Their skin had the springy tautness of a well-inflated balloon, so you had to be careful not to bite into it too violently! In restaurants, the ortolan eaters used to be completely shrouded with white sheets so as not to splash each other inadvertently with spurts of juice. It is now illegal in France to serve ortolans commercially, but I can still remember, as a boy, how utterly amazed I was to see six people sitting round a table in a Fleurance restaurant eating with sheets over their heads, looking for all the world like members of the Ku Klux Klan.

At the Oratoire we would eat about three or four ortolans each. The bones were very soft, and all the intestines had shrivelled up into a little ball. You could eat the whole bird without any difficulty, and if they had been fattened and killed in the traditional way, they were, as I have said, absolutely delectable.

At the time we were enjoying our ortolans, Marcel would be shooting the first partridges, and these were another source of culinary delight. In the weeks before the *vendange*, Camille would roast the younger ones and serve them with fresh grapes taken from the Oratoire vines. She might also mix the older and younger birds and cook them with cabbage, in the local way.

Perdrix aux Choux

YOUNG PARTRIDGE WITH CABBAGE—SERVES 4

2 old partridges

4 young partridges

200 g/7 oz duck fat

1 kg/2¼ lb green cabbages, quartered and hard core removed

150 g/5 oz onions

200 g/7 oz carrots

6 garlic cloves, peeled and left whole

1 small bouquet garni

300 ml/½ pt dry white wine

100 g/4 oz garlic sausage

100 g/4 oz toulouse sausages

150 g/5 oz salt pork

75 g/3 oz smoked bacon
1 clove
salt and freshly ground pepper

Preheat oven to 200°C/400°F/gas 6. Put the old partridges in a roasting pan, smear with 50 g/2 oz duck fat and roast in the preheated oven for 20 minutes. These birds are only used to give flavour to the cabbage and should not be served with the finished dish. Reduce the oven temperature to 180°C/350°F/gas 4.

Meanwhile, put the cabbage in a saucepan, cover with cold water, bring quickly to the boil and cook for 30 seconds to blanch it. Refresh in cold water and drain.

Cut the onions and carrots into 1 cm/½ in dice. Heat 100 g/4 oz fat in a flameproof casserole and gently sweat the onions and half the carrots for 15 minutes. Add the garlic, bouquet garni and wine and place half the cabbage on top.

Put in the 2 old partridges, the remaining carrots, both sausages, the pork, bacon and the clove. Season to taste. Put the rest of the cabbage on top, pour on 500 ml/18 fl oz boiling water and cover the casserole. Cook in the oven for 45 minutes, then remove and keep warm.

Raise the oven temperature to 200°C/400°F/gas 6. Smear the young partridges with the remaining fat and roast in the oven for about 30 minutes. They should still be pink. Leave to rest in a warm place for 10 minutes. Arrange the cabbage on a serving dish. Slice all the different meats and lay them on the cabbage. Top with the young partridges and pour over the cooking juices.

October and November were good months for pheasants. When we were children, we were always excited when Marcel came home with a pheasant or two among the partridges and hares. We loved the birds for their size and colour and for the fine feathers of the cocks. They made another welcome change from the usual chicken at the midday meal.

Young pheasants would be roasted, but Camille usually casseroled the larger ones, either with walnuts plucked from the Oratoire trees, or with celeriac from the kitchen garden and some floc, the Gascon aperitif which is made from freshly fermented grape juice mixed with armagnac.

Ragoût de Faisan aux Noix

PHEASANT WITH FRESH WALNUTS—SERVES 4

2 pheasants, each cut into 3 pieces

salt and freshly ground pepper

75 g/3 oz plain flour

100 g/4 oz duck fat

300 ml/½ pt dry white wine

1 bouquet garni

200 ml/7 fl oz double cream

100 g/4 oz shelled fresh walnuts

Season the pheasant pieces and roll them in the flour. Heat the fat in a flameproof casserole, put in the pheasant and seal until golden all over. Tip off the fat, pour in the wine and reduce by half. Add 100 ml/4 fl oz boiling water and the bouquet garni, cover and cook over low heat for 45 minutes, until the pheasant is tender.

Take out the pheasant and reduce the cooking stock to 100 ml/4 fl oz. Remove the bouquet garni and pour in the cream. Add the walnuts and return the pheasant to the casserole. Heat for about 5 minutes, until the sauce coats the pheasant. Check the seasoning and serve.

Faisan au Floc de Gascogne et au Céleri Rave

PHEASANT WITH FLOC & CELERIAC—SERVES 4

1 pheasant, drawn

100 g/4 oz duck fat

50 g/2 oz onions, diced

50 g/2 oz carrots, diced

25 g/1 oz butter

1 small celeriac

Stuffing

50 g/2 oz duck fat

75 g/3 oz cow's udder or veal sweetbread, soaked for 2–3 hours

salt and freshly ground pepper

1 small onion, finely chopped

25 g/1 oz breadcrumbs, soaked in water

2 egg yolks

100 g/4 oz fresh foie gras, cut into 5 mm/¼ in cubes

150 ml/5 fl oz floc de Gascogne or frontignan

Preheat the oven to 220°C/425°F/gas 7. To make the stuffing, heat the fat in a frying pan, put in the udder and cook gently for 5 minutes on each side. Season, remove from the pan, cut into 2.5 cm/1 in pieces and set aside.

Add the onion to the same frying pan and cook gently for 10 minutes, then put in a blender or food processor with the udder, breadcrumbs, egg yolks and seasoning and process for 1 minute until smooth and liquid. Take the stuffing out of the blender and stir in the foie gras and 50 ml/2 fl oz floc. Mix well and check the seasoning. Chill in the fridge until it begins to solidify, then stuff the pheasant with the stuffing and sew it up.

Heat 50 g/2 oz fat in a roasting pan and seal the bird on all sides. Turn it on to one leg and roast in the hot oven for 15 minutes. Turn it on to the other side and roast for another 15 minutes. Finally, turn the bird on its back, add the diced onions and carrots and roast for a further 10 minutes, basting from time to time throughout.

Pour off the fat from the pan and flame the pheasant with the remaining floc. Transfer to a dish, cover with greaseproof paper and keep warm.

Pour 200 ml/7 fl oz water into the roasting pan and reduce by one-third. Beat in the butter, check the seasoning and strain the sauce.

Peel the celeriac and cut four 1 cm/½ in slices. Heat the remaining fat and cook the celeriac gently until tender.

Carve the pheasant and place a slice of celeriac on each plate. Arrange the pheasant on top with a spoonful of stuffing beside each portion. Pour the sauce around the edge and serve.

The *Toussaint* holidays began after the *vendange*, at the end of October, and went on until about the second week in November. The far hills would then be tinged with a dull blackness that was already wintry; thick morning mists hung along the valley of the Gèle, veiling the mill of Escapat, and muffling the sound of the weir. The hedges burned with bunches of scarlet berries, the trees were almost bare, and only the leaves of the vines, stripped now of their harvest of grapes, still clung to their branches and drew lines of gold and yellow across the autumnal landscape.

At the Oratoire, as the evenings began to draw in, we would sit more and more round the fire; extra wood was brought up from the big barn behind the house and stacked up beside the fireplace. It was very important to ensure that the fire produced the correct degree of cooking heat at the right moment. You needed one sort of fire to roast a chicken on a spit; another to boil and simmer saucepans or earthenware casseroles or the big iron soup pot; another to keep the *four de campagne* at an even temperature, and so on. It was a difficult art, but Camille was skilful at it and managed very well.

Despite this, Marcel felt solely and totally responsible for the very life and existence of the fire. The fire of the house was sacred: he believed that he and no-one else should be in charge of it. If it went out, only Marcel could light it again. At night, only Marcel could bank it up with ashes so that it would still be alight in the morning. He alone had the right to rearrange the logs, or to add new ones. I think that the kitchen fire was the only thing about which my grandfather and I really disagreed. If ever I touched it, I was always criticized, so sometimes I could not resist teasing him by giving one of the burning logs a push with my foot just to watch his reactions. But, typically, he never changed his attitude, and was never prepared to share his fire with anyone else. It was, after all, the only source of heat in the whole house and therefore, in many ways, its heart.

At night, after we had spent the day harrowing or ploughing, and my feet were cold and blistered from leading the cows over the rough earth, it was wonderful to sit beside Marcel in front of the fire and to plunge our feet into bowls of hot water and sea salt. It was a joy to feel the relief to our feet and the warmth of the fire on our faces. As I listened to my grandfather's stories and *bêtises*, I felt so comfortable that I could almost forgive him for being so obstinate.

Another good moment during the first evenings of the *Toussaint* holiday was when Camille cooked us an omelette flambée, which she usually made with apples or blackberries, though sometimes she made them with grapes if it was at the time of the *vendange*, or with *Pruneaux d'Agen*. When we were children, we loved these omelettes with their blue flames, which leapt up so dramatically in the light of the fire. When my grandmother lit the *eau-de-vie*, we rushed to turn the lights out; and, if it happened to be lunch-time, we would close all the doors and shutters and draw the curtains to get the same exciting effect.

Omelette Flambée aux Mûres

FLAMBÉED BLACKBERRY OMELETTE—SERVES 4

8 eggs
150 g/5 oz caster sugar
250 g/9 oz blackberries
50 g/2 oz butter
100 ml/4 fl oz armagnac

Beat the eggs with 50 g/2 oz sugar. Put the remaining sugar in a saucepan with 250 ml/9 fl oz water and heat until the sugar has dissolved. Add the blackberries and warm them gently, then drain and set aside.

In a non-stick omelette pan, melt a quarter of the butter over a low heat, then increase the heat and add 2 eggs. Cook for 30 seconds, stirring with a wooden spatula, then leave for a few seconds until the omelette sets and the underside is lightly browned. Put a tablespoon of the blackberries in the middle and fold over the omelette. Roll it on to a warmed plate and spoon some more blackberries around the edge. Make 3 more omelettes in the same way.

Heat the armagnac in a saucepan and pour it over the top of the omelettes. Flame the alcohol in front of your guests and serve. The effect will be more dramatic if your dining room is dark, so draw the curtains if necessary.

After the ploughing and sowing and the maize harvest, Marcel would start to cut away some of the longer branches from the vines, which were now bare and leafless. These twisted, gnarled *sarments de vigne* would be stored away in the barn to dry, and would eventually be burned on the kitchen fire, where they would impart their own particular, subtle flavour to any food that was cooked on them. The earth round the trunk of each vine had to be broken up and turned over; Marcel did this with a small plough which was pulled between the rows of vines by a single cow.

At the same time, in October and early November, we would gather the pumpkins and water-melons which grew in the long fields on the other side of the Fleurance road. Most of these were sold to dealers and to the shop, but Camille kept some to make a whole variety of tarts, desserts and jams, or excellent savoury vegetable dishes.

Marmelade de Citrouille

PUMPKIN JAM

3 kg/6½ lb pumpkin, diced
700 g/1½ lb caster sugar
juice of 2 lemons

Cook the pumpkin with a little water until soft. Add the sugar and cook for another hour, stirring frequently. Add the lemon juice, pour the hot jam into sterilized jars, cool and seal.

Gratin de Citrouille

GRATIN OF PUMPKIN

800 g/1¾ lb pumpkin, diced
25 g/1 oz duck fat
100 g/4 oz cooked rice
100 ml/4 fl oz double cream
salt and freshly ground pepper
75 g/3 oz gruyère

Heat the fat in a saucepan, then put in the pumpkin and cook slowly until soft, stirring occasionally so that it does not stick. Add a little water if necessary.

Preheat the oven to 220ºC/425ºF/gas 7. Mash the pumpkin with a potato masher, then add the cooked rice and cream. Check the seasoning and pour the pumpkin into a gratin dish. Sprinkle the cheese on top and bake in the preheated oven for 15 minutes. Serve at once.

Early in November, we would start to spend the evening round the kitchen fire, stripping the covering leaves away from the maize cobs, detaching and collecting the big, yellow grains, and making a pile of the hard, inner core swhich we later burned as firewood. We had special wooden tools to strip away the leaves and a machine like a coffee-grinder to loosen the corn. As we worked, we would all talk and tell stories.

Marcel might tell about the wild ceps he had found that afternoon in the woods of La Plèche; we could imagine him wandering purposefully among the trees, a bag over his shoulder, gently and instinctively poking and exploring

the thick carpet of leaves with the end of a stick, until, suddenly, he started to uncover a large cep with a thick white, bulbous stalk. Bending down, he would cut it off at the base with his knife, carefully trim away all the earthy parts at the bottom, and place it reverently in his bag.

Some of the fresh mushrooms Camille would cook next day for lunch; others she would attach to a long string and hang up to dry, festooned across the kitchen fireplace. After drying, she would put them in jars and use them for cooking during the rest of the year. Nowadays, of course, you could freeze any ceps you are lucky enough to find. They are wonderful cooked straight from frozen and taste almost as good as fresh. Naturally, Camille did not have this option!

Tarte aux Cèpes

CEP FLAN—SERVES 4

Pastry

100 g/4 oz plain flour, sifted

50 g/2 oz lard or butter, softened

1 egg

a pinch of salt

Filling

100 ml/4 fl oz milk

2 egg yolks

1 egg

salt and freshly ground pepper

25 g/1 oz duck fat

300 g/11 oz fresh ceps, cleaned and sliced, or bottled ceps, drained

15 garlic cloves, peeled and left whole

First make the pastry. Put the flour on the work surface and make a well in the centre. Put all the other pastry ingredients in the well and mix and knead with your fingers until the dough is smooth. Add a few drops of cold water if it seems too dry. Roll into a ball, wrap in a cloth and leave to rest in the fridge for 30 minutes.

Preheat the oven to 200°C/400°F/gas 6. Next, prepare the filling. Mix together the milk, egg yolks, whole egg and seasoning, beat lightly with a fork and place in the fridge until needed.

Heat the fat in a frying pan, put in the sliced fresh ceps and garlic cloves, season and cook gently for about 10 minutes, until they begin to caramelize. If you are using bottled ceps, mix them with the garlic and heat for 5 minutes.

Roll out the pastry into a circle and use it to line a 20 cm/8 in flan dish. Put in the ceps and garlic, then pour in the filling and bake in the oven for 30 minutes, until the filling is set.

Daube de Cèpes

CEPS IN RED WINE

1 kg/2¼ lb small ceps

75 g/3 oz duck fat

50 g/2 oz shallots, chopped

120 g/4½ oz bayonne ham, diced

50 g/2 oz garlic, crushed

1 bottle of red wine

salt and freshly ground pepper

1 tablespoon chopped parsley

Clean the ceps and cut off the stalks. Finely slice and reserve them. Heat the fat in a small casserole, put in the cep caps and fry for 10 minutes, stirring halfway through. Take them out, put in the shallots and ham and fry for 5 minutes. Add the garlic and half the wine. Reduce by four-fifths, then pour in the rest of the wine. Return the cep caps, season and cover the casserole. Simmer very gently for 1 hour, adding the sliced stalks after 30 minutes. Before serving, add the parsley and check the seasoning.

Sitting round the fire, my grandmother might tell us the latest village news, like the goings-on between different families or about the farmer who had one daughter who was a university lecturer in Paris and another one who was mad and lived with him at his farm which was gradually falling into rack and ruin. She would tell us about another peasant who hated everyone and quarrelled with the whole village and who was known as 'the Bear'; his son, who was just as bad, was supposed to keep gold under his mattress – he was called 'the Little Bear', and never spoke to anyone. She might tell us about the Italian family who had settled in the village, or about the young gipsy girl she had helped and befriended.

I, in turn, would tell my grandparents about television, which they had never seen but which we had at Tarbes, or I might talk about Monsieur Georges, our black Senegalese neighbour at Tarbes, who had gone round the world as a merchant seaman and was so strong that we could swing on his outstretched arms without bending them; he could (we thought) tell what we had had for lunch just by looking at our tongues, and one day he punched the postman who had made advances to his wife. Or sometimes, if there was a haunch of venison for Camille to cook, Marcel would tell us about how the animal had been shot when he had gone out with my uncle in his car for a deer-hunting expedition.

Gigue de Chevreuil au Poivre

HAUNCH OF VENISON WITH PEPPERCORNS—SERVES 8–10

1 haunch of venison, about 2.7 kg/6 lb, trimmed

trimmings from the haunch

200 g/7 oz duck fat

50 g/2 oz ham shin

150 g/5 oz onions, chopped

20 g/¾ oz plain flour

1 bottle of red wine

1 bouquet garni

2 garlic cloves, crushed

15 black peppercorns, crushed

salt and freshly ground pepper

25 ml/1 fl oz armagnac

50 g/2 oz butter

Preheat the oven to 240ºC/450ºF/gas 8. Heat half the fat in a roasting pan. Season the haunch of venison and seal it in the hot fat, then roast in the preheated oven for about 1½ hours, depending on the size, basting from time to time. When the meat is cooked to your liking, leave to rest for 10 minutes in a warm place before carving.

To make the sauce, heat the remaining fat in a saucepan. When it is very hot, put in the venison trimmings and cook until golden. Lower the heat, add the ham shin and onions and cook for 5 minutes. Sprinkle over the flour and cook for 3 minutes, stirring continuously. Pour in the wine, add the bouquet garni, garlic and peppercorns and salt to taste. Cover and cook for 30 minutes.

Strain the sauce through a sieve into another saucepan and reduce it until it coats the back of the spoon. Add the armagnac and beat in the butter. Check the seasoning; it should be strong on pepper.

Sometimes my uncle might call in at the farm himself and spend the evening with us, sitting down and helping us with the maize. This often happened when he had been to Bordeaux and the Landes on insurance business, which he always managed to combine with some shooting, and had come back with a palombe. Palombes are wild pigeons which pass over the extreme south-west corner of France during their autumn migration to Africa. They are one of the most prized gastronomic delicacies of the area.

Palombe shooting is a fairly expensive sport, as it entails the upkeep of special, butt-like hides called *palombières*, which are often like small houses, built in the undergrowth at the edges of woods. Some even have their own kitchens, since the hunters often spend all day there, waiting for the birds to arrive. These hunters use trained live decoy birds, the flapping of whose wings in the branches, together with the plaintive imitation bird-calls made by the hunters, lure the palombes to their doom. Marcel never had the money or the time to shoot palombes, nor did he ever go to Bordeaux. It was more a sport for townsmen than for peasants, so we were always very pleased when my uncle gave us a bird.

Palombes à l'Armagnac

WILD PIGEON WITH ARMAGNAC — SERVES 4

4 wild pigeons, drawn and trussed

100 g/4 oz duck fat

salt and freshly ground pepper

12 shallots

12 garlic cloves, unpeeled

1 sprig of thyme

50 ml/2 fl oz armagnac

200 ml/7 fl oz dry white wine

25 g/1 oz butter

In a flameproof casserole, heat the fat until sizzling. Season the pigeons, put them in the casserole and seal on all sides. Lower the heat, add the shallots, garlic and thyme, cover the casserole and cook for 20–30 minutes, until tender. Tip out the excess fat, pour in the armagnac, quickly replace the lid and cook for 1 minute.

Transfer the pigeon to a serving dish and surround with the shallots and garlic. Pour the wine into the casserole, reduce by two-thirds, then add 200 ml/ 7 fl oz water and reduce by half. Check the seasoning and beat the butter into the sauce.

Toussaint on the 1st November, is the time when the French commemorate their dead and visit cemeteries to place flowers on their family graves. It was on a sombre, late autumn day in October or November, when I was seven years old, that I remember taking part in the funeral of Marcel's mother, my own great-grandmother. It was the only truly traditional peasant funeral I have ever seen. Nobody else in the family was ever buried like that again; the simple dignity of the occasion was unforgettable and very moving.

The hearse was the ordinary village hearse, which was kept in a barn near the church; it was really just like a farm cart which had been turned into a sort of four-poster bed, with an upright support at each corner and a roof of black cloth stretched between them. The wheels and all the woodwork were painted black; the coffin, covered with flowers, lay on the floor of wooden boards, and the hearse was drawn by two pale, sand-coloured cows. I remember how slow the journey up the hill towards the village seemed, and how the rolling walk of the cows kept its same, steady, regular pace without ever changing. When we first left the Oratoire, only the family followed the hearse, but as we reached the first houses in the village, little groups of people all dressed in black came out of every door we passed to join the procession, which gradually grew and grew until by the time we got to the church there were so many people behind us that the nave was completely full when the service started. Everybody in the village must have been there, I think.

After the burial, we walked back to the farm for the funeral meal, for which about ten or twelve people sat down round the dining-room table. The maize harvest had recently been gathered in and some of the cobs had already been stripped and shredded, so the lunch began with a nice maize soup. Then, since there were so many guests, Camille served a turkey as the main course, cooked with ceps and accompanied by a potato pie. This was followed by foie gras and the meal ended with an apple flan.

Even in those days, few peasants owned a car, so those people who had come by bus or train from villages a long way away stayed at the farm for two or three nights. Funeral meals, however, were not unhappy occasions. People soon forgot their sadness and began to reminisce about the person who had died; they told stories and laughed and joked, and ate and drank well. By the time the lunch was over and the bottles of armagnac and *eau-de-vie* were being passed round, there were not many people who were still crying.

Soupe de Maïs

MAIZE SEMOLINA SOUP—SERVES 4

1.7 l/3 pt chicken stock
100 g/4 oz carrots, finely diced
75 g/3 oz onions, finely diced
1 bouquet garni
1 salted pig's ear or duck's head
salt and freshly ground pepper
75 g/3 oz maize semolina
100 ml/4 fl oz double cream

Pour the stock into the saucepan, add the carrots, onions, bouquet garni, pig's ear or duck's head and a little salt, bring to the boil, then cover and simmer for 20 minutes.

Sprinkle the semolina into the pan like rain and cook, stirring continuously, for 20 minutes. Remove the bouquet garni and ear or head, check the seasoning and stir the cream into the soup before serving.

Dindonneau Rôti aux Cèpes

ROAST TURKEY WITH CEPS—SERVES 10–12

1 young turkey, about 4.5 kg/10 lb

1 kg/2¼ lb fresh ceps, cleaned

250 g/9 oz duck fat

400 g/14 oz sausage meat

50 g/2 oz fresh breadcrumbs

100 g/4 oz fresh foie gras, cut into 5 mm/¼ in dice

2 egg yolks

salt and freshly ground pepper

100 g/4 oz carrots, chopped

100 g/4 oz onions, chopped

4 garlic cloves, crushed

2 tablespoons chopped parsley

500 ml/18 fl oz dry white wine

Preheat the oven to 200°C/400°F/gas 6. To make the stuffing, cut off the cep stalks and fry them in 50 g/2 oz hot fat until golden, then chop finely. Leave until cold, then mix them with the sausage meat, breadcrumbs, foie gras, egg yolks and seasoning. Stuff the turkey with this mixture and sew up the opening.

In a roasting pan, heat 150 g/5 oz fat until sizzling. Put in the turkey and seal on all sides until golden. Lay the bird on one leg and roast in the preheated oven for 45 minutes, basting frequently. Turn the bird on to the other leg and roast for another 45 minutes, still basting often.

Turn the turkey breast-side up, add the carrots and onions to the pan and cook for a final 20–30 minutes, until the juices run clear when you insert a thin knife into the thickest part of the thigh. Lay the turkey on a serving dish, breast-side down. Forty-five minutes before the turkey is cooked, heat the remaining fat in a deep frying pan until sizzling, put in the cep caps, then lower the heat, cover the pan and cook gently for 20 minutes. Turn the ceps over and cook for another 20 minutes on the other side. Season to taste. Finally, add the garlic and parsley and cook gently for 5 minutes.

When the turkey is ready, tip off the fat from the roasting pan, pour in the wine and reduce completely. Add 500 ml/18 fl oz water and reduce by half. Check the seasoning, then strain the sauce into a sauce boat. Turn the turkey the right way up, arrange the ceps around it and serve.

Tourte de Pommes de Terre à l'Ail

POTATO PIE IN PUFF PASTRY—SERVES 4

400 g/14 oz puff pastry

flour, for dusting

500 g/1 lb 2 oz potatoes, very thinly sliced

2 garlic cloves, finely chopped

2 tablespoons chopped parsley

salt and freshly ground pepper

egg wash (1 egg yolk lightly beaten with 1 tablespoon milk)

100 ml/4 fl oz double cream

1 egg yolk

Preheat the oven to 200°C/400°F/gas 6. On a lightly floured surface, roll out three-quarters of the pastry and use it to line a gratin dish.

Put the potatoes, garlic, parsley and seasoning in a bowl, mix well, then place in the gratin dish. Roll out the rest of the pastry and place it on top of the potatoes to make a lid. Carefully seal the edges and brush the top with egg wash. Cut a hole in the lid to let the steam escape and bake the pie in the preheated oven for 55 minutes.

Mix together the cream and egg yolk and, using a funnel, pour this mixture into the pie through the hole in the pastry. Return the pie to the oven for 5 minutes, then serve.

Tarte aux Pommes

APPLE FLAN—SERVES 4

800 g/1¾ lb cooking apples

150 g/5 oz caster sugar

1 vanilla pod

250 g/9 oz Pâte à tarte sucrée (recipe page 142)

Peel and core the apples. Cook half of them very gently with 100 g/4 oz sugar and the vanilla pod until puréed and almost caramelized. Leave to cool.

Preheat the oven to 200°C/400°F/gas 6. Roll out the pastry into a circle to fit a 25 cm/10 in flan dish and line the dish with the pastry. Prick the bottom with a fork to prevent it from rising. Fill with the cooked apples. Slice the remaining apples and arrange them attractively on top of the purée.

Bake in the oven for 15 minutes, then sprinkle the top of the flan with the remaining sugar and return to the oven for about 20 minutes, until the apples are lightly browned. Serve hot or cold.

I have said how I remember my great-grandmother sitting by the kitchen fire, very old and silent, and always in black. To me she was more a presence than a person, but of course to Marcel and Camille she was very much more than that. I sometimes wonder what my grandmother's feelings were at the time of the funeral. I know that her mother-in-law was a difficult person, who did not make the early years of Camille's married life as easy or as happy as they ought to have been. She was very jealous of Camille, and would not allow her to help in the house or to do any cooking. She insisted instead that Camille should spend her day working on the farm, in the fields, or looking after the poultry.

The young married couple lived in one of the small rooms below the corn loft. Marcel spent most of the time out in the fields; even his father, the very tall Pierre, does not seem to have supported his young daughter-in-law very much, though Camille always talked of him with admiration. She used to tell us that my great-grandfather owned a set, in several imposing volumes, of the illustrated Larousse dictionary; every evening before going to bed, he would sit down at the kitchen table with one of the volumes, select a page at random and read it right through from beginning to end, irrespective of its contents. In those days, peasants had no money for books and never read them, so Pierre's erudition struck Camille as being quite remarkable. In later years, she often used to complain to Marcel that things would be so much better if only he had been a reader like his father.

What really helped Camille at this difficult time of her life, in the early 1920s, was, I think, the great friendship she had with two other women of Saint Puy. One of them, Louise, was a widow who lived in a farmhouse near the wood of La Plèche. I can just remember her, when I was a boy, coming to help Camille with the cooking at the time of the harvest or the *vendange*. The other friend was called Madame Lefèvre. She lived on the left-hand side of the wide street which climbs up towards the *château*, not far from Monsieur Taste's abattoir.

Madame Lefèvre was not a native of Saint Puy, and was regarded with great respect by everyone in the village because she had once been a Paris dressmaker. Camille used to see a lot of her; it was she who really taught my grandmother to embroider and crochet and made her persist with her cooking. She encouraged Camille's interest in learning new things, gave her sympathy and understanding and equipped her well for the time when Marcel's mother at last became too old and weak to run the house. Then Camille had to assume all responsibility for the housekeeping and cooking, besides continuing to look after the poultry, the ducks and the rabbits.

Camille looked after Marcel well, seeing that he had the little things he wanted and always cooking him the food he liked best. She also gave shape and structure to his life. Without Camille, I think my grandfather could well have become a sort of tramp, or, at best, just a very ordinary sort of peasant. My grandmother often used to say that she hoped Marcel would die before she did, because she could not imagine him coping without her.

As it happened, Camille died first, in 1979. Marcel lived on alone at the Oratoire until he, too, died three years later, in 1982. He refused to leave the farm. My uncle and aunt used to visit him and bring him his food, until, one morning, they found him dead. It was how he wanted to die, I think. Without Camille, he did indeed become lost and bored, and sat all day in his chair listening to the radio. In some ways, Marcel's whole life had been spent in a cloud of blissful unreality; but if he ever reflected honestly about his past life before he died, and totted up all the hours he had spent shooting and fishing, telling stories and enjoying drinks with his friends at the Saint Puy café, he can only have told himself that, despite all his grumbles, it really had been a very happy one.

I have already mentioned Marcel's hatred of the Church and his dislike of the curé. At the time it was an unusual attitude, since most peasants, though not particularly religious, always went to mass on a Sunday and did have a certain respect for the Church. Marcel had none. Neither he nor Camille ever went to mass; the very sight of the curé was enough to evoke an outburst of some of my grandfather's worst oaths, and when the curé called at the Oratoire just to have a chat with Camille, Marcel would leave the house and hide in the barn or the stables until he had gone. Yet neither Marcel nor Camille ever said anything against the Church to other people whose religious susceptibilities they might offend, and Marcel always followed the country custom of sending some wine to the curé at the time of the *vendange*, or of giving him a piece of pork when a pig was killed.

The curé, in those days, was always *un monsieur* in a country village, but the curé of Saint Puy was also something of an eccentric. He was a small man, about sixty years old, whose hair was completely white and who always wore a cassock. He had a brusque, rather nervous manner, and was certainly not the sort of priest who would spend much time getting to know his flock or talking to them. If you met him in the street, he just said 'bonjour' politely and walked straight on without stopping. His attitude to church services was equally brusque; his aim was always to get them over as quickly as possible. He could knock off a marriage in twelve minutes, perform mass in twenty, and take confession in about thirty seconds: he devised one single omnibus question, which included every sin you might possibly have committed, to which you just had to answer in the affirmative and then the confession was over.

Every village curé has his maid, who lives in the presbytère and acts as his cook and housekeeper. The curé of Saint Puy was no exception in this respect, but what really was rather unusual was the fact that his 'maid' was a young man, about half the curé's age, called Monsieur Louis. Monsieur Louis was small, like the curé, but here all resemblance between them ended.

The 'maid' was cheerful, smiling, gregarious and very amusing. He rode about the village on a mobilette, and talked to everyone; he gossiped endlessly and knew everyone's business. He often came to buy groceries at my aunt's shop and would always stay for some conversation. I suppose the curé got to know so much about the village from his 'maid' that he himself had no need to talk to anyone. At one time, disapproving speculations were made about the nature of their relationship, and reports were even sent to the diocesan authorities, but nothing ever came of it.

In the autumn of 1972 I married Annie Barrau, whom I had first met in England not long after I had started working there. Annie was born at Bellegarde, in Haute-Savoie, but all her family came from Bordeaux, and so her real background, like mine, was that of south-west France. It seemed natural that we should decide to have our wedding at Saint Puy.

The curé knew that I lived and worked in England, and when I went to see him to arrange about the service, he turned out to be a furious anglophobe. He asked if any English people would be coming to the wedding; when I said there might be just one or two, he was relieved, and said: 'Well, I suppose that's all right. The English poisoned Napoleon and burnt Joan of Arc, and I just can't stand them.' I think if there had been more than just one or two English

guests, he really would have refused to marry us. I know that his sentiments led him sometimes to attack the English during a sermon, if the congregation happened to include the notary's daughter, who was a teacher of English and often visited London.

Eventually our wedding went off perfectly. The civil ceremony was conducted at the mairie by my uncle, who was still mayor; then the curé got us through the church service in a brisk fifteen minutes. We were married in the afternoon, but before that, at midday I had my last lunch at the Oratoire as a bachelor. It was one of Camille's best meals – so good, in fact that no-one wanted to hurry it and I was almost late for my own wedding. I particularly remember the quails cooked in vine leaves. I think they were the last real, wild quails I ever ate; they were delicious, and I have never forgotten their special taste.

Cailles aux Feuilles de Vigne

QUAIL WRAPPED IN VINE LEAVES—SERVES 4

4 quails

4 vine leaves, soaked in water and drained

4 thin rashers of bacon

50 g/2 oz duck fat

1 shallot, finely chopped

100 ml/4 fl oz dry white wine

1 large bunch of grapes

Wrap each quail in a vine leaf, then in a rasher of bacon. Heat the fat in a casserole and when it is very hot, put in the quails and cook for 10 minutes, turning them halfway through. Do not add seasoning, as the bacon is already salty.

Remove the quails from the casserole and keep warm. Pour off the fat from the casserole, then put in the shallot and sweat until soft. Pour in the wine and reduce by two-thirds, then add 200 ml/7 fl oz water and reduce by half. Add the grapes to warm through, then pour the sauce over the quails and serve.

When at last we arrived at the mairie, Annie was already there, waiting anxiously and wondering what had delayed us. She had been so busy getting ready that she had had no time to eat any lunch; so when the ceremony started I was feeling thoroughly contented after my wonderful meal, but poor Annie was dying of starvation. She had a long wait, too, since our big wedding dinner did not take place until late in the evening. It was not held at Saint Puy, but at my friend Bernard Ramounéda's restaurant, Le Florida at Castéra-Verduzan, not very far away. The menu included local recipes such as roast leg of lamb with ceps and a *croustade aux pommes*, but there was also a superb *turbotin Cambacérès*, which is one of the great classical dishes of French 19th-century *haute cuisine*.

My last, and in some ways, one of my most favourite autumn memories of Saint Puy, is of a visit Annie and I paid to my grandparents not long after we had opened La Tante Claire. Marcel and Camille had invited another neighbouring family of farmers to lunch and in order, perhaps, to redeem a little of the great culinary debt I owed my grandmother, I offered to cook the meal – but only on condition that I could prepare anything I liked, and that I could make it the sort of meal I would serve at La Tante Claire. I really wanted to give them pleasure and to offer them a meal such as they had never had before: this is the menu I cooked.

Soupe de Grenouilles au Cresson

FROGS' LEGS SOUP WITH WATERCRESS—SERVES 4

300 g/11 oz frogs' legs, deboned, bones reserved
40 g/1½ oz butter
2 shallots, finely chopped
1 medium leek, chopped
200 ml/7 fl oz dry white wine
1 l/1¾ pt chicken stock
2 bunches of watercress, trimmed and washed
100 g/4 oz potatoes, thinly sliced
1 garlic clove, peeled and left whole
100 ml/4 fl oz noilly prat
salt and freshly ground pepper
100 ml/4 fl oz double cream

Melt half the butter in a saucepan, put in the chopped shallots and leek and sweat until soft. Add the bones from the frogs' legs and cook for 5 minutes. Pour in the white wine, reduce by half, add the chicken stock and simmer this stock for 20 minutes, skimming the surface frequently.

In another saucepan, melt the remaining butter, add the boned frogs' legs and cook gently for 5 minutes. Remove the frogs' legs. Add the watercress to the pan and cook for 3 minutes, then add the potatoes, garlic, noilly prat and strain in the cooking stock. Cook until the potatoes are disintegrating, season with salt and pepper, purée in a blender for 3 minutes, then pass through a sieve.

Check the seasoning. Divide the frogs' legs between 4 soup plates, pour over the soup and finish with a swirl of cream.

Mousseline de Volaille au Citron et aux Carottes

MOUSSELINE OF CHICKEN WITH CARROTS & LEMON SAUCE—SERVES 4

150 g/5 oz chicken breast

½ egg white

375–400 ml/13–14 fl oz double cream

salt and freshly ground pepper

1 teaspoon butter

50 g/2 oz sugar

150 g/5 oz carrots, shredded

juice of 2 small lemons

juice of 1 orange

Remove the skin and sinews from the chicken. Put the meat in a food processor and purée for 1 minute. Add the egg white and process for 1 more minute. Rub the purée through a sieve into a bowl and place in the freezer until it begins to crystallize at the edges. At the same time, chill the bowl of the food processor in the fridge.

Return the chicken to the food processor and process for 1 minute, then slowly add 150 ml/5 fl oz cream. Switch off the motor and scrape the chicken from the edges of the bowl into the purée, then switch on and add another 75 ml/3 fl oz cream more quickly. Season with salt and a little pepper.

Test the mousseline by poaching a small spoonful in simmering salted water; it should be soft, but holding together. If it is too hard, add a little more cream.

Melt the butter in a saucepan, add 2 teaspoons sugar and the carrots and cook slowly until tender.

Bring a large saucepan of salted water to the boil. Form the mousseline into oval shapes, using a large spoon, and poach them in the simmering water for 10 minutes, turning them over halfway.

Put the remaining sugar and the lemon juice in a small saucepan and cook until caramelized. Add the orange juice and 150 ml/5 fl oz cream and cook gently until the sauce is thick enough to coat the back of a spoon.

To serve, put the carrots in a dish, arrange the mousselines on top and pour over the sauce.

Civet de Homard au Madiran

BRAISED LOBSTER IN RED WINE—SERVES 4

4 lobster portions, 450 g/1 lb each
50 g/2 oz carrots, finely diced
50 g/2 oz mushrooms, finely diced
25 g/1 oz fennel, finely diced
1 celery stalk, finely diced
25 g/1 oz shallots, finely diced
50 ml/2 fl oz olive oil
1 small bouquet garni
1 garlic clove, crushed
3 anchovy fillets, soaked to remove the salt, drained and chopped
1 teaspoon tomato purée
1 l/1¾ pt red madiran wine
salt and freshly ground pepper
1 teaspoon plain flour
20 g/¾ oz butter, softened
50 ml/2 fl oz armagnac

In a saucepan, sweat all the diced vegetables with half the oil for 5 minutes. Add the bouquet garni, garlic, chopped anchovies, tomato purée and wine, season with salt and pepper and cook gently for 20 minutes.

Cut the lobsters into pieces. Collect the corals and mix them into a small ball with the flour and softened butter.

Heat the remaining oil in a large frying pan. When it is hot, put in the lobster pieces and sauté on all sides until the shell has turned red. Pour in the armagnac and flambé, then put the lobster pieces in the sauce and cook gently for 8 minutes.

Lift out the lobster with a slotted spoon and keep warm. Whisk the coral mixture into the sauce and simmer gently for 3 minutes. Check the seasoning, put the lobster back into the sauce and serve.

Paupiettes d'Agneau aux Feuilles de Poireau

STEAMED FILLET OF LAMB IN LEEK PARCELS—SERVES 4

2 lamb fillets from the best end, cut lengthways into 2 pieces
(keep the bones to make a juice for serving)
50 g/2 oz duck fat or butter
4 large leek leaves, blanched
roasted garlic and french beans, to serve

Stuffing
50 g/2 oz mushrooms, very finely chopped
2 shallots, very finely chopped
1 tablespoon butter
100 g/4 oz dried breadcrumbs
1 tablespoon chopped parsley
a pinch of thyme or marjoram leaves
1 garlic clove, chopped
1 egg yolk
500 g/1 lb spinach, chopped

Heat the duck fat in a frying pan, put in the lamb and seal on all sides.

Put the chopped mushrooms, shallots and butter in a frying pan and sweat until very soft. Cook the spinach in a pan of boiling water, drain and squeeze dry. Add with all the other stuffing ingredients and mix to a firm paste. Halve the mixture, place each half between 2 sheets of cling film and flatten with a rolling pin into a sheet large enough to wrap around two pieces of meat. Remove the top sheet of cling film.

Cut the 2 sheets of stuffing and cling film in half, place a piece of lamb in the centre of each piece and use the cling film to mould the stuffing around the meat. Cut out 4 more pieces of cling film, lay a leek leaf on each, place the coated meat on top and wrap very lightly in the cling film. Twist the ends tightly to make 4 'sausages'.

Prepare a steamer with boiling water. Steam the lamb for 10 minutes, then leave to rest in a warm place for another 10 minutes. Remove the cling film, carve each piece of lamb into 2 slices and serve with roasted garlic, steamed french beans and a juice made from the lamb bones.

Galettes de Foie Gras aux Echalotes Rôties

POTATO CAKES WITH FOIE GRAS & SHALLOTS—SERVES 4

12 shallots, of equal size

75 g/3 oz butter

1 large potato

4 tablespoons oil

salt and freshly ground pepper

75 ml/3 fl oz sauternes

4 slices of foie gras, 100 g/4 oz each

Preheat the oven to 200º/400ºF/gas 6. Wrap all the shallots together in foil with 15g/½ oz butter and bake in the oven for about 40 minutes until tender and pale golden. You must do this before cooking the foie gras. Keep warm.

Prepare the potato galettes: finely grate the potato on a mandoline and squeeze out all the moisture with your hands. Heat 1 tablespoon oil in a small frying pan, put in one-quarter of the potato and spread it out, pressing down hard with a fish slice or spatula so that it coheres into a flat cake. Cook for about 2 minutes until the underside is crisp and golden, then turn over the galette, salt lightly and cook until the other side is crisp. Drain on absorbent paper. Wipe out the pan with kitchen paper, pour in another spoonful of oil and make 3 more galettes in this way. Keep warm.

To make the sauce, pour half the sauternes into a saucepan and reduce to 2 tablespoons. Add the remaining wine and reduce by half. Whisk in the remaining butter, a little at a time, taking care that the sauce does not boil again.

Season the foie gras, put it in a frying pan without adding any fat (it will give off a huge quantity of its own) and cook for 1 minute on each side, until the outside is golden and the inside very slightly pink.

Place the potato galettes on hot plates, top each with a slice of foie gras and place the shallots around the edge. Pour the sauce around and serve immediately.

Soufflé aux Pistaches

PISTACHIO SOUFFLÉ—SERVES 6

100 ml/4 fl oz milk

50 g/2 oz pistachio paste

1 whole egg

1 egg yolk

50 g/2 oz caster sugar

40 g/1½ oz plain flour

20 g/¾ oz butter, softened

50 g/2 oz grated chocolate

6 egg whites

Preheat the oven to 230°C/450°F/gas 8. Boil the milk with the pistachio paste. Beat together the egg, yolk and half the sugar for 2 minutes, then add the flour and mix for 1 minute. Pour on the milk mixture, transfer to a saucepan and cook for 4 minutes, whisking continuously. Pour the mixture into a bowl, cover with foil and keep in a warm place.

Grease the inside of 6 individual soufflé dishes with the softened butter and coat with grated chocolate.

Beat the egg whites very stiffly, add the remaining sugar and beat until firm. Whisk the pistachio mixture for a few seconds, then add one-quarter of the egg whites and whisk it in vigorously. Add half the remaining egg whites, stirring quickly with a spatula to make sure there are no lumps. Quickly stir in the rest of the egg whites in the same way. Pour the soufflé mixture into the prepared dishes and bake in the preheated oven for 10 minutes.

Camille was delighted at the thought of this meal, but when Marcel came in and heard what was going to happen, he turned awkward and began to grumble, refusing to eat anything except his ordinary soup and chicken. When I served up the meal, Marcel was disappointed and suspicious, and we had to coax him to eat. But by the time he had finished the chicken mousseline, he liked it so much that he asked for a second helping. 'Do you like it?' he asked the other farmer in patois. 'Yes I do,' replied the farmer. 'Do you know what it is?' asked Marcel. 'No,' said the farmer. 'It's chicken,' said Marcel, 'and do you know, it's the very first chicken I have ever eaten which had no bones in it.'

Souvenir de famille.

Winter

In December Camille began to fatten her ducks and geese for Christmas, and in January the pigs were killed. Their hams and *confits* would last us through the year. In the biting cold we bathed in a tub by the kitchen fire. After Christmas lunch and the midnight supper on New Year's Eve came Epiphany, with a bean hidden in the cake and the crowning of kings and queens.

WINTER AT SAINT PUY was a season of silent fields and frozen ponds. Though the winters were cold, we did not often have snow. The colours of the landscape were usually those of black woods, dull green pastures and the brown, lumpy earth of ploughed fields. The smell of wood smoke on a cold afternoon meant that everybody was living and working as much as possible indoors, either round the kitchen fire or inside one of the farm buildings. At the Oratoire, for example, Marcel would probably be in the barn, sawing the big logs which dried there in neat, square stacks, then chopping and splitting them with a heavy long-handled axe. Sitting in the warm kitchen, we could hear the dull thuds of the axe and also my grandfather's spasmodic commentary of oaths which nearly always accompanied them; or we would listen to the sounds made by his hammer and file as he repaired the haycutter or the harrow or one of the carts.

If there was any building work outstanding, such as a stall or a sty to be mended, or a window to be put in or painted, or new rabbit-cages to be erected, Marcel had to do these tasks in winter. Another of his jobs at this time was to mend the straight-backed, straw-seated chairs we had at the farm, and, if necessary, to make new ones. He also made all the besoms with which Camille would sweep the house during the coming year, binding new thin brown branches on to the wooden handles. In the evenings we sat round the fire, peeling and stripping the corn cobs, reminiscing and telling each other stories; in the afternoons, my grandfather had ample time to ride up to the café and spend an hour or two with his friends over a few glasses of wine and a game of cards.

The church clock, which like the clock in our kitchen had been made by Monsieur Duprom, still sounded each hour twice, just in case you had miscounted the number of strokes the first time you heard them, but they rang over a deserted countryside. Harvesters, *vendangeurs* and ploughmen had all vanished, and no-one came out to work when the clock struck twelve at 6 o'clock in the morning, or hastened back to lunch when it struck twenty-four strokes at midday. The animals had vanished as well. Marcel's cows, brought in from the fields, spent the winter in the stables, lying on some of the straw which had been spewed out of the threshing-machine in July. They were fed on maize and on the hay that was forked down into their mangers from the loft above their heads.

When the weather was fine, and there were days of bright winter sunshine, Marcel would go out to the vines to continue pruning them and cutting away their branches, the *sarments*. Some of these he brought back to the barn to be dried for firewood, and some of them he burned in little bonfires whose slim, blue columns of smoke could be seen from right across the valley, rising above the vineyards like wispy feathers.

There were always three days every winter when my grandfather, like the other peasants of Saint Puy, was obliged to work at repairing and cleaning the minor roads and lanes round his farm. The work was not hard; it consisted mostly of filling in the holes with stones and digging out the ditches, but it was unpaid. This was a due the landowning peasants owed to the commune in accordance with local custom; it was, in fact, a continuation of the old *corvée*, the compulsory labour on the road which 18th-century peasants performed annually for their feudal landlords. Otherwise, apart from going off with his gun to shoot woodcock and wild duck, Marcel was not very active out of doors in winter; he just did his work at the farm and, as I have said, spent a good deal of time at the café.

I shall never forget how bitterly cold the Saint Puy winters could be. The only warm room in the farm was the kitchen, where we spent as much time as possible. It was here that we made a supper of eggs cooked in the hot embers of the fire when we came home from visiting my aunt on dark Sunday evenings. We used to put our eggs under the very hot ashes and leave them for 3 minutes or so, then dip pieces of bread into the delicious soft yolks.

It was here, in front of blazing logs, that we all took our baths, standing or sitting in a wide metal tub of heated water. Our bedrooms were on the other side of the passage, beyond the dining-room, and they were like ice-houses. The cold seemed to cling remorselessly to the whole of your body, and once you had left the kitchen there was little you could do to get rid of it. In the evening we heated our beds with warming pans called *moines*, or 'monks', which consisted of a closed pan full of red-hot embers from the wood fire, and a sort of metal cage which fitted above it to prevent the sheets from getting burned. On waking up in the morning we would often find the well frozen, and would have to break the ice before we could draw any water.

To protect himself from the cold, Marcel used to put on massively heavy underwear, which he wore like a suit of armour. His thick shirt and even thicker flannel vest were both as long as nightdresses, and he tucked them down into his trousers as far as he could, over the old-fashioned woollen drawers which went right down to below his knees. His wooden *sabots* were stuffed with extra felt, and when the wind was particularly cold or there was rain or snow, he used to wear a potato sack cut down one of its seams over his head, which made him look like a mediaeval friar.

In those days, we either grumbled about the cold or accepted it philosophically, and kept warm as best we could; but of course in the past, winter conditions in that part of France were often far worse than anything I, or perhaps even my grandparents, ever knew. When I was browsing through the old volumes of parish records in the *mairie*, I came upon Monsieur Dubarry's account of how the village was affected by the terrible winter weather which spread all over France in January 1709. Snow fell at Saint Puy for two weeks on end, and the drifts were so deep that all the roads out of the village were blocked. The wine froze in its barrels and burst the wood; large oak trees were split into two or three pieces by the cold; the desperately hungry sheep tried to eat each other, and nearly all of them died; and most of the vines perished and had to be pulled up, with catastrophic consequences for that year's *vendange*.

Snow did not fall every year, though the Gèle valley was often white with a heavy frost which lay on the hedges and on the branches of the trees in deep, powdery layers, vague and obscure at first in the early morning fog, but suddenly as precise as lace when the winter sun broke through the haze and illuminated everything with dazzling highlights and dark shadows. It was on these cold, bright, blue-skied mornings that Marcel would leave the Oratoire early with his gun and his dog and set off in search of snipe, woodcock and wild duck.

He would find the duck along the rivers and around the ponds, where, sometimes, if the water had frozen during the night, he would come upon birds trapped in the ice by their legs. Though it was not a very sporting thing to do, perhaps, because the ducks were defenceless, Marcel could never resist the temptation to kill them and bring them home in his bag, along with the other game he had shot in a more conventional manner. Once Camille had cooked them, it did not seem to matter very much how the ducks had died; they were all good to eat!

Canards Sauvages au Suc d'Orange

WILD DUCK WITH ORANGE JUICE—SERVES 4

2 wild ducks

3 seville oranges

salt and freshly ground pepper

50 ml/2 fl oz Pousse rapière *(see page 254)* or cointreau

200 ml/7 fl oz white wine

20 g/¾ oz butter

segments of 2 seville oranges, to serve

Preheat the oven to 230ºC/450ºF/gas 8. Squeeze the 3 seville oranges, reserve the juice and stuff the ducks with the skins. Truss and season.

Roast the ducks in the hot oven for 45 minutes–1 hour; they should be slightly underdone. Pour off the fat from the roasting pan and flame the duck with the *pousse rapière.* Place them on a dish, breast-side down, and keep in a warm place.

Drain any remaining fat from the roasting pan, deglaze with the wine and reduce completely. Add the orange juice, reduce by half, then beat in the butter and check the seasoning.

Carve the ducks, arrange them on a serving dish with the orange segments and coat with the sauce.

Snipe and woodcock, with their long beaks and their jerky, irregular flight, darting up suddenly from beneath the hedges or from behind water reeds, are very difficult to hit, and it was a proof of my grandfather's skill with a gun that he was able to shoot as many woodcock as he did, though he always did best when the weather was very cold. There were far fewer woodcock when the winter was mild.

Once he had brought the birds back to the Oratoire, Marcel had his own special way of cooking them. He first hung them up by their beaks in the larder, and left them there until a sort of whitish liquid began to ooze out of them and drip down into a plate below. When this happened, the woodcock were ready for cooking. It took about a week for the liquid to materialize, and by then the birds had begun to give out quite a strong smell, but we knew how good they were going to taste when we ate them so nobody complained.

Marcel then plucked the birds, taking great care not to tear their skins, and roasted them. He tied a piece of string to their beaks, and hung the birds up over the fire so that they revolved slowly while they cooked and as they did so, the juice which dripped out of them fell on to a piece of bread. When they were roasted, he emptied them and threw away the crop, which usually contained a lot of sand. Then he chopped up the rest of the intestines very finely, adding shallots, garlic, salt, pepper and a drop or two of armagnac. He spread this mixture in the slices of bread, which were already soaked with the cooking juices. He toasted these a little in the embers of the fire, and we ate them with the woodcock.

Prepared like this, the birds are absolutely delicious, but, of course, like Marcel, you do have to like your game high. If you do not, you can always follow Camille's recipe for the excellent *salmis* of woodcock which she used to make in one of her big iron casseroles.

Salmis de Bécasse

SALMIS OF WOODCOCK

4 woodcock

50 g / 2 oz duck fat

50 ml / 2 fl oz armagnac

salt and freshly ground pepper

4 slices of bread, toasted

4 shallots, sliced

1 bottle of red wine

1 garlic clove, sliced

1 sprig of thyme

50 g / 2 oz butter

Preheat the oven to 240°C/475°F/gas 9. Truss the woodcock. Heat the duck fat in a roasting pan until it spits, put in the woodcock and roast in the oven for about 15–20 minutes. Pour off any excess fat from the pan, pour in the armagnac and flambé. Lay the birds on a dish, breast-side down. Remove the guts, chop and season them. Spread on the toasted bread and bake in the oven for 5 minutes.

Using the same pan in which you cooked the woodcock, sweat the shallots over low heat for 5 minutes. Meanwhile, cut off the legs and breasts from the birds and keep in a warm place. Finely chop the carcass meat and add to the shallots. Cook gently for 5 minutes, stirring occasionally.

Add the red wine, garlic, thyme and pepper to taste and reduce by half. Pass the sauce through a strainer and beat in the butter. Put a bird on each croûton and pour over the sauce.

Winter was rather rich in feasts. There was, of course, Christmas, and this was followed by the *fête de Saint Sylvestre* with its midnight *réveillon* on New Year's Eve. Then, on the first Sunday in January came Epiphany and the *galette des rois*, a special Twelfth Night cake with a bean hidden in the centre, and finally, on 16th January, we celebrated the *fête de Saint Marcel*, when my grandfather became the hero of the day and received cards and congratulations, and Camille cooked him a special lunch. But the first really important winter feast at Saint Puy came before all of these, and was held on 4th December, which is Saint Barbara's day.

Saint Barbara, whose protection against flames and thunderstorms is considered to be especially efficacious, is the patron saint of all French firemen. At Saint Puy, her feast day was marked by the firemen's banquet at midday, followed by a fair outside the fire station during the afternoon, and by the *bal des pompiers*, the firemen's ball, in the evening.

The fire brigade numbered about twelve members, one of whom was Marcel. He held the rank of sergeant, and my uncle Capuron, the mayor, was captain. My grandfather was immensely proud of being a fireman; it was as important to him as being an *ancien combattant* or *garde-chasse* or *garde-pêche*. He became a *pompier* when he was quite a young man, before 1939, and remained one until he was really quite old. I often wonder whether his enthusiasm for the fire service did not have something to do with a fire which broke out at the Oratoire when he was still a boy, and which destroyed the barn and half the house. The place was rebuilt afterwards, but the traumatic memory of the fire may well have remained in Marcel's mind all his life.

Whether or not this was really the origin of his vocation as a fire-fighter, I do not know, but I well remember his pride in his two uniforms, which were always kept ready for use in the bedroom wardrobe. The working uniform was a blue overall suit with a stout belt and a magnificent fireman's helmet in burnished brass, which Camille used to polish until it shone like gold. The ceremonial uniform was of dark blue serge, with silver buttons and red stripes down the trousers; with it, my grandfather wore a *képi* with red piping round the top and a silver badge.

This ceremonial uniform was Marcel's special delight and, shortly before his death, he told my uncle that his last wish was to be buried in it. When he died, his wish was respected, and he was placed in his coffin wearing his best uniform, with his *képi* resting on his breast and all his buttons polished. This was quite illegal and contrary to all fire service regulations, since the uniform was state property and should have been returned to the authorities, but no-one paid attention to this aspect of the affair, and, at any rate, it all seemed charmingly typical of my grandfather's character. After the funeral everyone said that Marcel must have been the only fireman in the whole of France ever to be buried in his uniform.

The fire station at Saint Puy occupied the whole of the lower storey of the *salle des fêtes*, opposite the butcher's shop and almost next door to the bakery of Monsieur Trille. Behind the wide double doors, the village fire engine, all scarlet and chrome, stood ready for instant action at any moment of the day or night. Rather surprisingly, it was the largest engine in the whole of the *département* of the Gers, and it was a source of justifiable pride to all the inhabitants of Saint Puy that it was often borrowed by larger villages or even towns, when their own engines were not powerful enough to fight a particularly difficult fire. All the firemen worked on a voluntary basis, and none of them received any sort of fixed salary.

There was a siren on the roof of the *salle des fêtes*; whenever the duty fireman received news of a fire, he sounded the siren to call the other firemen to leave whatever they might be doing at the time, and to assemble immediately at the fire station.

Farm fires nearly always started at night, when, usually, the hay had started to ignite or a lamp had fallen over in one of the barns or stables. At 2 or 3 o'clock in the morning the siren would suddenly start wailing, and Marcel would jump out of bed, put on his uniform and helmet, rush down to his *mobilette* and set off in the direction of the fire station.

We children would all get up in a state of great excitement, and so would Camille, who used to stand by the front door to see which way the engine went when it drove out of its garage. It could take the road to Condom, on the far side of the village or go southwards in the direction of Auch; it could take the turning towards Lectoure, near the accident black-spot by the cross; or, most thrilling and dramatic of all, it could drive straight down the hill towards the Oratoire, on the Fleurance road.

By now we would all be standing at the door, as the huge yellow headlights and the heavy sound of the motor came nearer and louder, until, at last, the engine plunged past us, and we saw, for an instant, in the patch of light which spilled out on to the road from the Oratoire doorway, the helmeted faces of my uncle and my grandfather as they sped away into the darkness. Camille had friends who owned farms on all the roads out of Saint Puy and, whichever way the firemen went, she would stand in horror, her hand to her cheek, exclaiming: *'Mon Dieu! Mon Dieu!* I do hope it isn't Monsieur So-and-so's farm, or Madame Somebody's! I do hope it isn't Passy, or Frescatis, or la Bourdette' – or whatever farm came into her mind.

When silence fell, we children went back to bed, but my grandmother stayed up all the rest of the night, anxiously awaiting Marcel's return. Sometimes he was back in an hour or two, but if the fire was a serious one and buildings, corn, hay and even animals burned, it might take the *pompiers* about five or six hours to put it out. On these occasions my grandfather would come back about 9 or 10 in the morning, and, over breakfast, he would tell us all the news of the fire. Once he returned much later even than that, after a particularly dangerous fire in which a child had died; Camille was so relieved to see him safely back at home that she cooked us all a special lunch which included a baked stuffed cabbage with tomato sauce. And it must have been an exceptionally good one, for I have never forgotten it!

Gâteau de Choux

BAKED STUFFED CABBAGE—SERVES 4

1 savoy cabbage

1 kg/2¼ lb hock and belly of pork

2 egg yolks

1 tablespoon chopped parsley

2 garlic cloves, chopped

100 ml/4 fl oz dry white wine

salt and freshly ground pepper

Sauce tomate *(see next recipe), to serve*

Preheat the oven to 200°C/400°F/gas 6. Cut the cabbage stalk to free the leaves and blanch them in boiling water for 2 minutes. Refresh and drain.

Mince the pork, using a medium blade. Add the egg yolks, parsley, garlic, wine and salt and pepper to taste and mix thoroughly.

Line the bottom and sides of a 20 cm/8 in cake tin or pudding basin with cabbage leaves, put in one-quarter of the stuffing, then a layer of cabbage and so on, until you have used all the stuffing. Cover with cabbage leaves. Place in a bain-marie and bake in the oven for 1½ hours.

Unmould the cabbage 'cake' on to a serving dish and pour the tomato sauce round the edge.

Sauce Tomate

TOMATO SAUCE

700 g/1½ lb tomatoes, deseeded and chopped
25 g/1 oz duck fat
50 g/2 oz carrots, chopped
50 g/2 oz onions, sliced
20 g/¾ oz bayonne ham, diced
15 g/½ oz plain flour
2 garlic cloves, chopped
1 bouquet garni
salt and freshly ground pepper

Put the fat into a thick saucepan, add the carrots and onions and cook for 5 minutes. Add the ham, cook for 5 more minutes, then stir in the flour and cook for 3 minutes, stirring with a wooden spoon.

Pour in 200 ml/7 fl oz water, add the garlic, bouquet garni and tomatoes and season to taste. Simmer gently for 1 hour, then rub through a coarse sieve.

In the daytime the *pompiers* were often called out to local accidents. Road accidents were dealt with by the police and the ambulance service, but the siren above the *salle des fêtes* often sounded when a farmer had injured his leg with a scythe, or a child had fallen into a lake or a river and was thought to be drowned, or someone had been electrocuted after touching a live cable. Marcel never told us much about these accidents, but I know that some of the things were quite unpleasant.

All these dramas were remembered and celebrated each year on Saint Barbara's day. The festivities started at midday with music by the firemens' band and a formal parade of all the firemen, including Marcel, in their best uniforms. After the parade they sat down at a long table to enjoy their annual banquet, at which, despite the patronage of Saint Barbara, no woman was ever permitted to be present.

The main room of the little restaurant under the arches near the market hall was hired for the occasion, and Monsieur and Madame Dassain worked from the crack of dawn in their kitchen to produce the menu which, over the years, had become traditional. The banquet began with melon, enhanced by the addition of a couple of spoonsful of *floc*, the local aperitif; the soup was always mutton and chestnut; the fish course was a *brandade* of salt cod; the main dish was a *civet* and finally, after the foie gras, came a fruit tart or light sponge cake.

Soupe de Mouton aux Châtaignes

MUTTON SOUP WITH CHESTNUTS—SERVES 12

500 g/1 lb 2 oz mutton or lamb breast, cut into 4

50 g/2 oz duck fat

4 l/7 pt boiling stock or water

150 g/5 oz carrots, diced

100 g/4 oz onions, diced

1 bouquet garni

2 cloves

3 garlic cloves, crushed

salt and freshly ground pepper

700 g/1½ lb chestnuts, peeled and skinned

300 g/11 oz savoy cabbage, shredded and blanched

200 g/7 oz french bread

mustard and gherkins, to serve

In a large pot, fry the mutton in the fat until golden on both sides. Pour over the hot water, then add the carrots, onions, bouquet garni, cloves and garlic and season. Cook for 1½–2 hours. After 45 minutes, add the chestnuts, then, 20 minutes later, the cabbage. Check the seasoning.

Cut the bread into chunks, place in a large soup tureen and pour over the soup, keeping the meat aside. Leave the soup to infuse for 5 minutes before serving. The meat can be served after the soup with mustard and gherkins.

Brandade de Morue

CREAMED SALT COD

500 g/1 lb 2 oz salt cod, soaked overnight under running water

250 g/9 fl oz milk

1 sprig of thyme

1 bay leaf

150 g/5 oz duck fat or oil

3 garlic cloves, crushed

1 tablespoon chopped parsley

500 g/1 lb 2 oz potatoes, boiled and mashed

freshly ground pepper

croûtons or crusty bread, to serve

Put the soaked cod in a saucepan and add the milk, 250 ml/9 fl oz water, thyme and bay leaf. Bring to the boil, take the pan off the heat and leave the fish to cool in the cooking liquid. Strain off the cooled liquid and reserve it. Flake the cod.

Heat the fat or oil in the saucepan. When it is sizzling, add a little of the cod and stir well with a wooden spoon. Add a little more cod, stir well and repeat until you have used all the cod. Make sure the fat stays very hot and that the fish absorbs it all. Stir in the garlic and parsley and mix well.

Mix the fish into the mashed potatoes; the mixture should be very creamy. If it is not, add some of the cooking stock. Check the seasoning; the pepper flavour should be very pronounced, but you will almost certainly not need to add salt. Serve the *brandade* in a deep dish with croûtons or crusty bread.

Civet de Lièvre

HARE IN RED WINE—SERVES 4

1 mature hare, cut into serving pieces, liver reserved

salt and freshly ground pepper

75 g/3 oz plain flour

180 g/6 oz duck fat

500 g/1 lb 2 oz onions, thinly sliced

3 garlic cloves, sliced

1 bouquet garni

1 l/1¾ pt red wine

15 g/½ oz bitter chocolate

120 g/4½ oz bayonne ham rind

Season the hare pieces and roll them in the flour. Heat 100 g/4 oz fat in a large frying pan and seal the hare pieces on all sides.

In a flameproof casserole, heat the remaining fat, put in the onions and sweat gently for 15 minutes, then add the garlic and bouquet garni. Put the hare in the casserole with the onions. Tip off the fat from the frying pan and reserve, and pour the wine into the pan. Bring to the boil, then pour it into the casserole.

Add the chocolate and ham rind, cover and cook over low heat or in a low oven (140ºC/275ºF/gas 1) for about 2½ hours, until the hare is very tender.

Meanwhile, heat a tablespoon of the reserved fat in a small roasting pan, put in the hare liver and seal on all sides. Drain then cook it in the oven until very dry, then grate on the fine side of a cheese grater.

When the hare is cooked, skim off the fat from the surface, check the seasoning, stir in the grated liver and serve.

Tarte aux Pruneaux

PRUNE FLAN—SERVES 4

250 g/9 oz prunes

3 tea bags

250 g/9 oz Pâte à tarte sucrée (recipe page 142)

250 ml/9 fl oz whipped cream, to serve

Pastry Cream

300 ml/½ pt milk

70 g/2½ oz caster sugar

1 egg yolk

40 g/1½ oz plain flour

The night before, put the prunes in a saucepan, cover with water and add the tea bags. Boil for 5 minutes, then take the pan off the heat, cover and leave overnight. The next day, drain the prunes and stone them.

Prepare the pastry cream: bring the milk to the boil. Beat the sugar with the egg yolk until pale, then mix in the flour. The mixture should be like very fine breadcrumbs. Gradually pour on the boiling milk, stirring continuously. Pour the mixture into a saucepan, heat it until it bubbles,

then cook gently for 5 minutes, stirring all the time. Pour into a bowl, cover and leave to cool completely.

Preheat the oven to 220°C/425°F/gas 7. Line a 25 cm/10 in flan dish with the pastry and prick the bottom with a fork. Put in the cold pastry cream and arrange the prunes on top; the pastry case should be three-quarters full. Bake in the preheated oven for 30 minutes.

Leave the cooked tart to cool completely and serve with whipped cream on the side.

Gâteau Mousseline

LIGHT SPONGE CAKE—SERVES 4

120 g/4½ oz caster sugar
finely grated zest of 1 orange or 1 lemon, or 25 g/1 oz ground hazelnuts
4 eggs, separated
50 g/2 oz plain flour
75 g/3 oz potato flour
butter and flour for the tin

Beat together the sugar, zest or hazelnuts, and egg yolks until very creamy. Gradually beat in the 2 flours with a wooden spoon. Beat the egg whites until stiff and very delicately fold them in.

Butter and flour an 18 cm/7 in cake tin or a traditional fluted conical mould and pour in the sponge mixture. Bake in the preheated oven for 40 minutes. Leave the cake to cool in the tin, then unmould on to a wire rack. It will remain very light and airy.

In the afternoon there was a village fair on the open space in front of the *salle des fêtes*. The band, the *fanfare des pompiers*, played more music, and stalls were set up at which the women of Saint Puy sold numerous items of home-made food. All profits were donated to the firemen. You could buy *confits*, pancakes, *beignets*, sweets, *galantines* and *conserves* of every kind. Trade was brisk, and there was always a good sum of money for the *pompiers* at the end of the evening. I remember that Camille, helped by one of her friends, once made over a thousand pancakes for the *fête des pompiers*. It took them several days to do it, but they sold every one of them.

The fair ended with a dance in the village hall above the garage of the fire engine, and the feast of Saint Barbara was prolonged, with a good deal of noisy enjoyment, well into the early hours of the following morning.

Generally speaking, our meals at the Oratoire were comparatively unvaried during the early part of winter, and without many special highlights. We depended a good deal on the fruit and vegetables which Camille had preserved or bottled in the late summer and autumn and, of course, we ate her *galantines* and her *confits* of duck and pork. On Sundays Marcel always insisted on his roast chicken, but during the week, to vary our diet a little, my grandmother used to send me to my aunt's shop in the village to buy some noodles or macaroni along with whatever other groceries she might want at that moment.

During these winter morning excursions, the narrow little streets were empty and silent and it was too cold for people to prolong a chance meeting by standing about to gossip and laugh. The absence of leaves on the trees would reveal unexpected or previously unnoticed details and corners of old buildings, which, like Monsieur Dubarry's handwriting, brought village history vividly back into my thoughts.

Turning into the little square of the war memorial, I passed an old corner house with an arched doorway, projecting wooden beams, massive stone corbels and the date 1686 carved within a stone medallion above the window. Further on, near the *mairie*, there was a round mediaeval tower with a pointed, conical roof, and from inside my aunt's shop, through the shelves in the window, I could just see the beginning of the lane which curled itself along the side of the church like a shadow, and beyond, above the houses, the sharp tip of the east window, whose flamboyant gothic tracery was usually hidden by the foliage of the trees.

Once my basket was filled with groceries, there was no time to hang about, and I had to get back quickly to the Oratoire before my grandfather could start complaining that lunch was late. If it was nearing noon, I would find him standing outside the door of the farm, tapping at his watch and calling out in a sort of measured litany of hungry irritation: '*L'heure, c'est l'heure; après l'heure, ce n'est plus l'heure.*' (Time is time and late is late.)

However, I was usually home with the groceries in good time, and the simple winter soup was firmly on the table long before the last stroke of midday had sounded from the kitchen clock. Camille, at this time of year, usually put the macaroni into a stew of chicken giblets, but occasionally she might just cook this straight away with some foie gras as the main dish of the meal.

Tourain Blanchi à l'Ail

ONION & GARLIC SOUP—SERVES 4

400 g/14 oz onions, sliced

75 g/3 oz garlic, sliced

50 g/2 oz duck fat

1 bouquet garni

1.5 l/2½ pt duck or chicken stock

2 eggs

1 tablespoon wine vinegar

salt and freshly ground pepper

120 g/4½ oz french bread, sliced

Heat the fat in a casserole, add the onions and cook for 15 minutes, until golden, stirring from time to time. Add the garlic, bouquet garni and stock, season, bring to the boil and simmer gently for 20 minutes.

Separate the eggs and mix the vinegar with the yolks. Put the bread into a tureen, pour the soup, then gently stir in the egg yolks and whites. Serve at once.

Ragoût d'Abattis de Volaille

CHICKEN NECKS, WINGS & GIBLETS STEWED IN
WHITE WINE WITH MACARONI—SERVES 4

4 chicken necks, halved

8 chicken wings, cut at the joint

4 chicken gizzards

4 chicken hearts

50 g/2 oz duck fat

200 g/7 oz carrots, very thinly sliced

100 g/4 oz onions, very thinly sliced

200 ml/7 fl oz dry white wine

3 garlic cloves, crushed

1 bouquet garni

salt and freshly ground pepper

300 g/11 oz macaroni

In a frying pan, heat the fat until sizzling, put in the chicken necks, wings, gizzards and hearts and seal until golden all over. Transfer the meat to a saucepan or flameproof casserole.

Fry the carrots in the same fat until golden, then add the onions and sweat for 10 minutes. Pour in the wine and boil for 3 minutes. Put the vegetables on top of the meat, pour on enough hot water to cover the vegetables and bring to the boil. Add the garlic and bouquet garni and season. Cover the pan and cook gently for 20 minutes, then add the macaroni and cook for another 10–15 minutes. Check the seasoning and serve.

Winter suppers were equally simple, but I looked forward to them eagerly because afterwards we would sit by the great log fire and listen to Camille's wonderful stories about Saint Puy as it was hundreds of years ago. She had a great fund of these tales and I felt transported back in time whenever she told them.

I have spent about half my life in England, and for most of that time I have lived in London, where I have created and developed La Tante Claire and Koffmann's at The Berkeley. England has been a good home to me, but whenever I think of my own English connections, I always remember Camille talking about the important mediaeval link between England and the town of Saint Puy which lasted for about three hundred years, and which, lingering somewhere in a corner of my memory since childhood, may have exerted a sort of unconscious influence on the course of my life.

When Henri d'Anjou became king of England as Henry II in 1154, he was already Duke of Aquitaine and the possessor of the whole of south-western France. Thus it was that from the middle of the 12th century until the end of the Hundred Years' War, about halfway through the 15th, Saint Puy was sometimes under English control, sometimes under French, and sometimes under the control of both sides at the same time. Somehow, even four hundred years later, the Englishness of Saint Puy persisted as folklore in the popular mind, and found a place in the stories Camille used to tell us when we sat round the kitchen fire in the evening.

The great siege of 1272 was the subject of another of my grandmother's stories, although, of course, she always told it as a legend and not as history. By the middle of the 13th century, Saint Puy had developed into a fortified *bastide* – a walled, commercial town with an important market, a strong castle on the top of the hill and a second fort to the south, near the church. In 1272 its prosperity aroused the jealousy of the Count of Armagnac, who marched from Lectoure to attack it, but his army was badly defeated and he was obliged to retire. He was encouraged to make a second attempt (and this was the part of the story which always appealed to Camille) by another Gascon baron called Raymond de Tillac, who was desperately in love with the beautiful daughter of the *seigneur* of Saint Puy, who had rudely refused to accept him as a suitor.

In open defiance of the orders of the French king, Philip the Bold, the two allies with their combined armies now besieged Saint Puy for a second time. The town was defended by an English garrison and French officers, but after a heroic defence, which lasted eight days and in which all the inhabitants took part, the place was finally taken when the Armagnacs catapulted huge fireballs over the walls which set alight the thatched roofs of the houses. Saint Puy and all the surrounding countryside was sacked and pillaged, vines and crops were destroyed, and many of the inhabitants were massacred.

Camille used to tell us that a busy suburb, standing outside the town walls and surrounding a large abbey (later the site of Marcel's farm), was totally razed to the ground and never rebuilt. This district has always been known as 'the Oratoire', and perhaps the name is that last vestige of the abbey and its oratory which once stood there.

Another name from Saint Puy's historical past, which we all knew well, was that of Blaise de Monluc, the 16th-century soldier and man of letters. Really he was as much a face to us as a name, since his wood-engraved portrait was on the label of every bottle of *vin de monluc*, the familiar sparkling wine which is made at Saint Puy; this was the wine in which Camille used to macerate her strawberries during the summer. The expression on the old warrior's face as he looks out from beneath the brim of his round hat is stern and unflinching, and well reflects his indomitable, irascible character. He led a bloody and warlike life, and after fighting in the Italian wars and the Wars of Religion, during which half his face was blown away, he retired to Saint Puy, where he dictated his famous *Commentaires.* The old soldier died in 1577, quite possibly at Saint Puy, aged about seventy-five. His castle, overlooking the village, was rebuilt in the early 18th century, when it took on the appearance it has now. The present owners, René and Mireille Lassus continue to produce the sparkling wines of Monluc and also to make a special armagnac liqueur called *pousse rapière* ('rapier thrust'), which is a blend of various armagnacs mixed with orange essence. A judicious mixture of the sparkling wine with a little of the liqueur makes a delicious cocktail, and the liqueur also gives an excellent flavour to game.

Pintade aux Pruneaux d'Agen et à la Pousse Rapière

GUINEA FOWL WITH AGEN PRUNES & POUSSE RAPIÈRE—SERVES 4

1.2 kg/2¾ lb guinea fowl

12 large moist Agen prunes

salt and freshly ground pepper

75 g/3 oz duck fat

20 g/¾ oz shallots, finely chopped

50 ml/2 fl oz Pousse rapière (see page 254) or cointreau

juice of 4 medium oranges

25 g/1 oz butter

If the prunes are dry, pre-soak them for several hours, then drain. Preheat the oven to 200°C/400°F/gas 6.

Season the guinea fowl, smear it with duck fat and roast in the preheated oven for 45–55 minutes, until the juices run clear when you insert a skewer into the thickest part of the thigh, basting every 5 minutes. This is vital!

Tip out the fat from the pan, add the shallots and sweat for 3 minutes. Flame with the *pousse rapière*. Take the guinea fowl out of the pan and leave in a warm place. Add the orange juice to the pan and scrape up all the congealed juices, then pass through a sieve into a saucepan. Add the prunes to the juice and simmer for 5 minutes.

Cut the guinea fowl into 8 pieces and place on a serving dish. Beat the butter into the sauce, check the seasoning and pour it over the guinea fowl.

Early in December, when the remains of Monluc's battlements and the long, low silhouette of the castle seemed very stark behind the clumps of leafless trees which surrounded them, Camille, at the Oratoire, would be thinking about fattening her ducks and geese so that they could be sold at Christmas for their plump breasts and their delicious livers. Nowadays most birds are fattened industrially; feeding machines are used and the production of *magrets* (breasts), *confits* and foie gras is continuous throughout the year, but in those days, on the farms, the fattening only took place in winter.

My grandmother always kept about a hundred ducks, but only about ten geese, since for her a goose was never as profitable as a duck. Firstly, a goose tends to eat a great deal and is therefore more expensive to keep and secondly, though its breast and liver are larger, they were much too large for my grandparents who always like to keep a few birds for themselves. A goose *magret* contains too much meat for only one or two people and has a great deal of fat, whereas a *magret de canard* is just right. The only real advantage of a goose for Camille was the fact that its liver contains very little fat compared to a duck's and is therefore much better for preserving.

Only mature birds could be force-fed, and all Camille's ducks were at different stages of development. Nevertheless she knew her flock like the back of her hand, and remembered at a glance the precise age of each duck. She organized the fattening and slaughtering of them by batches. The first batch, which consisted of about fifty birds, had to be ready for selling at Fleurance market on the last Tuesday before Christmas. The process of fattening took precisely three weeks, so she was able to calculate the exact day on which it should begin. Immediately after Christmas, the fattening of the second batch of about thirty ducks would start so that they would be ready for the market at the end of January.

Some years, there would even be a third batch of another thirty to be fattened for the end of February. It was in arranging these batches, and in selecting the right birds to put into each of them, that my grandmother's knowledge of their ages was so important. She could tell at once if a bird which was too young in December would be right or not for January or February.

Those birds which were too young to be fattened, or which were destined to wait their turn as members of the next batch, were still allowed their freedom in the open air, together with the cocks, hens and turkeys. They would sit or stand in the yard, puffing out their white feathers and enduring the cold with an expression of stoic, defiant indignation.

Once the ducks of a particular batch had been selected, they were locked up in one of the dark rooms near the stable, and the only light they saw was the light of my grandmother's lamp at dawn or at dusk, when they were fed. Some people used to feed their ducks three times a day, but Camille insisted that it was best to feed them only twice, once early in the morning and once in the evening. She used to sit astride an old wooden box with a hole cut in the top. She would put a duck inside the box with its neck and head protruding from the hole which was just in front of her. Then she would insert a metal funnel very carefully into the bird's beak, and push the maize down it with a small round stick.

Force-feeding was a skilled art, which was only learned after long experience. Camille could feed a duck completely in two or three minutes, but a clumsy person might take a quarter of an hour just to get the funnel down the duck's throat. If you pushed the maize down too quickly, the bird could not breathe and it suffocated; each bird had its own characteristic way of swallowing, and you had to discover what this was and respect it. All through the feeding time, Camille's hand would run up and down the duck's throat, softly and judiciously feeling it and pressing it to see how the bird was taking the maize, whether the funnel was in the right place and whether the crop was full and the duck could eat no more. At that point she would release the duck from the box, and choose another to take its place.

When you had thirty or forty ducks, the work took up several hours every day. At the end of the three-week feeding period, the ducks were so fat that they could hardly walk, and some of them could hardly even breathe. The time had come for them to be slaughtered.

The killing and plucking of an entire batch of ducks involved a great deal of work – far too much for Camille to do on her own. Even with the help of three or four of her friends, who came every year to help her, it often used to take a couple of days before everything was finished. It required two people to kill a duck or goose. The first person stood holding the bird by its legs, one in each hand, while the second, bending down or sitting, held the head and the beak in the left hand so that the right hand was free to make a small incision with a knife in the outstretched neck. The birds died fairly quickly and quietly; the blood was collected in a dish on the ground and mixed with herbs and garlic. It was later used to make a *sanquette* (see page 113).

After the killing came the plucking, which was a very lengthy process. If you want to pluck a duck quickly, you just boil it and the feathers will come away quite easily, but you cannot do this if, like Camille, you want to keep the down for filling cushions, pillows and eiderdowns, because the hot water will damage the down. At the Oratoire, Camille and her friends first used to pull off the larger feathers in the ordinary way; then, in the evening sitting round the fire, they would heat little flat-irons near the embers and pass them carefully over a damp cloth laid across the white down on the ducks' bodies. After a gentle warming the down came away quite easily, but again the work was very time-consuming. The sight of four women sitting round a fire and ironing some thirty or forty ducks as though they were so many handkerchiefs was certainly an unusual one.

Lunches on these days always included traditional dishes made from one or two of the ducks which had just been killed. Duck carcasses, after the liver and the flesh of the breast have been removed, are called *demoiselles* in Gascony. If you leave enough meat on the bones and grill them carefully so that they are not too dry and burnt, they are absolutely delicious, and as you suck and chew the pieces in your mouth, you really feel you are eating the very essence of a duck. Or we might be given some of the breasts, the *magrets*, which Camille would grill over a handful of glowing vine branches if there were some ready in the kitchen, just to give the meat that special taste. With them we might eat some of the dried haricots we had threshed in the autumn, and which were now cooked in red wine. Best of all, as a special treat, my grandmother might cut some slices from one of the livers, and we would have foie gras with eggs.

Magrets de Canard aux Sarments de Vigne

DUCK BREASTS GRILLED OVER VINE BRANCHES—SERVES 4

4 boneless duck breasts
salt and freshly ground pepper
50 g/2 oz shallots, finely chopped
dried vine branches (if you can't find these, charcoal will do)

Season the duck breasts and cook them over a fire made from dried vine branches or, failing that, charcoal, until done to your liking. Place the duck in a dish and spread the shallots on top. Place another dish on top of the first to make a sort of box and stand it near the fire for 10 minutes to keep it hot. Spoon the juices over the meat from time to time, then serve.

Haricots au Vin Rouge

HARICOT BEANS IN RED WINE

250 g/9 oz dried haricot beans
600 ml/1 pt red wine
100 g/4 oz carrots, diced
100 g/4 oz onions, diced
75 g/3 oz bayonne ham, diced
1 bouquet garni
salt and freshly ground pepper

Soak the beans in water overnight, then drain them. Place in a saucepan with the wine, vegetables, ham, bouquet garni and some pepper (but no salt at this stage) and cook gently for 2½–3 hours. Check the seasoning and serve.

A goose liver is considerably larger than that of a duck; it can weigh as much as a kilo, whereas a duck's liver may weigh only 500 or 600 grams. My own preference is for goose if you want to eat your foie gras cold; but if you prefer it hot and freshly cooked, then I would always recommend the liver of a duck.

Camille really specialized in ducks' livers, and had built up a very good local reputation for the excellent quality of her foie gras. Some of her ducks were sold at Fleurance market, but she sold most of them to local people who often ordered them several months in advance. The doctor, for example, might order ten, the *notaire* six, and the postman four. Camille could always tell when one of her birds had a particularly large liver, because after death the fat of a duck hardens but the liver remains soft, so, by feeling the bird with her fingers, she could detect at once the extent and consistency of the foie gras.

After each killing, some of the ducks, as I have said, were always kept for us to eat at the farm; their livers were lowered down into the well to keep them fresh until they were wanted. I remember that Camille sometimes used to cook a liver for about an hour, very slowly, on the low heat of the small embers right at the side of the fire. The foie gras was of such good quality that hardly any fat came out of it. If you were to cook today's commercially produced foie gras in that way, it would be disastrous – you would be left with a great pool of fat.

One of Marcel's eccentricities over food was his point-blank refusal ever to eat any foie gras that was not freshly cooked and hot. The rest of us always enjoyed the duck livers which Camille bottled, but my grandfather would never touch them. Naturally this meant that Marcel did not eat foie gras very often, but, when he did, I must say that he really enjoyed it. Here are three of Marcel's favourite recipes.

Foie Gras de Canard aux Maïs et Pommes

DUCK FOIE GRAS WITH SWEETCORN & APPLES—SERVES 4

4 slices of duck foie gras, 1 cm/½ in thick (about 100 g/4 oz each)

4 reinette apples, peeled, cored and cut into 6

50 g/2 oz butter

25 ml/1 fl oz armagnac

salt and freshly ground pepper

100 ml/4 fl oz dry white wine

40 g/1½ oz sweetcorn kernels

Fry the apples in half the butter, turning occasionally, until light golden but still slightly firm. Flame with the armagnac and keep warm.

Season the foie gras and cook it in a non-stick frying pan without added fat for 1 minute on each side, or until it feels slightly soft when you press it with your finger. Transfer to a serving dish.

Tip off the fat from the pan, pour in the wine and reduce completely. Add 50 ml/2 fl oz water and beat in the remaining butter, then add the sweetcorn to the sauce. Arrange the apples around the foie gras and pour the sauce over the top.

Oeufs au Plat au Foie Gras

FRIED EGGS WITH FOIE GRAS—SERVES 4

4 slices of fresh foie gras, 1 cm/½ in thick (about 100 g/4 oz each)

salt and freshly ground pepper

4 fresh farm eggs

red wine vinegar

Season the foie gras with salt and pepper from the mill. Heat 4 individual flameproof gratin dishes on the hob without adding any fat. When they are very hot, put a slice of foie gras in each dish. It will give off a great deal of fat; you may prefer to pour some off at this stage. Crack the eggs into the dishes beside the foie gras, cook for 1 minute, then turn over the foie gras and cook for 1 more minute. Pour a few drops of vinegar around the edge and serve at once.

Foie Gras de Canard aux Raisins

DUCK FOIE GRAS WITH GRAPES—SERVES 4

4 slices of duck foie gras, 1 cm/½ in thick (about 100 g/4 oz each)
salt and freshly ground pepper
4 slices of toasted french bread
300 ml/½ pt sweet jurançon wine
50 g/2 oz butter
20 large grapes, peeled

Season the foie gras. Heat a non-stick frying pan and cook the foie gras for 1 minute on each side or until it feels slightly soft when you press the top with your finger. Do not add any fat; the foie gras has more than enough of its own.

Place a slice of foie gras on each slice of toast. Pour off the fat from the pan, add the wine and reduce by half. Beat in the butter and add the grapes. Pour the sauce and grapes around the foie gras and serve.

Each duck killing was followed by days when my grandmother prepared the bottles of rendered duck and goose fat which were kept in the dining-room cupboard and would play such an important part in her cooking during the coming year. She also made large jars of *confits de canard*, or preserved duck, which was equally important for her cooking and which is one of the most traditional gastronomic products of south-west France.

You can put all the best parts of a duck into a *confit* – that is to say the *magrets*, the legs and the wings – then eat these all through the year, but you can also put in almost everything else, such as the feet, neck, giblets, head and other less attractive parts, which even if you do not eat them (although the peasants always did) can still be used to give a very good flavour to stews and soups. But, whatever you put in a *confit*, it must first be salted, in order to get rid of any blood or gall that may still be attached to the different parts of the duck, and to give it that very special *confit* flavour. Camille used an iron *marmite* into which she put alternate layers of salt and duck, then the duck was left to cure in the salt overnight for about twelve hours.

In the morning each piece was taken out, rubbed with a cloth, and put into a cooking pot which contained some melted duck fat. The *confit* was then cooked very slowly over a corner of the fire where it was not very hot, since too much

heat would turn the duck brown and spoil it. The simmering went on for about three hours, but my grandmother would only consider the cooking finished when the pieces of meat were so tender that she was able to pierce them with a bit of straw.

The *confit* was now left for another night to get completely cold and, in the morning, Camille would take out the pieces of duck by hand, put them into their earthenware jar, and pour over some melted duck fat. It was important that no piece of duck should ever touch the side of the jar and that none of the juice which had collected at the bottom of the cooking pot should find its way there, because it would deteriorate rapidly; however, this juice was excellent when spread on a slice of toast.

Other things which my grandmother made from the birds we kept for ourselves included *graisserons*, which were the little bits of meat and skin which had got left behind in the pot in which fat for the *confit* had been cooked; and *gahuzagues*, a dish made of finely minced goose tripe, which is very good, but which is nowadays completely forgotten, perhaps because of the enormous amount of time and work involved in cleaning and scraping the tripe. The recipe also calls for a bottle of *bourrit* left over from the time of the *vendange*, which is not something everybody has easily to hand. And I shall never forget how good a stuffed duck's neck could be when Camille cooked it.

Confit de Canard

PRESERVED DUCK

1 force-fed duck, plucked and drawn
300 g/11 oz coarse sea salt

Cut the duck into pieces – legs, breasts, wings and neck. Keep the feet, head, heart and neck. Skin the neck and keep the skin to stuff, if you like (see below). Trim off and any excess fat from the duck pieces and reserve them. Clean the gizzard. Put all the duck pieces in a bowl with the gizzard, feet, heart and head and mix well with the coarse salt. Cover with a tea towel and refrigerate for 12 hours.

Cut the reserved fat and skin into very small pieces. Put 50 ml/2 fl oz water in a saucepan, bring to the boil, then add the fat and cook as slowly as possible for 1½ hours. Strain the liquid fat through a sieve and keep the small solid pieces to make *graisserons* (see below). Keep the strained fat in a cool place until needed.

Remove the duck pieces from the salt and wipe off the excess salt and salty juices with a cloth. You may find that you do not have enough fat to cover all the duck; in this case, cook it in 2 batches – first the smaller pieces (neck, feet, gizzard, head and wings), then the legs and breasts.

Put the first batch of duck into the fat and cook for about 1 hour, skimming the surface from time to time. The meat is ready when you can pierce it easily with a wooden skewer. Take the meat out of the fat and cover it to prevent it from drying out. Add the second batch of duck and cook in the same way for about 1½ hours.

Leave the duck to cool completely in the fat, then put the smaller pieces into one stone jar and the legs and breast into another. Do not pack the pieces too tightly into the jars, as the fat must run in between them. Ladle in the fat, taking care not to pour in any cooking juices, as these will not keep. Keep the *confit* in a cool place until the next day, then cover with greaseproof paper and store in the fridge or a cold place.

If you prefer, you can sterilize the *confit* by boiling the jars in water for 30 minutes; it will then keep for many years (even unsterilized, it will keep for up to a year).

To make the *graisserons*, fry the lumps in a pan for about 5 minutes without adding any more fat. Season and add some chopped garlic and parsley. Do not overcook the *graisserons* or they will become dry. Eat them when cold.

You can also stuff the skin from the duck neck with sausage meat, secure both ends and cook as for *confit*.

I have already mentioned how we might eat a grilled *magret* at lunch on one of the days when the birds were killed. This is almost as traditional a Gascon delicacy as a *confit*. We used to eat this dish all through the rest of the winter, depending, of course, on when exactly each batch of birds was slaughtered. Besides grilling them, my grandmother used to cook *magrets* with pepper or wild mushrooms, or she sometimes tied them up with string and poached them suspended in a specially prepared stock.

Magrets de Canard au Poivre

DUCK BREASTS WITH PEPPER—SERVES 4

2 large boned duck breasts

salt

1 tablespoon black peppercorns, crushed

50 g/2 oz duck fat

50 g/2 oz shallots, chopped

1 tablespoon white wine vinegar

50 ml/2 fl oz armagnac

100 ml/4 fl oz double cream

With a sharp knife, make several incisions in the duck skin. Sprinkle with salt and press the peppercorns into the meat, making sure that they stick.

In a frying pan, heat the duck fat over low heat. Put in the duck breasts, skin-side down, and cook slowly for 10 minutes, until most of the fat runs out of the duck breasts and the skin is golden and crispy. Turn the duck over and cook for 3 minutes on the other side. Transfer to a serving dish and keep warm.

Pour off most of the fat from the pan, add the shallots and cook for 1 minute. Add the vinegar and cook until it has completely evaporated. Pour in the armagnac and cream and boil for about 1 minute, until the sauce coats the back of a spoon. Check the seasoning.

Slice the duck breasts, pour the sauce around the edge and serve.

Magrets de Canard, Sauce aux Cèpes

DUCK BREASTS WITH CEP SAUCE—SERVES 4

2 large boned duck breasts

salt and freshly ground pepper

50 g/2 oz duck fat

50 g/2 oz shallots, chopped

50 ml/2 fl oz armagnac

100 ml/4 fl oz dry white wine

200 ml/7 fl oz madeira

50 g/2 oz dried ceps, soaked

25 g/1 oz butter, diced

Make several incisions in the duck skin and rub in some seasoning. Heat the duck fat in a frying pan over low heat, put in the duck breasts, skin-side down, and cook for 8 minutes. Turn them over and cook for 6 minutes on the other side. Transfer the duck to a serving dish and keep warm.

Pour off most of the fat from the pan, put in the shallots and cook gently for 2 minutes. Mix together the armagnac, wine and madeira and pour half into the pan. Reduce completely over fairly high heat, then add the rest of the alcohol and the ceps. Reduce by half, add 200 ml/7 fl oz water and cook slowly for 10 minutes. You should be left with 150 ml/5 fl oz sauce.

Slice the duck and add the juices to the sauce. Pass the sauce through a conical sieve, beat in the butter and pour round the duck. Serve immediately.

Magrets de Canard à la Ficelle

DUCK BREASTS COOKED ON A STRING—SERVES 4

4 duck breasts, skinned and boned, bones reserved

1 chicken carcass

120 g/4½ oz carrots, quartered

100 g/4 oz onions, halved and singed over an open flame

4 small leeks

4 small turnips

1 bouquet garni

1 clove

10 black peppercorns

salt

mustard, gherkins or salt, to serve

Prepare the stock by boiling the duck bones and chicken carcass with 4 l/7 pt water. Skim well, then add the vegetables, bouquet garni, clove, peppercorns and salt and cook for 30 minutes. Pass the stock through a sieve and keep the vegetables for the garnish.

Tie a piece of string round each duck breast and cook them in the simmering stock for 7–8 minutes if you like the meat rare (allow a little longer if you prefer it better done). Slice the cooked duck, place on individual plates and arrange the vegetables beside it. Spoon over 4 tablespoons of stock and serve with mustard, gherkins or coarse salt.

It was always a moment of intense happiness and excitement when we arrived at the Oratoire at the beginning of the Christmas holidays. We had come all the way from Tarbes, squashed uncomfortably together in the car, but the welcome from Camille and Marcel seemed warmer than ever, and at once we were regaled with the habitual walnut leaf aperitif, ham and fresh bread. My parents stayed at the farm over Christmas and the New Year, and slept in the spare room with the imitation bamboo furniture which so impressed me when I first saw it. My father enjoyed being at the farm, but my mother hated it; after two days, she always started agitating to get back to Tarbes.

By the time we had all settled in, and the barking of Rex, the dog, had subsided, and we children had been down to see the cows and rabbits and to discover if any changes had taken place since our last visit, my grandmother would have put the soup on the table, and lunch would be ready.

Camille regarded the first lunch of the Christmas holidays as already something of a festive occasion. After the soup, instead of roast chicken, she often gave us a shin of veal if a calf had recently been slaughtered, or else a potato and bacon pie, which would be followed by a salad; then, as a dessert, she would make us some special pancakes. Marcel would pour out a bottle of the Oratoire red wine which he had drawn from one of the *barriques* in the dimly lit cellar, and after the meal, he and my father would sit at the table and chat over a glass or two of *eau-de-vie* which had been distilled on the farm.

Jarret de Veau aux Carottes

SHIN OF VEAL WITH CARROTS—SERVES 4

2.5 kg/5½ lb shin of veal, trimmed

150 g/5 oz duck fat

salt and freshly ground pepper

300 g/11 oz ham or bacon rind

1 kg/2¼ lb onions, cut into large dice

500 ml/18 fl oz white wine

1 bouquet garni

4 garlic cloves, peeled and left whole

1.2 kg/2¾ lb carrots, thinly sliced

2 tablespoons chopped parsley

Preheat the oven to 200°C/400°F/gas 6. Heat the fat in a flameproof casserole. Season the veal and seal it in the hot fat until golden brown all over. Add the ham or bacon rind and sweat gently for 10 minutes. Add the onions, cover the casserole and sweat very gently for another 45 minutes, stirring occasionally and skimming the surface as necessary.

Pour in the wine and boil for 5 minutes. Add 2 l/3½ pt boiling water, the bouquet garni and garlic, and season to taste. Bring back to the boil, cover and cook in the oven for 1 hour. Remove the shin of veal and strain the stock. Put the veal and stock back into the casserole, set over high heat and boil, uncovered, until only 600 ml/1 pt stock remains, skimming the surface if necessary. Add the carrots, cover and cook gently until tender.

Place the veal on a serving dish, arrange the carrots around it and sprinkle over the parsley.

Tourte de Pommes de Terre au Lard

POTATO & BACON PIE—SERVES 4

400 g/14 oz new potatoes

salt and freshly ground pepper

25 g/1 oz butter

2 medium onions, sliced

75 g/3 oz streaky bacon, diced

2 garlic cloves, crushed

250 ml/9 fl oz double cream

5 egg yolks

7 lean bacon rashers, derinded

Wash the potatoes and cook them in their skins in salted water until soft. Drain, peel and slice them thickly.

Heat the butter in a frying pan, add the onions and cook slowly for 10 minutes, stirring frequently. Add the diced bacon and garlic, fry over medium heat for 3 minutes, then pour in the cream. Boil for 1 minute, transfer to a bowl and leave to cool.

Heat the oven to 180°C/350°F/gas 4. When the cream mixture is almost cold, stir in the egg yolks and season with pepper, then add the sliced potatoes. Line the bottom and sides of a 900 g/2 lb terrine with the bacon rashers and put in the potato mixture. Cover with greaseproof paper.

Stand the terrine in a bain-marie and bake the pie in the preheated oven for about 55 minutes, until fairly firm. Turn out on to a plate and serve very hot.

Crêpes au Vin Blanc

WHITE WINE PANCAKES—SERVES 4

150 g/5 oz plain flour

3 eggs

a pinch of salt

50 g/2 oz sugar, plus extra to serve

250 ml/9 fl oz white wine

25 g/1 oz butter, melted

a piece of pork back fat, for cooking the pancakes

Place all the ingredients except the back fat in a blender and blend for 2 minutes, making sure that the flour is well mixed. Pass the batter through a sieve and leave to rest for 1 hour.

To make the batter by hand, sieve the flour into a bowl and make a well in the centre. Put all the other ingredients in the well and stir with a whisk, gradually drawing in the flour. When the batter is smooth, leave it to rest for 1 hour.

Heat an iron crêpe pan and grease it with a piece of back fat held on a fork. Stir the batter and pour a small quantity into the pan, lifting and tilting the pan so that the base is covered with a very thin layer of batter. Cook over medium heat until the underside of the pancake is light golden, then turn or toss it and cook until the other side is golden.

As you cook each pancake, put it on a plate and sprinkle with sugar while hot. Fold into 4 and keep the pancakes warm until you are ready to eat them.

These pancakes are lighter than those made with milk. You can also make them with equal quantities of milk and beer.

Christmas celebrations were centred strongly on the big family lunch which we ate in the dining-room. We never had the usual French *réveillon* on Christmas Eve, largely I think because Marcel, with his deep antipathy towards the Church, always refused to go to midnight mass, and therefore all our fun started as early as possible on Christmas morning. When we came into the kitchen, we found our stockings hanging from the mantelpiece above the fire. On each of them Camille had embroidered our names and a little picture of a duck or a cockerel. Inside the stockings were traditional Christmas goodies like nuts and tangerines, oranges and sweets.

Our presents were always small, but they meant a lot to us. Besides the usual toys and handkerchiefs with embroidered initials, we were sometimes given gifts of a practical nature, intended perhaps to encourage us towards some particular trade or activity. I remember, for example, that one Christmas I was given a little saw and plane. Perhaps my grandmother though that, since I was good at painting her walls, I might also turn out to be a good carpenter.

At Christmas lunch we were always joined by my uncle Ivan Capuron and my aunt Marraine. Although I have mentioned their grocery shop, and that my uncle was captain of the fire brigade and an insurance agent, and how he was for many years mayor of Saint Puy, I have not said how much my uncle helped my grandparents in several very practical ways. He was a tall, dark-haired man, full of energy, and when Marcel grew too old to cope with the farm, my uncle bought a tractor, and with it did almost all of the hard physical work in the fields. He was also able to arrange a small state pension for my grandparents; left to their own devices they would never have known how to apply for this, since, like many peasants, they were terrified and confused by any kind of printed form or official document. The presence of the Capurons, therefore, completed our family circle in a particularly happy way. Christmas lunch started with a soup and this was followed by a roast turkey. Camille usually kept a few turkeys in the Oratoire poultry yard, but she did not regard them as being of much importance commercially; as with her capons, she just sold them or gave them to friends and acquaintances in the village. But she always made certain there was a good one ready for the family feast on Christmas Day, when there were plenty of people to eat it.

The turkey was served with salsify fritters, then came a salad in which some of Camille's conserved artichokes were combined with foie gras. The meal ended with a *gâteau à la broche*, a favourite Christmas dessert, which is made by pouring a sweet batter mixture over a wooden cone as it revolves on a spit above an open fire.

Dinde Rôtie aux Marrons

ROAST TURKEY WITH CHESTNUT STUFFING—SERVES 12

1 turkey, about 4.5 kg/10 lb

300 g/11 oz boneless chicken

200 g/7 oz pork back fat

100 g/4 oz breadcrumbs, soaked

2 egg yolks

salt and freshly ground pepper

24 chestnuts, cooked and skinned (frozen or canned are fine)

100 g/4 oz duck fat

50 g/2 oz carrots, diced

75 g/3 oz onions, diced

200 ml/7 fl oz dry white wine

Preheat the oven to 220°C/425 °F/gas 7. Prepare the stuffing by mincing the chicken and back fat. Add the breadcrumbs and egg yolks and season. Stir in the chestnuts and stuff the turkey.

Heat the duck fat in a roasting pan, put in the turkey and seal on all sides. Lay it on one leg and roast in the preheated oven for 45 minutes, then turn it on to the other leg and roast for another 45 minutes. Turn the bird on to its back, add the vegetables and roast for a further 40 minutes, or until the juices run clear when you pierce the thickest part of the thigh with a skewer, basting from time to time.

When the turkey is ready, place it breast downwards on a serving dish while you make the sauce. Tip off the fat from the roasting pan, pour in the wine and reduce by two-thirds. Add 200 ml/7 fl oz water and reduce by half. Check the seasoning, strain the sauce, turn the turkey breast-side up and serve.

Salsifis en Beignets

SALSIFY FRITTERS

600 g/1¼ lb salsify

1 tablespoon vinegar

oil, for deep-frying

Batter
250 g/9 oz plain flour
a pinch of salt
2 tablespoons oil
2 eggs, separated

Prepare the batter 2 hours in advance. Put the flour in a bowl and make a well in the centre. Put the salt, oil, egg yolks and a little water in the well and mix slowly with a wooden spoon, gradually drawing in the flour little by little. When the batter is homogenous, add more water (about 150 ml/5 fl oz altogether) and mix until smooth and creamy. Leave the batter in a warm place until needed.

Peel the salsify and drop it into water acidulated with the vinegar. Cut into even 3 cm/1¼ in lengths and cook in boiling salted water until tender. Drain and leave to cool.

To make the fritters, beat the egg whites until stiff and gently fold into the batter. Fill a deep frying pan with oil and heat until very hot. Dip the salsify into the batter and fry in batches until the fritters are golden and puffed up. Drain the fritters on kitchen paper and serve very hot.

Although Camille had to use her preserved artichokes for this salad, since of course artichokes were not in season at Christmas, it is much nicer made with fresh artichokes, as in the version I give here.

Artichauts en Salade avec Foie Gras et Jambon

SALAD OF ARTICHOKES, BAYONNE HAM & FOIE GRAS—SERVES 4

4 small artichokes
2 little gem lettuces
300 g/10 oz trimmed green beans, blanched
100 ml/4 fl oz mild vinaigrette
4 slices of bayonne ham
200 g/7 oz Ballotine de foie gras *(recipe page 105)*

Trim the artichokes and cook in plenty of boiling salted water. They are cooked when you can pull out a leaf easily. Take the artichokes out of the water and stand them upside down to drain.

Take 4 plates and arrange the little gem leaves round the plates like a rosette. Pull out the artichoke leaves and hairy chokes and place the hearts in the centre of the plates, discarding the leaves. Mix the green beans with the viniagrette and arrange on top. Lay the ham around the edge of each heart. Thinly slice the foie gras and arrange it on top. The finished dish should look like a flower.

Gâteau à la Broche

'STALAGMITE' CAKE COOKED ON THE SPIT—SERVES 12

500 g/1 lb 2 oz plain flour, sifted

500 g/1 lb 2 oz caster sugar

24 eggs, separated

500 g/1 lb 2 oz butter, melted

100 ml/4 fl oz rum

1 teaspoon salt

150 g/5 oz shelled walnuts

crème anglaise, *to serve*

Put the flour, sugar, egg yolks, egg whites and butter in 5 separate bowls. Beat the egg whites until stiff.

Take another bowl large enough to hold all the ingredients and put in a spoonful of each at a time, mixing all the time. You really need two people for this operation, so that one can add the ingredients while the other mixes. When everything is well mixed, add the rum and salt. (The walnuts will be added when three-quarters of the batter has been cooked.)

Tightly wrap a wooden cone in greaseproof paper and place it on the spit. Stand in front of an open fire and drop some of the batter on to the cone, turning the spit as you go. Add the walnuts to the batter when you have used up three-quarters. As the spit turns and the batter drips, the cake will look like stalagmites. Cook until you have used up all the batter.

Leave the cake to cool, then cut off the bottom to remove the wooden cone. Serve the cake with a *crème anglaise*.

This recipe is not easy to do in a modern kitchen!

New Year's Eve was always celebrated at the Oratoire with a *réveillon*, at which Camille often served one of the wonderful duck dishes she reserved for important occasions. Once again, the whole family ate together round the dining-room table and we raised glasses of wine or *eau-de-vie* and drank to the New Year as Monsieur Duprom's clock rang out the strokes of midnight.

Daube de Cuisses de Canard aux Pruneaux

BRAISED DUCK LEGS WITH PRUNES—SERVES 12

12 duck legs
salt and freshly ground pepper
100 g/4 oz duck fat
200 g/7 oz onions, diced
2 bottles of full-bodied red wine
1 bouquet garni
10 black peppercorns
3 garlic cloves, crushed
75 g/3 oz smoked bacon, diced
24 large moist prunes
2 duck livers, cleaned
25 ml/1 fl oz armagnac

Season the duck. In a flameproof casserole, heat the fat until sizzling, put in the duck legs and fry until golden all over. Add the onions, lower the heat and cook gently for 10 minutes.

Pour off the fat, pour the wine into the casserole and bring to the boil. Add the bouquet garni, peppercorns, garlic, diced bacon and some salt and cook for about 30 minutes, adding the prunes 5 minutes before you stop cooking.

Skim off any trace of fat from the sauce and check the seasoning. Pound the duck livers with the armagnac and add to the sauce, stirring continuously until the sauce is smooth. Serve immediately.

After New Year, on the first Sunday in January, came Epiphany, the night of the Three Kings, when we ate the round, crown-shaped *galette des rois* containing the hidden bean which entitled its finder to crown the king or queen of his or her choice. To us children, finding the bean was a truly magical moment. Camille always bought her *galette* from Monsieur Trille; she said that she could never make one as good as his. The beans were always real local dried broad beans which had been threshed in the summer; they were never the little plastic or ceramic images that lurk inside so many modern *galettes*.

In early January, when Camille's force-feeding of the second lot of ducks was well under way, it was time to fix the date on which Monsieur Montaud, the Saint Puy pig-killer, would come to the Oratoire to kill Marcel's pigs. This was a great annual event and a long day of very hard work – a ceremony with all its own customs and traditions and also something of a family feast, which we used to enjoy hugely when we were children.

So, on a carefully chosen day in January, when his services were not required elsewhere and when the moon was on the wane, Monsieur Montaud arrived at the Oratoire with his five assistants. My grandfather used to keep two pigs, one of which was always named after the President of the Republic and the other after some prominent politician; they lived in a sty with a small square window next to the stables. Sometimes they managed to loosen their gates and then they escaped into the fields and had to be chased back. This was an event which we greatly enjoyed when we were children, but it was not enjoyed by the adults, especially not by my grandfather, whose running and thwacking and breathless shouting and swearing had to be heard to be believed.

The annual slaughter of the pigs was an important happening, since every scrap of the animals would be used in some way or other, and nothing would be wasted. Hams, *confits*, sausages and fat would be eaten and used all through the year. In addition to Monsieur Montaud's team, three or four women friends of my grandmother's came to help as well, probably the same women who helped with the duck killing. There was plenty of work, enough usually to last for two days at least, and each day there were about a dozen people to be fed at lunch.

It took six very strong men to kill one pig, and both our pigs were killed on the same day. Four men were needed to get a pig out of its sty, each man being put in charge of a different leg; once outside, the pig was rolled over on to its back, its legs were tied together, and everybody hoisted it up until it lay, flat on its back, on the top of a special low, upturned wooden trough. Once the animal was in position, Monsieur Montaud, wearing a black beret and white apron, came forward with his knife and expertly, and in just the right place, cut a thin slit down the side of the upturned throat. Immediately the pig set up a raucous, screaming yell, and blood started to pour from the wound in torrential spurts. It was the job of the sixth man to catch the blood in a large pan.

Once the bleeding had stopped and the pig was finally quiet and dead, the wooden trough was turned right way up and the pig was placed in it to be covered with boiling water from the wash-house copper. All six men then worked together in a huge cloud of steam to scrape its hair off, until at last the animal's skin was absolutely soft, white and clean. Then the pig was heaved up against the wall and attached by its back legs to an iron hook. Monsieur Montaud executed another swift, skilful cut right down the length of the animal's belly, and suddenly the great heap of intestines fell out, steaming, into the winter air.

The women had already taken the blood away into the kitchen, and were busy with their first task of the day of a slaughtering: this was always to make the black pudding and to clean and prepare the right pieces of intestine into which the pudding had to be pushed in order to turn it into a *boudin noir*. *Boudin* was traditionally the main dish at the lunches, and Camille always served it with a potato purée flavoured with duck fat. It was also the day when she mixed some of the blood with cornmeal to make a special version of the little maize cakes called *miques* (see page 191).

Boudin Noir

BLACK PUDDING

100 g/4 oz duck fat

300 g/11 oz onions, finely chopped

200 ml/7 fl oz double cream

4 l/7 pt pig's blood

2 tablespoons finely chopped fresh or 2 teaspoons dried mixed herbs

salt and freshly ground pepper

5 m/6 yd sausage casing

Peau de porc croustillante *(recipe page 289) and sautéed apple, to serve*

Stock

1 pig's head, boned

150 g/5 oz onions, halved

200 g/7 oz carrots, halved

200 g/7 oz leeks, tied together

20 peppercorns

1 large bouquet garni

salt

4 l/7 pt water

Prepare the cooking stock the day before by boiling all the ingredients for 2½ hours. When the pig's head is cooked, take it out of the stock and cut into 5 mm/¼ in pieces.

In a large saucepan, melt the duck fat and cook the chopped onions very gently for 20 minutes. Add the cream and cook for 5 minutes. Put in the chopped meat from the head and warm through, stirring continuously. Add the blood, herbs and seasoning and bring to a temperature of 40°C/104°F. Do not let the mixture get any hotter than this, or it will spoil.

Take the pan off the heat, fill the sausage casing with the *boudin* mixture by pushing it through a piping bag fitted with a large nozzle, and tie the ends (this may be easier if you have someone to help you). This recipe will make two 2.5 kg/5½ lb *boudins*. Heat the stock to 85°C/185°F, put in the *boudins* and poach for 20 minutes. Leave to cool in the stock before serving sliced and pan fried with *Purée de pommes de terre* (see next recipe), *Peau de porc croustillante* and sautéed apple.

Purée de Pommes de Terre a la Graisse de Canard

PURÉED POTATOES WITH DUCK FAT

800 g/1¾ lb potatoes, peeled and cut into chunks

salt and freshly ground pepper

200 ml/7 fl oz milk

70 g/2½ oz duck fat

Cook the potatoes in boiling salted water until soft, then drain and mash. Boil the milk and pour it on to the potatoes, add the duck fat and mix well. Check the seasoning and serve very hot.

The second day was the charcuterie day. Outside, down by the stables, Monsieur Montaud and his assistants started to cut up the two pigs, which were now quite cold. As all the various bits and pieces were brought up to the kitchen, they were piled on to the table, and Camille and her friends were kept hard at work with

herbs and spices and knives and choppers and mincers and, now and then, a touch of armagnac, to produce pâtés, sausages, hams, *confits*, *rillettes*, *couennes* and all the other countless products and by-products of the annual pig.

Rillettes de Porc

PORK RILLETTES

1 kg/2¼ lb pork fillet
salt and freshly ground pepper
300 g/11 oz pork fat, melted
1 bouquet garni
4 garlic cloves, peeled and left whole
100 ml/4 fl oz dry white wine

Cut the pork into 5 cm/2 in cubes and sprinkle with 25 g/1 oz salt. Leave to marinate overnight.

The next day, gently warm the fat, add the meat, bouquet garni, garlic and wine and bring to simmering point. Cover and cook very gently for 3–4 hours, stirring occasionally with a wooden spoon, until the meat disintegrates. Leave to cool.

Remove the bouquet garni and garlic and work the meat and fat together with your fingers until very well mixed. Adjust the seasoning; go easy on the salt and be generous with the pepper. Put the *rillettes* in an earthenware pot and keep in the fridge for up to 2 weeks.

Terrine de Foie Gras

TERRINE OF FOIE GRAS

1.5 kg/3 lb 5 oz raw foie gras (2 duck foie gras)
1 tablespoon armagnac
salt and freshly ground pepper

Soak the livers in a large bowl of lightly salted warm water for 3 hours.

Preheat the oven to 170°/325°F/gas 3. Lay the livers on the work surface and peel off the thin membrane which encloses them. Open up each lobe and, with the point of a knife, remove all the veins and nerves and the parts which have touched the greenish gall.

Sprinkle the armagnac into a 25 x 10 cm/10 x 4 in terrine. Season the livers and put them in the terrine. Place in a bain-marie and bring the water to the boil, then cover the terrine with foil and cook in the preheated oven for 45 minutes.

Take the terrine out of the bain-marie and leave to cool for 1 hour. Lay a wooden board wrapped in foil on the foie gras, tip off the fat and juices into a bowl and refrigerate. Place a weight on the board (a brick is ideal for this) and put the terrine in the fridge to firm up for 12 hours.

Remove the hardened fat from the bowl, scrape off any juices which are sticking to the bottom and melt the fat. Pour it over the terrine to seal it and leave to harden before serving.

Jambonneau de Porc en Bocal

BOTTLED SHIN OF PORK

1 shin of pork, boned

4 garlic cloves, halved

salt and freshly ground pepper

haricot bean and onion salad, to serve

Insert the garlic into the boned pork and season the meat with salt and pepper. Place in a large preserving jar and seal. Boil in a pan of water for 2¾ hours and leave to cool in the water.

The jar will be full of delicious jelly from the meat. Serve it cold with a salad of white haricot beans with onions.

When all the work was over, and Monsieur Montaud and his assistants had left the Oratoire, and Marcel had sent his customary piece of pig to the curé, it was time for us to sit down on our own at the kitchen table to enjoy our first meal of fresh pork. This was often a pork chop, accompanied by pickled gherkins and a purée of chick peas; though, when I think of pork dishes, I always like to suggest my own Tante Claire recipe for stuffed pigs' trotters, which I serve with a purée of split peas.

RIGHT: CÔTES DE PORC AUX CORNICHONS (P. 286)

Côtes de Porc aux Cornichons

PORK CHOPS WITH GHERKINS—SERVES 4

4 pork rib chops
50 g/2 oz duck fat
75 g/3 oz onions, thinly sliced
1 sprig of thyme
3 garlic cloves, thinly sliced
salt and freshly ground pepper
Cornichons au vinaigre, to serve (recipe page 64)

Heat the duck fat in a frying pan, put in the chops and cook for 4 minutes on each side. Transfer to a dish and keep in a warm place.

Tip off half the fat from the pan, add the onions to the pan and cook until soft. Add the thyme and garlic, cover and cook for about 8 minutes until soft.

Place the chops on the vegetables and heat through for 3 minutes. Check the seasoning, stir in the gherkins and serve.

Purée de Pois Chiches

CHICK PEA PURÉE

500 g/1 lb 2 oz chick peas
salt and freshly ground pepper
100 g/4 oz bayonne ham
50 g/2 oz green leek leaves, washed
1 bouquet garni
250 g/9 oz potatoes, cut into chunks
100 g/4 oz butter

Place the chick peas in a casserole, cover with cold water and bring to the boil. Skim, season and add the ham, leeks and bouquet garni. Cook at a slow boil for 2 hours, then add the potatoes and cook for another 30 minutes, until soft.

Rub through a sieve and beat in the butter. Check the seasoning and serve. A split pea purée can be cooked in exactly the same way.

Pieds de Cochon aux Morilles

STUFFED PIGS' TROTTERS WITH MORELS—SERVES 4

4 pigs' back trotters, boned
100 g/4 oz carrots, diced
100 g/4 oz onions, diced
150 ml/5 fl oz dry white wine
1 tablespoon port
150 ml/5 fl oz veal stock
225 g/8 oz calf's sweetbreads, blanched and chopped
75 g/3 oz butter
20 dried morels, soaked until soft and drained
1 small onion, finely chopped
1 chicken breast, skinned and diced
1 egg white
200 ml/7 fl oz double cream
salt and freshly ground pepper
Purée de pommes de terre (recipe page 281) and Peau de porc croustillante (recipe page 289), to serve

Place the trotters in a casserole with the diced carrots and onions, wine, port and veal stock. Cover and braise in the oven at 160ºC/325ºF/gas 3 for 3 hours.

Meanwhile, fry the sweetbreads in 70 g/2½ oz butter for 5 minutes, add the morels and chopped onion and cook for another 5 minutes. Leave to cool.

Purée the chicken breast with the egg white and cream and season with salt and pepper. Mix with the sweetbread mixture to make the stuffing.

Take the trotters out of the casserole and strain the cooking stock, keeping the stock but discarding the vegetables. Open the trotters out flat and lay each one on a piece of foil. Leave to cool. Fill the trotters with the chicken stuffing and roll tightly in the foil. Chill in the fridge for at least 2 hours.

Preheat the oven to 220ºC/425ºF/gas 7. Place the foil-wrapped trotters in a steamer and heat over simmering water, or put them in a casserole, add 100 ml/4 fl oz water and heat in the preheated oven for 15 minutes.

Transfer the trotters to a serving plate and remove the foil. Pour the reserved stock into the casserole, reduce by half, add the remaining knob of butter, pour the sauce over the trotters and serve with *Purée de pommes de terre* and *Peau de porc croustillante*.

Peau de Porc Croustillante

CRISPY PIG SKIN

500 g / 1 lb pork skin
salt and freshly ground pepper
1 mirepoix *of vegetables, including 1 carrot (finely diced), 1 leek, 1 onion,*
1 clove and 1 celery branch
1 bouquet garni

Roll up the pork skin, tie tightly with string and add to a large pan filled the water. Season and simmer slowly being careful not to let the water boil. Skim the surface as necessary. Add the *mirepoix* of vegetables and the bouquet garni and very slowly for 2–3 hours, or until tender. Leave the rolled pork skin to cool in the liquor then remove the string, roll tightly in cling film and chill until set.

Slice the skin very thinly using a meat slicer. Lay the slices on a baking tray lined with greaseproof paper, cover with another sheet of greaseproof paper and weigh down with another baking tray. Bake at 160°C/325°F/gas 3 until golden and crispy.

In winter my grandparents hardly ever left the farm, except to go to the village or to take the bus to Fleurance on market days. But then I realize that, all through their lives, they hardly ever left the countryside around Saint Puy (except, of course, when Marcel went to war). I know that Camille came to Tarbes in my father's car to help when my sisters and I were born, but Marcel did not come, and I am certain that neither of my grandparents ever saw Bordeaux or Toulouse. Like most peasants at that time, they calculated all journeys in terms of hours, never in kilometres. When I was small and visited Camille's mother in another village on a Sunday, we went by horse and cart; it took most of the morning to get there and most of the afternoon to get back.

News came to my grandparents via the radio or occasional copies of the local newspaper, and through the postman and the roadmender. The roadmender was a fantastic character. He came from another part of France, and talked with a different accent from ours, so we regarded him as a total foreigner. He was a traveller, always on the move, who picked up gossip everywhere. He was a wild and dramatic story-teller, who could make us laugh or cry, just as he chose. It was the custom at Saint Puy that wherever the roadmender stopped working

at midday, he was asked to share the meal at the nearest farm. Needless to say, when he stopped outside the Oratoire Camille always gave him a good lunch and I always loved to listen to him. One of his favourite meals was *crépinettes* with a gratin of jerusalem artichokes.

Crépinettes de Joue et Queue de Boeuf

OXTAIL AND OX CHEEK FAGGOTS—SERVES 6

1 oxtail, jointed
2 ox cheeks, cleaned and soaked in salted water for 2 hours
100 g/4 oz duck fat
salt and pepper
200 g/7 oz baby onions
2 garlic cloves, chopped
1 bouquet garni
2 bottles of red wine
75 g/3 oz bacon, diced
4 egg yolks
50 g/2 oz fresh breadcrumbs
4 x 10 cm/4 in squares of pig's caul
Purée de pommes de terre (recipe page 281) and carrots, to serve
chopped parsley, to garnish

In a frying pan, heat the fat until it sizzles. Season the meat and seal on all sides in the hot fat. Remove the meat from the pan, put in the onions and fry until brown, then add the garlic, bouquet garni and the meat. Pour in the wine, bring to the boil and check the seasoning. Put in the ham shin, cover the pan and cook in the oven for 3 hours, until the meat is starting to disintegrate.

Leave to cool completely, then take the meat out of the stock and shred it into a bowl. Add the egg yolks and breadcrumbs and mix well.

Preheat the oven to 180°C/350°F/gas 4. Lay the squares of caul on the work surface, put one-quarter of the meat mixture on each square and wrap in the caul. Reheat the cooking stock, put in the *crépinettes* and cook over gentle heat for about 20 minutes, turning them over at least once.

Transfer the *crépinettes* to a serving dish, reduce the stock to make a good gravy and serve with *Purée de pommes de terre* and carrots, garnished with parsley.

Gratin de Topinambours

GRATIN OF JERUSALEM ARTICHOKES

1 kg/2¼ lb jerusalem artichokes
15 g/½ oz butter
15 g/½ oz plain flour
250 ml/9 fl oz milk
salt and freshly ground pepper
50 g/2 oz gruyère cheese, grated

Peel the jerusalem artichokes and slice them very thinly. Cover with a cloth and set aside.

Prepare a béchamel sauce by melting the butter in a saucepan. Add the flour and stir continuously for 2 minutes over low heat to make a roux. Boil the milk and pour a little on to the roux, stirring with a whisk, then whisk in the rest of the milk and cook gently for 10 minutes.

Sieve the sauce on to the jerusalem artichokes and mix well. Season to taste and place in a gratin dish. Sprinkle the gruyère on top and bake in a slow oven at 150°C/300°F/gas 2 for 1 hour.

It must have been about 1968 that my father bought my grandparents a television set. Though they quite liked the news and variety programmes with popular singers, they could never get used to films, especially westerns. Camille was never quite convinced that she was just watching actors who were only pretending to shoot each other. Each time somebody was killed, it all seemed so real to her that she let out a piercing scream of horror.

But if the television was only moderately successful in mitigating their winter solitude, the celebration of Saint Marcel's Day on 16th January did much more to bring my grandparents in touch with a wider world. On that day Marcel was fêted like a king; everybody in the village came to see him and the postman brought what seemed to him an immense quantity of letters and postcards, which reminded him of friends and relations all over the country, whom he knew he would probably never see again. Of course, Camille would cook Marcel a special lunch for his saint's day. I remember that one year she gave him a veal tongue with lentils and a salad of cabbage and duck giblets, although of course, he insisted on one of his favourite soups to start with.

Soupe aux Pois Cassés

SPLIT PEA SOUP—SERVES 4

400 g/14 oz split peas
100 g/4 oz leeks, thinly sliced
1 small onion, thinly sliced
100 g/4 oz duck fat
100 g/4 oz preserved pork or duck (see Confit de canard, page 263)
2 garlic cloves, peeled and left whole
1 small bouquet garni
200 g/7 oz bread, diced
salt and freshly ground pepper

Wash the split peas in cold water, put them in a pan of cold water and bring to the boil. Rinse in cold water and drain.

In a saucepan, sweat the leeks and onions in half the duck fat for 5 minutes, add the salt pork or duck, the drained peas, garlic, bouquet garni and 1.5 l/2½ pt water. Bring to the boil and simmer gently for 1½ hours.

Meanwhile, fry the bread in the remaining duck fat to make croûtons. When the split peas are tender, remove the pork or duck and dice it. Purée the soup in a blender, then pass through a fine sieve. Season generously with salt and pepper and serve very hot, garnished with the diced pork or duck and the croûtons.

Langue de Veau aux Lentilles

CALF'S TONGUE WITH LENTILS—SERVES 4

1 calf's tongue
1 small bouquet garni
salt and freshly ground pepper
500 g/1 lb 2 oz onions, halved
500 g/1 lb 2 oz carrots, halved
1 kg/2¼ lb leeks, split lengthways
400 g/14 oz lentils
50 g/2 oz duck fat
2 garlic cloves, chopped
2 tablespoons chopped parsley

Pour 7 l/12 pt water into a huge pot, add the tongue and boil for 20 minutes, skimming the surface very thoroughly until it is quite clear. Add the bouquet garni, season and simmer gently for 1½ hours. Add the vegetables and cook for another 45 minutes. Add the lentils and cook for 25 minutes.

Remove the tongue and peel it, then slice and arrange on a serving dish. Drain the lentils with a slotted spoon, reserving the stock and vegetables. Stir the duck fat, garlic and parsley into the hot lentils and add 200 ml/7 fl oz stock. Pour the lentils around the tongue.

Purée the remaining vegetables and stock in a blender to make a delicious soup, or serve the vegetables with a vinaigrette and use the cooking liquid for stock.

Salade de Choux et Gésiers de Canard Confits

SALAD OF CABBAGE & PRESERVED DUCK GIZZARDS—SERVES 4

500 g/1 lb 2 oz white cabbage
salt and freshly ground pepper
100 ml/4 fl oz oil
100 g/4 oz carrots, shredded
25 g/1 oz shallots, finely chopped
1 garlic clove, crushed
25 ml/1 fl oz vinegar
8 preserved duck gizzards (see Confit de canard, *page 263)*

Shred the cabbage very thinly and place in a bowl. Season with salt and pepper. In a saucepan, heat the oil without letting it get too hot, add the carrots and cook until still crunchy, then add the shallots, garlic and vinegar to taste, and pour this mixture on to the cabbage. Cover the bowl and leave to marinate for 1 hour. Adjust the seasoning, place the cabbage in a serving dish and surround with the duck gizzards.

I always enjoyed the nameday occasion, and I liked the blissful pleasure it gave my grandfather. When Saint Marcel's day fell on a Saturday or Sunday, there was no trouble about getting away from school and I was very pleased; but when it was over, I knew that my next visit to Saint Puy would not be until the spring, and I was sorry that the winter had come to its end.

Service militaire
à Toulon.

Epilogue

I LEFT SCHOOL in the summer of 1963, and that autumn I started a three-year cookery course at the *Collège d'Enseignement Technique Reffye* at Tarbes. This choice of career was a natural one. All my life, almost without knowing it, I had been interested in and curious about cooking; I can even remember that one afternoon when I was about eight years old and had been playing with four or five other children in the village, I invited them all back to the Oratoire for a meal. My grandparents were both out of the house at the time, but I opened up one of the jars of *confit*, heated up its contents over the fire and served them a very good supper. When Camille came back she found me standing at the head of the table with an expression of complete happiness on my face as I watched the other children eating away with a hearty appetite. 'Just think,' she used to say later on, 'it was your very first restaurant!' It was also the occasion when I first made the important discovery that you can only cook well for people if you sincerely want to make them happy with the food you give them.

While I was a student there was no difficulty about keeping in contact with Saint Puy and my grandparents. Besides weekends and the usual college holidays, we also had one day off every week, so my visits to the Oratoire went on just as before. The course at Tarbes was excellent. We were given a good basic knowledge of cooking in general, and also a thorough grounding in the art of French classical *haute cuisine*. I have always been grateful to the school for what it taught me, and I have never thrown away the printed instruction cards we had as text-books because of the clear and detailed way in which the recipes were written. I think that my training was much sounder than that given to many students today. When I ask a young cook to make me something quite basic and straightforward, like a veal stock or a *sauce béarnaise*, I am often surprised to find that he is not quite sure how to do it, and I have to show him. In our case there was never any need for a further lesson.

My personal experience of working in hotel and restaurant kitchens began with the summer jobs I took while I was still at the cookery school. In 1964, I worked a *stage* at the Chalet Hotel at Cauterets, the famous mountain spa surrounded by the snow-capped Pyrenees, and the following year I went to the nearby Argèles-Gazost. In 1966 I finished my course, and took my first real job in the kitchen of L'Aubette at Strasbourg. It was the first time I had ever left Gascony, but I think Marcel was pleased I was going to Strasbourg because, when I went to Saint Puy to say goodbye, he told me once more all the stories of his wartime adventures there.

After Strasbourg I worked for a short time at Juan-les-Pins, and then from 1968 to 1969 I did my national service as a cook in the French navy. The following year I worked at Ouchy, on the shores of the lake of Geneva, and also at Marseilles and La Ciotat. Over a period of about seven years I had jobs in quite a variety of kitchens; each experience was useful to me, each job taught me something different, and the moment I felt that I had gained all I possibly could from a particular kitchen or a particular chef, I moved on at once to another.

At school I had always been a very keen rugby player; one of my most constant dreams was to be able to watch as many matches as possible at Twickenham which, of course, seemed then to be a very long way from Saint Puy. In the summer of 1970, when I left Lausanne, I decided that the easiest way for me to get from France to Twickenham would be to find a job somewhere in London. When a suitable opportunity was offered me by the Roux brothers, who had recently started La Gavroche, I grabbed it with great enthusiasm.

To my delight, I not only enjoyed the rugby at Twickenham even more than I expected, but I also began to like London and English life so much that I wanted to stay there permanently. In 1972, the year of my marriage, Albert Roux asked me to take over the kitchen at the Waterside Inn at Bray; and with the exception of a brief period when I went back to France, I stayed there until 1976. In 1977 I took on the challenge of opening my own restaurant, La Tante Claire, in Chelsea. Incidentally, I never actually had a *Tante Claire* of my own! The eponymous lady was actually the aunt of a friend of mine, whom I had never met.

Through all this period I was never out of touch with Camille and Marcel. While I was still in France I was able to buy my first car, and I could drive Camille to Fleurance market. I have already described how Annie and I were married at Saint Puy, and how, in 1978, I surprised my grandfather with a complete menu from La Tante Claire. We visited the Oratoire almost every summer, and usually at Christmas as well. Marcel adored Annie, and he was at his happiest and most irrepressible when she was there.

The next few years were marked by the deaths of both my grandparents. At about the same time my uncle Capuron ceased to be mayor, and he and my aunt retired from their grocery business, though they still lived in the house at the corner of the little square near the *mairie* and the war memorial. Nearly all the land which Marcel used to farm has now been sold, but the farmhouse still belongs to the family, and is the home of my uncle's son, my cousin Jean-Pierre Capuron.

The interior of the farmhouse has been completely altered, and the kitchen I knew no longer exists. Nevertheless the old long-case clock is still there, with its *vendange* scene round the dial, and we have reverently preserved one of Marcel's shotguns. Outside, a few bits of twisted rusty iron are all that is left of Camille's arbour where we used to sit in the summer evenings; sadly, where her neat kitchen garden was, there are now only mounds of rough grass overgrown with bushes.

The barn where the wheat was piled up at the *dépiquage* has been converted as part of the house, but the pigsty is still there, as are the stables with their stalls and mangers, although these will never see another cow. In the dark work-room below the kitchen there is an old plough, a rusty collection of Marcel's tools and implements hanging on the wall, and nearby you can see a large pile of *matoles*, the traps he used for catching ortolans. The well, the copper in which Marie-Jeanne boiled the washing and the concrete tree trunks round the *foudres* are all still there as well, though the latter are now somewhat battered and chipped.

One summer evening, during one of our last visits to Saint Puy, I remember standing outside the house with Camille while Annie and Marcel were laughing and joking in the kitchen. My grandmother turned to me and said, 'One day, you know, you will come to the Oratoire, and Marcel and I will not be here any more.' It was a moment of sadness. It cannot have been very long after this that she died, so perhaps it was her way of saying goodbye to me. At the time of her death Camille was seventy-five, and Marcel, when he died, was eighty-four; they had both come to the end of their long lives, but for me, in my heart, they will always go on living, and I shall never forget them.

Index

Acacia flower fritters 37
Adour salmon cooked in goose fat
52, 54
Adour salmon poached with
vegetables 52, *53*
Agen prunes in rum *188*, 189
Alicot d'oie aux légumes d'hiver
176–7
Alouettes sans têtes 185, *186*
Anguilles au vin rouge 45–7, *46*
Apéritif aux feuilles de noyer 24–5
Aperitifs:
  Orange aperitif 120, *121*
  Walnut leaf aperitif 24–5
Apple:
  Apple flan *213*, 214
  Creamy apple tart 177–8
  Flaky croustade of caramelized
  apples 145–7, *146*
Apricot coulis 111
Armagnac:
  Armagnac-flavoured pancakes 38, *39*
  Calves' testicles with armagnac 80–81
  Greengages in armagnac 90, *91*
  Wild pigeon with armagnac 208–9
*Artichauts en salade avec foie gras et
  jambon* 274–6, *275*
Artichoke:
  Fricassée of rabbit with
  artichokes 151–3, *152*
  Gratin of jerusalem artichokes 293
  Salad of artichokes, bayonne ham
  and foie gras 274–6, *275*
Asparagus omelette 59, *60*

Bacon:
  Potato and bacon pie 268–9
  Trout cooked with bacon 48, *49*
Ballotine de foie gras au jurançon 105
Bayonne ham tart with garlic *109*, 110
Bean:
  Broad bean soup 58
  Dried french beans 96
  French beans in cream 174
  Haricot beans in red wine 257–8
  Toulouse sausages with white
  beans and tomatoes 167
  White bean soup 166
Beef:
  Gascon boiled meats with
  vegetables 32, 34
Beignets 55
*Beignets de fleurs d'acacia ou de
  citrouille* 37
Biscuits de maïs 193
Black pudding *279*, 280–1
Blackberry:
  Blackberry jelly *163*, 164
  Flambéed blackberry omelette *200*, 201
Blanquette d'agneau 73, 74
Boudin noir 279, 280–81

Boudins verts 123–4
Bouilli 32, 34
Brandade de morue 243, 245
Bread 128–31:
  'Corkscrew' loaf *129*, 130
  French bread sticks *129*, 131
  Gascon bread 128–30, *129*
  Oil bread *129*, 130–31
Brioche 122–23
Broad bean soup 58
Brochet au vinaigre et au poivre
  148–50, *149*

Cabbage:
  Baked stuffed cabbage 239–41, *240*
  Salad of cabbage and preserved
  duck gizzards 295
  Spring cabbage soup 56–8
  Stuffed cabbage 123
  Young partridge with cabbage 194–5
Cailles sur la cendre 117, 118
Cailles aux feuilles de vigne 218,
  219–20
Cakes:
  Light sponge cake 248
  'Stalagmite' cake cooked on the
  spit 276
Calf's tongue with lentils 294–5
Calves' testicles with armagnac 80–1
Camille's special garbure 27–9, *28*
Canard aux olives 135, *136*
Canard aux pêches 135, 137
Canard au sang 137
Canards sauvages au sue d'orange
  234, *235*
Carp with potatoes and herbs *50*, 51
Carpe à la boulangère 50, 51
Carrot:
  Shin of veal with carrots *267–8*
Cassoulet de morue 168, 169
Cassoulet de morue á la Tante Claire
  169–70
Cep:
  Cep flan 204–6, *205*
  Ceps in red wine 206
  Duck breasts with cep sauce 265–6
  Roast turkey with ceps 212
Chestnut:
  Mutton soup with chestnuts 242
  Roast turkey with chestnut
  stuffing *271*, 272
Chick pea purée 286
Chicken:
  Chicken liver pâté with capers
  114, *115*
  Chicken necks, wings and giblets
  stewed in white wine with
  macaroni 250–1
  Cooked chicken blood 113
  Cockerel in madiran wine 187
  Gascon boiled meats with
  vegetables 32, 34
  Grilled spring chicken with
  shallots and vinaigrette 68–9

Mousseline of chicken with
  carrots and lemon sauce 221–2
Stuffed chicken in the pot with
  stuffed cabbage and poached
  brioche 122–4
Civet de homard au madiran 222
Civet de lièvre 244, 245–6
Cockerel in madiran wine 187
Cod:
  Creamed salt cod *243*, 245
  Salt cod cassoulet à la Tante
  Claire 169–70
  Traditional salt cod cassoulet
  168, 169
Confit de canard 262, 263–4
Confiture de noix vertes 96
Confiture aux prunes 162, *163*
Confiture de tomates vertes 164
Coq au madiran 187
Cornichons au vinaigre 64
Cornmeal biscuits 193
Cornmeal cakes 191, *192*
Cornmeal porridge 124
Côtes de porc aux cornichons 285, 286
Courgette:
  Gratin of courgettes 177
Crayfish in white wine 150–1
Creamed salt cod *243*, 245
Creamy apple tart 177–8
Crème brûlée à la gasconne 76, *79*
Crème de petits pois 59
Crêpes à l'armagnac 38, *39*
Crêpes au vin blanc 269
Crépinettes de joue et queue de boeuf
  290, 291
Crispy pig skin 289
Croustade de confit de canard 35–7
*Croustade de pigeonneaux à la
  gasconne* 88–9
Croustade aux pommes caramélisées
  145–7, *146*
*Cuisses de grenouilles aux
  champignons* 153–4

Dandelion salad with bacon and
  poached eggs *33*, 34
*Darne de colin aux câpres, safran et
  tomates* 100, 101
Daube de cèpes 206
*Daube de cuisses de canard aux
  pruneaux* 277
Dinde rôtie aux marrons 271, 272
Dindonneau rôti aux cèpes 212
Duck:
  Braised duck legs with prunes 277
  Duck with blood sauce 137
  Duck breasts with cep sauce 265–6
  Duck breasts cooked on a string 266–7
  Duck breasts grilled over vine
  branches 257
  Duck breasts with pepper 265
  Duck foie gras with grapes 261
  Duck foie gras with sweetcorn
  and apples *259*, 260

INDEX

Preserved duck *262*, 263–4
Preserved duck legs in
    featherlight pastry 35–7
Roast duck with olives 135, *136*
Roast duck with peaches 135, 137
Salad of cabbage and preserved
    duck gizzards 295
Terrine of duck 134–5
Wild duck with orange sauce 234, *235*
Dumpling with kidneys and morel
    sauce 126

Easter waffles 76, *77*
Écrevisses au pacherenc 150–1
Eels in red wine 45, *46*
Egg:
    Asparagus omelette 59, *60*
    Dandelion salad with bacon and
        poached eggs *33*, 34
    Flambéed blackberry omelette
        200, 201
    Fried eggs with foie gras 260
    Garlic and breadcrumb patty 58
    Gudgeon omelette 43
    Poached egg whites with vanilla
        custard *101*, 102
    Spring onion omelette 69–70
    Wild mushroom omelette 85
Épaule d'agneau à la boulangère
    143, *144*
Estouffade de sanglier 179, *180*

Faisan *au floc de gascogne et au*
    céleri rave 196, 198
'Fantasy' fritters 40
Farce à tout faire 124
Farci aux oeufs 58
Flaky croustade of caramelized
    apples 145–7, *146*
Flambéed blackberry omelette
    200, 201
Flan de pêches de vigne au vin doux 161
Flans *see* Tarts and flans
Foie gras:
    Ballotine of foie gras with sweet
        jurançon wine 105
    Duck foie gras with grapes 261
    Duck foie gras with sweetcorn
        and apples 260
    Fried eggs with foie gras 260
    Potato cakes with foie gras and
        shallots 225
    Salad of artichokes, bayonne ham
        and foie gras 274–6, *275*
    Spring vegetables with foie gras
        61–2
    Terrine of foie gras 283–4
    Foie gras de canard aux maïs et
        pommes 260
    Foie gras de canard aux raisins 261
Fraises au vin de Monluc et au poivre
    140, *141*
French beans in cream 174
French beans, dried 96

Fricassée de lapin aux artichauts
    151–3, *152*
Fricassée de pintade à l'ail 132, *133*
Fricassée de veau 80
Fritters:
    Acacia or pumpkin flower fritters 37
    'Fantasy' fritters 40
    Fritters 55
    'Rat's tail' fritters 38, 40
    Salsify fritters 272–4, *273*
Frogs' legs with oyster mushrooms 153–4
Frogs' legs soup with watercress 220–1
Fruit. *See also individual names*
    Summer fruits in red wine 142

Galettes de foie gras aux échalotes
    rôties 225
Garbure de fête 27–9, *28*
Garbure de gascogne 26–7
Garlic and breadcrumb patty 58
Gascon boiled meats with
    vegetables 32, 34
Gascon bread 128–30, *129*
Gascon crème brûlée 76, *79*
Gascon leg of lamb 72
Gasconnade de gigot d'agneau 72
Gâteau à la broche 276
Gâteau de choux 239–41, *240*
Gâteau de foies de volaille aux câpres
    114, *115*
Gâteau mousseline 248
Gâteau de riz aux abricots 111, *112*
Gâteaux aux fers 76, *77*
Gelée de coings 162, *163*
Gelée de mûres 163, *164*
Gherkin:
    Pickled gherkins *63*, 64
Gigot pascal en croûte 75
Gigot de quatre heures 106
Gigue de chevreuil au poivre 207–8
Goose:
    Goose giblets with root vegetables
        176–7
    Vegetable soup with preserved
        goose 26–7
Grapes, duck foie gras with 261
Gratin de citrouille 202, *203*
Gratin de courgettes 177
Gratin d'haricots verts 173, *174*
Gratin de poireaux au roquefort 70, *71*
Gratin de topinambours 293
Green sausages 123–4
Green tomato jam 164
Green walnut jam 96
Greengages in armagnac 90, *91*
Gudgeon omelette 43
Guinea fowl:
    Fricassée of guinea fowl with
        garlic 132, *133*
    Guinea fowl with Agen prunes
        and *pousse rapière* 253, 254

Hake with capers, saffron and
    tomatoes 100, 102

Ham:
    Bayonne ham tart with garlic *109*, 110
    Salad of artichokes, bayonne ham
        and foie gras 274–6, *275*
Hare:
    Hare in red wine 244, *245*–6
    Roast hare with mustard and
        beetroot 171–2
    Stuffed hare in white wine 172
Haricot bean:
    Haricot beans in red wine 257–8
    Toulouse sausages with white
        beans and tomatoes 167
    White bean soup *165*, 166
Haricots verts secs 96
Haricots au vin rouge 257–8
'Headless larks': stuffed veal
    escalopes 185, *186*

Jambon de mouton 116
Jambonneau de porc en bocal 284
Jams and jellies:
    Blackberry jelly *163*, 164
    Green tomato jam 164
    Green walnut jam 96
    Plum jam 162, *163*
    Pumpkin jam 202
    Quince jelly 162, *163*
Jarret de veau aux carottes 267–8
Jerusalem artichokes, gratin of 293

Kidney:
    Dumpling with kidneys and morel
        sauce 126

Lamb:
    Gascon leg of lamb 72
    Lamb cured like ham 116
    Lamb stew in a white sauce 73, 74
    Leg of lamb cooked for 4 hours 106
    Paschal lamb in pastry 75
    Shoulder of lamb with potatoes
        143, *144*
    Steamed fillet of lamb in leek
        parcels 223, 224
Langue de veau aux lentilles 294–5
Lapin farci aux herbes 65, 66
Leek:
    Gratin of leeks with roquefort 70, *71*
    Steamed fillet of lamb in leek
        parcels 223, 224
Lentils, calf's tongue with 294–5
Levraut rôti à la moutarde et aux
    betteraves 171–2
Lièvre à la royale 172
Lobster:
    Braised lobster in red wine *222*

Magrets de canard à la ficelle 266
Magrets de canard au poivre 265
Magrets de canard aux sarments de
    vigne 257
Magrets de canard, sauce aux cèpes 265–6
Maize semolina soup 210, *211*

Marmelade de citrouille 202
Melon flan *139*, 140–1
Merveilles 40
Milhas 124
Mique à la royale 125, 126
Miques de maïs 191, *192*
Morel:
    Dumpling with kidneys and morel
        sauce *125*, 126
    Stuffed pigs' trotters with morels
        287, *288*
Mousseline de volaille au citron et
    aux carottes 221–2
Mousserons en persillade 84
Mushroom. *See also* Cep, Morel
    Frogs' legs with oyster
        mushrooms 153–4
    Sweetbreads with mushrooms 100
    Wild mushroom omelette 85
    Wild mushrooms with parsley 84
Mutton soup with chestnuts 242

Oeufs à la neige 101, 102
Oeufs au plat au foie gras 260
Oil bread *129*, 130–1
Olives, roast duck with 135, *136*
Omelette aux asperges 59, *60*
Omelette flambée aux mûres 200, 201
Omelette aux goujons 43
Omelette aux mousserons 85
Omelette aux oignons nouveaux 69–70
Omelettes:
    Asparagus omelette 59, *60*
    Flambéed blackberry omelette
        200, 201
    Gudgeon omelette 43
    Spring onion omelette 69–70
    Wild mushroom omelette 85
Onion:
    Onion and garlic soup 250
    Rabbit with baby onions 64
Orange:
    Orange aperitif 120, *121*
    Wild duck with orange juice 234, *235*
Oxtail and ox cheek faggots 291
Oyster mushrooms, frogs' legs with
    153–4

Pain baguette *129*, 131
Pain gascon 128–30, *129*
Pain à l'huile 129, 130–1
Pain tordu du Gers 129, 130
Palombes à à l'armagnac 208–9
Pancakes. *See also* Fritters
    Armagnac-flavoured pancakes 38, *39*
    White wine pancakes 269
Partridge:
    Young partridge with cabbage 194–5
Paschal lamb in pastry 75
Pastry:
    Pastis pastry 35–6
    Savoury flan pastry 110–1
    Sweet flan pastry 142
    Pastry cream 246–8

Pâte à tarte 110–1
Pâte à tarte sucrée 142
Pâté:
    Chicken liver pâté with capers
        114, *115*
    Terrine de foie gras 283–4
Paupiettes d'agneau aux feuilles de
    poireau 223, 224
Pea:
    Pea soup 59
    Split pea soup *292*, 294
Peach:
    Roast duck with peaches 135, 137
    Vineyard peach flan with sweet
        wine 161
Perdrix aux choux 194–5
Petits gris farcis au vin rouge 83
Petits gris gros sel 82
Peau de Porc Croustillante 289
Pheasant:
    Pheasant with *floc* and celeriac 196, 198
    Pheasant with fresh walnuts 196, *197*
Pickled gherkins 64
Pieds de cochon aux morilles 287, *288*
Pies:
    Potato and bacon pie 268–9
    Potato pie in puff pastry 214
Pigeon:
    Pigeon in traditional Gascon
        pastry 88–9
    Young pigeon with thyme and
        garlic *86*, 87–8
    Wild pigeon with armagnac 208–9
Pigeonneaux au thym et à l'ail 86, 87–8
Pigs' trotters:
    Stuffed pigs' trotters with morels
        287, *288*
Pike steaks with wine vinegar and
    crushed peppercorns 148–50, *149*
Pintade aux pruneaux d'Agen et à la
    pousse rapière 253, 254
Pissenlits au lard avec oeufs mollets
    33, 34
Pistachio soufflé *226*, 227
Plum jam 162, *163*
Porcelet cuit à la broche 89–90
Pork:
    Baked stuffed cabbage 239–41, *240*
    Bottled shin of pork 284
    Pork chops with gherkins *285*, 286
    Pork rillettes *282*, 283
    Sucking pig cooked on a spit 89–90
Potato:
    Potato and bacon pie 268–9
    Potato cakes with foie gras and
        shallots 225
    Potato pie in puff pastry 214
    Puréed potatoes with duck fat 281
    Shoulder of lamb with potatoes
        143, *144*
Poule au pot 122–4
Poulet grillé à la vinaigrette
    d'échalote 68–9
Preserved duck *262*, 263–4

Preserved duck legs in featherlight
    pastry 35–7
Prune:
    Agen prunes in rum *188*, 189
    Braised duck legs with prunes 277
    Guinea fowl with Agen prunes
        and *pousse rapiere 253*, 254
    Prune flan 246–8, *247*
Pruneaux d'Agen au rhum 188, 189
Puddings:
    Acacia or pumpkin flower fritters 37
    Agen prunes in rum *188*, 189
    Apple flan *213*, 214–5
    Armagnac-flavoured pancakes *38*, *39*
    Creamy apple tart 177–8
    'Fantasy' fritters 40
    Flaky croustade of caramelized
        apples 145–7, *146*
    Flambéed blackberry omelette
        200, 201
    Gascon crème brûlée 76, *79*
    Melon flan *139*, 140–1
    Moulded rice pudding with
        apricot coulis 111, *112*
    Pistachio soufflé *226*, *227*
    Poached egg whites with vanilla
        custard *101*, 102
    Prune flan 246–8, *247*
    'Rat's tail' fritters 38, 40
    Strawberries in sparkling wine
        with pepper 140, *141*
    Summer fruits in red wine 142
    Traditional Easter waffles 76, *77*
    Vineyard peach flan with sweet
        wine 161
    Walnut flan *183*, 184
    White wine pancakes 269
Pumpkin:
    Gratin of pumpkin 202, *203*
    Pumpkin flower fritters 37
    Pumpkin jam 202
Purée de pois chiches 286
Purée de pommes de terre à la graisse
    de canard 281

Quail:
    Quail wrapped in vine leaves
        218, 219
    Quails cooked over the embers
        117, 118
Queues de rat 38, 40
Quince jelly 162, *163*

Rabbit:
    Fricassée of rabbit with
        artichokes 151–3, *152*
    Rabbit with baby onions 64
    Rabbit stuffed with herbs *65*, 66
Ragoût d'abattis de volaille 250–1
Ragoût de faisan aux noix 196, *197*
Ragoût de légumes nouveaux au foie
    gras 61–2
'Rat's tail' fritters 38, 40
Reine Claude à l'armagnac 90, *91*

Rice:
  Moulded rice pudding with
    apricot coulis 111, *112*
Rillettes de porc 282, 283
Ris de veau à la forestière 100
Rognons blancs à l' armagnac 80–1
Roquefort, gratin of leeks with 70, *71*

Salad:
  Dandelion salad with bacon and
    poached eggs *33*, 34
  Salad of artichokes, bayonne ham
    and foie gras 274–6, *275*
  Salad of cabbage and preserved
    duck gizzards 295
  *Salade de choux et gesiers de canard
    confits* 295
Salmis de bécasse 236–7
Salmon:
  Adour salmon cooked in goose fat 52, 54
  Adour salmon poached with
    vegetables 52, *53*
Salsifis en beignets 272–4, *273*
Salsify fritters 272–4, *273*
Salt cod *see* cod
Salt cod cassoulet *168*, 169
Salt cod cassoulet à la Tante Claire
  169–70
Sanquette de poulet 113
Sauce tomate 241
Saucisses aux haricots et tomates 167
*Saumon de l'Adour confit à la graisse
  d'oie* 52, 54
*Saumon de l'Adour etuvé aux
  légumes* 52, *53*
Sausages:
  Green sausages 123–4
  Toulouse sausages with white
    beans and tomatoes 167
Snail:
  Snails grilled with coarse salt 82
  Stuffed snails in red wine 83
Soufflé aux pistaches 226, 227
Soup:
  Camille's special garbure 27–9, *28*
  Frogs' legs soup with watercress 220–1
  Maize semolina soup 210, *211*
  Mutton soup with chestnuts 242
  Onion and garlic soup 250
  Pea soup 59
  Split pea soup *292*, 294
  Spring cabbage soup 56, 58
  Vegetable soup with preserved
    goose 26–7
  White bean soup 166
Soupe aux broutes 56, 58
Soupe aux fèves 57, 58
Soupe de fruits au vin rouge 142
Soupe de grenouilles au cresson 220–1
Soupe de haricots blancs 166
Soupe de maïs 210, *211*
Soupe de mouton aux châtaignes 242
Soupe aux pois cassés 292, 294
Split pea soup *292*, 294

Spring cabbage soup 56, 58
Spring chicken, grilled, with
  shallots and vinaigrette 68–9
Spring onion omelette 69
Spring vegetables with foie gras 61–2
'Stalagmite' cake cooked on the
  spit 276
Strawberries in sparkling wine
  with pepper 140, *141*
Stuffed chicken in the pot with
  stuffed cabbage and poached
  brioche 122–4
Stuffed hare in white wine 172
Stuffed pigs' trotters with morels
  287, *288*
Stuffed snails in red wine 83
Stuffing (all-purpose) 124
Sucking pig cooked on a spit 89–90
Summer fruits in red wine 142
Sweet flan pastry 142
Sweetbreads with mushrooms 100

*Tanches braisées à la tomate et
  moutarde* 42
Tarte aux cèpes 204–6, *205*
Tarte au jambon et à l'ail 109, 110
Tarte au melon 139, 140–1
Tarte aux noix 183, 184
Tarte aux pommes 213, 214–5
*Tarte aux pommes et à la crème de
  lait* 177–8
Tarte aux pruneaux 246–8, *247*
Tarts and flans. *See also* Pastry
  Apple flan *213*, 214–5
  Bayonne ham tart with garlic
    109, 110
  Cep flan 204–6, *205*
  Creamy apple tart 177–8
  Melon flan *139*, 140–1
  Prune flan 246–8, *247*
  Vineyard peach flan with sweet
    wine 161
  Walnut flan *183*, 184
Tench, braised, with tomato and
  mustard 42
Terrine de canard 134–5
Terrine de foie gras 283–4
Tomato:
  Green tomato jam 164
  Tomato sauce 241
Tongue:
  Calf's tongue with lentils 294–5
Toulouse sausages with white beans
  and tomatoes 167
Tourain blanchi à l'ail 250
Tourte de pommes de terre à l' ail 214
Tourte de pommes de terre au lard 268–9
Tripe:
  Veal tripe 80
Trout:
  Trout cooked with bacon 48, *49*
  Trout with watercress 48
Truites au cresson 48
Truites au lard 48, *49*

Turkey:
  Roast turkey with ceps 212
  Roast turkey with chestnut
    stuffing *271*, 272

Vanilla custard *101*, 102
Veal:
  'Headless larks': stuffed veal
    escalopes 185, *186*
  Shin of veal with carrots 267–8
  Veal tripe 80
Vegetables. *See also individual
  names*
  Adour salmon poached with
    vegetables 52, *53*
  Goose giblets with root vegetables 176
  Spring vegetables with foie gras 61–2
  Vegetable soup with preserved
    goose 26–7
Venison:
  Haunch of venison with
    peppercorns 207–8
Vin d' orange 120, *121*
Vinaigrette 34, 61–2, 68–9
Vineyard peach flan with sweet
  wine 161

Waffles:
  Traditional Easter waffles 76, *77*
Walnut:
  Green walnut jam 96
  Pheasant with fresh walnuts 196, *197*
  'Stalagmite' cake cooked on the
    spit 276
  Walnut flan *183*, 184
  Walnut leaf aperitif 24
Watercress:
  Frogs' legs soup with watercress 220–1
  Trout with watercress 48
White bean soup 166
White wine pancakes 269
Wild boar casserole 179, *180*
Wild duck with orange juice 234, *235*
Wild mushroom omelette 85
Wild mushrooms with parsley 84
Wild pigeon with armagnac 208–9
Woodcock:
  Salmis of woodcock 236–7

Acknowledgements

I would like to thank the entire staff of Koffmann's at The Berkeley, especially Craig Burrows, Christian Edwardson, Joe Fordyce, Yik Hoi Ng, Katherine Kokot, Christopher Lindsay, Lixi Lineas, Tiffany Lo, Ian McMillan, Ben Murphy, Anna Quaile, Parnpim Sasipibool, Mark Silvester, Kim Sin Tae and Jeremy Trehout. Special thanks and gratitude go to my wife Claire, whose guidance and help in reviving this book was invaluable.

Memories of Gascony
by Pierre Koffmann with Timothy Shaw

An Hachette UK Company
www.hachette.co.uk

First published in Great Britain in 1990 by Mitchell Beazley, a division of Octopus Publishing Group Ltd
Carmelite House, 50 Victoria Embankment, London EC4Y 0DZ
www.octopusbooks.co.uk

Revised edition 2012
This edition published in 2016

ISBN: 978 1 78472 223 4

A CIP record for this book is available from the British Library
Printed and bound in China

10 9 8 7 6 5 4 3 2 1

Publishing Director: Stephanie Jackson
Art Director & Design: Jonathan Christie
Editor: Stephanie Milner
Proofreader: Joanna Smith
Production Manager: Peter Hunt
Photographer: Laura Edwards
Prop Stylist: Twig Hutchinson

Koffmann's at The Berkeley, Wilton Place, London SW1X 7RL

+44 (0)20 7235 1010 | koffmanns@the-berkeley.co.uk | www.the-berkeley.co.uk/koffmanns.aspx

For the first edition

The authors wish to thank the parents of Pierre Koffmann and also his uncle and aunt, Ivan and Yvonne Capuron, for being able to provide them with many useful items of infomation. The friendship of Bernard Ramounéda and his informed approach to Gascon cooking have been another source of stimulation. At Saint Puy René and Mireille Lassus introduced us to the château and evoked the life and times of Blaise de Monluc, its most illustrious seigneur; and we are greatly indebted to Raymond Puech for sharing with us his wide knowledge of local history and for allowing us to see his collection of historical documents and early photographs. Finally, this book would never have been written without the generous support and good advice of Annie Koffmann and Maryse Shaw, nor without the enthusiasm, encouragement and unfailing help of Jeremy Cooper.

Commissioned by Lewis Esson | Editorial Direction: Joanna Lorenz | Editor: Kate Whiteman

A GRIEVING DAUGHTER'S HEART

A Grieving Daughter's Heart

Majella Quinlan Duignan

VERITAS

First published privately 2020
This edition published 2021 by
Veritas Publications
7–8 Lower Abbey Street
Dublin 1, Ireland
publications@veritas.ie
www.veritas.ie

ISBN 978-1-84730-997-6

10 9 8 7 6 5 4 3 2 1

A catalogue record for this book is available from the British
Library.

Cover designed by Colette Dower
Printed in Ireland by SPRINT-print Ltd, Dublin

*Veritas books are printed on paper made from the wood pulp of
managed forests. For every tree felled, at least one tree is planted,
thereby renewing natural resources.*

Contents

Acknowledgements 9

Never Have I Ever 11
Introduction 15
Sad 44
Numb 50
Isolated 55
Guilt 64
Grief 70
Vulnerable 76
Desperation 81
Anger 87
Love 94
Fear 100
Anxious 108
Gratitude 114
Resilience 124
Proud 129
Hope 135
A Day like No Other 141

For my Dad
Mike Joe Quinlan

Acknowledgements

THIS BOOK IS DEDICATED TO THE MEMORY OF MY Dad. It starts and ends with a poem. The first was an outcry of the utter despair I experienced after he died. The second, written on the first month anniversary of his passing. Essentially in between is the memoir of a heartbroken daughter, as I struggle with the phenomenon of my own grief in isolation. I am fulfilling a solemn promise I made to Dad that I would find my voice again and I would pursue my passion for writing.

I need to thank my precious daughter, Molly, and my supportive husband, Conor, who nurtured and encouraged me as I embarked on this, my maiden voyage. They were resolute in their belief in me even when I didn't believe in myself. Personally, this was a cathartic experience. In writing this book, I was honouring the first man I loved in my life: my Dad. His unconditional love, his unwavering support and his faith in me, inspired me to embark on this journey.

To my Mom, Bridie, and my brothers, Joe and John, I need to say I love you forever. As Dad said as he approached the end of his life, 'I think we have the makings of a great family!'

I believe family first is the way forward for all of us. So, as we remember the past with Dad and live in the present without him, we look forward to a future where we can honour his legacy by living our best life.

Love you all, Majella x

Never Have I Ever

Never have I ever, felt such SADNESS and DESPAIR.
Never have I ever, been so overwhelmed by the
    calm of a lonely air.
Never have I ever, felt such NUMBING of the heart.
Never have I ever, been so VULNERABLE and have
    fallen apart.

Never have I ever, felt GRIEF like this pain.
Never have I ever, felt an ache so quite insane.
Never have I ever, believed tomorrow may never come.
As in my world my new reality was no fun.

Never have I ever, felt as cold as cold could be.
Never have I ever, felt as though just lost at sea.
Never have I ever, cried such solemn tears.
Never have I ever, lamented more for bygone years.

Never have I ever, called so loud and no one heard.
Never have I ever, known the true meaning of being
    part of a herd.

Never have I ever, seen the world with such dark eyes.
Never have I ever, hoped my Dad would be my
guiding light.

Never have I ever, felt such contempt and despair
combined.
Never have I ever, known grief could make you blind.
Never have I ever, needed friendship more.
Never have I ever, missed the familiar knocking at
the door.

Never have I ever, seen such loneliness in my eyes.
Never have I ever, played such a game of pure disguise.
Never have I ever, felt an ache so intense.
Never have I ever, known a loss so immense.

Never have I ever, felt a LOVE so Divine.
Never have I ever, known a Dad quite like mine.
Never have I ever, felt as cross as cross could be.
Never have I ever, known the solution would be in me.

Never have I ever, resented the world I lived in
more.
Never have I ever, loved my Dad so much more.
Never have I ever, learnt such lessons of the heart.
Never have I ever, known the true importance of
living apart.

Never have I ever, believed so much in God and all
his might.
Never have I ever, thought he would give us such
guidance in our worldly fight.
Never have I ever, FEARED so much for what might
be.
Never have I ever, felt there was a sinner as
ISOLATED as me.
Never have I ever, yearned so much for what cannot
be.
Never have I ever, come to terms with just let it be.
Never have I ever, felt such HOPE and PRIDE
combined.
Never have I ever, thought such ANXIOUS vibes
were mine.

Never had I ever, thought such ANGER would reside
in me.
Never have I ever, succumbed to such GUILT to
bring me to my knees.
Never have I ever, witnessed such a RESILIENT
version of me.
Never have I ever, realised that my GRATITUDE
would be my magic key.

Never have I ever, been just a sad little girl like ME.

Introduction

WE ARE ALL CONFINED AND EVEN DEFINED BY numbers: our money in the bank, our debt, our age, our medical statistics, our weight. Numbers, numbers, numbers everywhere! Never has this been more apparent than in the world we live in today: our life going forward will be forevermore referred to as pre/post Covid-19. We are bombarded on a daily basis with the number of new cases and daily death total in our country and worldwide. Now a new phenomenon known as the 'the COVID stone' is a term that is being used in all forms of media and social media platforms. It refers to the weight we could all potentially gain in this stressful time of isolation, if we haven't already gained the weight. Emotional eating has always been my nemesis. It is as virulent in my life as the virus that was infecting our world. This was an impetus for my writing, as it became abundantly clear that I was primed and at the ready to gain over fourteen pounds with the greatest of ease at this time. However, the premise to my writings, have a more organic nature rather than the vanity that is associated with weight. For me it became apparent that it was the onslaught of emotions rather than food that were my personal version of the 'COVID-19 stone'. Even though my 'COVID kilos' had both a physical and emotional weight attached to them, it was most certainly the latter that was the most excruciating of them. So, in an effort of self-preservation, survival of the species so to speak, and in a desperate attempt to make sense of the world I was living in, my world, I began to write. I was like a human Petri dish of emotions – a plethora of them but I focused on the fifteen that had most prevalence in my life at this time. So, in order to make sense of their existence, the scientist in me needed to know more. I essentially needed to extrapolate the data so I could make sense of it all. Each emotion had its own origin, had its strengths and weaknesses, had traits and idiosyncrasies that made it unique. In isolation, they could be compartmentalised but when they co-existed their virulence and might was often insurmountable. Truthfully in the absence of people, namely my immediate family, this was my only lifeline. I began to write in an attempt to make sense of my new reality, to cope with my tremendous loss and to try to unburden my heart somewhat. This was my cry for help in a world that was crying too. This was my attempt at preservation of the species ... namely myself.

IN THE PREVIOUS SIX MONTHS I HAD LOST THE business that I had worked tirelessly on for over fifteen years. This had happened overnight without warning. I was recuperating at home after shingles when I received a call from a concerned colleague of mine. Her concern, superseded by sheer discomfort when she realised I was unaware of what had happened and was oblivious to the reality of it all. At that moment I thought my life was over, that this was the worst day of my life. I was broken, shell-shocked, angry, dismayed, frightened, vulnerable and afraid. Little did I know that the worst was yet to come as three weeks later my precious Dad was diagnosed with terminal cancer! This was the day essentially that my heart started to disintegrate, as I knew what was to come. I had that eerie realisation that our life would never again be the same. I was aware that our family as we knew it would be irrevocably changed, compromised and incomplete forevermore. This was the third time my Dad had faced this deadly opponent, but unfortunately, even though he fought and fought very hard for over four months, this time the beast fought too and the beast won.

Now I am embroiled in the reality of losing my precious Dad in the midst of this pandemic, and the restrictions and isolation that has ensued has made writing my escapism and the cathartic friend I needed at this time. In retrospect, this was my antidote to the guttural loss I was feeling. There are no guidelines to help with grieving through a pandemic. This was unprecedented in the world as we knew it. I was isolated and restricted by all of these extenuating circumstances. I needed help. I needed a way out. So, this was essentially my attempt at survival. I did not want to be another casualty of this virus. I did not have a preconceived notion of writing about grief. However, my repertoire of coping mechanisms was inadequate to deal with my new reality. Desperate times call for desperate measures. Essentially, this was a desperate attempt to try to cope with my new life and in lieu of friends, my laptop became my trusty companion and my confident of sorts.

I am a very tactile person. I love the expression of human touch and the emotive response it invokes in your body; a hug, a warm embrace, a strong handshake. All of these were absent in my new world. All now restricted, even condemned, and replaced by smiling eyes over a mask from two metres away. How can this be so? This new phenomenon of social and physical distancing was a violation of my core values. I had a visceral need for human interaction and contact, a need for what our country is synonymous with when we are in mourning. Our pedigree for how we mourn supreme the world over. Our traditional wakes epic, but, more importantly, a necessary component in grieving.

I was so perplexed by the complexity of my dilemma as it seemed the newness of grief needed the oldness of traditions to ease its burden. However, such a luxury was now off limits to me and all those dealing with grief at this time. The absence of people, namely mourners, catapulted me into a state of suspended grief. My grief was so real, yet it was as if inanimate because its expression was suppressed, even appearing somewhat unreal, elusive at this time. In reality, my grief had been deferred, temporarily put on hold, along with so many other mass gatherings around the world. In my capacity to rationalise this, I felt I was obsolete as such. My rationale was that you cannot have a concert without a crowd and in my world, I felt I could not grieve without people. The traditionalist in me needed the formalities of a real funeral. I needed the mourners to essentially help me mourn. So, in reality their absence had caused what felt like an abscess to fester within me. One I know that when it bursts it will implode with such gusto and might. I am in no doubt, there will be certain carnage in its wake. There is a great anticipation associated with all rescheduled events and in my wisdom, I knew the same is true for my grief. It is not cancelled only deferred to a later date due to the Covid-19 pandemic restrictions. In retrospect, I feel that Dad was instrumental in guiding me to write. This was his way of protecting his little girl, safeguarding me from the enormity of grieving that is without doubt in my future. Such a process may dilute the onslaught of emotions that are most certainly welling up within the confines of my body. So under the guidance of Dad's watchful eye and in a mammoth show of self-preservation, I decided to share my feelings, emotions, thoughts and personal perspective on grieving at this time.

The emotions I write about are specific to my journey, and are honest and real. I have an affinity to certain dates and numbers that are pivotal in my world and those I share with you too. This is my version of events, my life's experience; it is fact not fiction, it is not a self-help book but rather the honest ramblings of a disillusioned, vulnerable, sad woman who lost so much in a short space of time and who just needs an outlet to share her story. On my behalf, this is the greatest show of love for the blessing of my own life, because by doing this I can only hope that I will heal my broken heart, rescue all the pieces, and with the love of family and friends, and with the luxury of time, rebuild my life once again. My world is akin to that of a patchwork quilt – each piece beautiful on its own, but its real beauty only evident when all its pieces are mended together like that of my broken heart. It is an act of love, of dedication, a laborious task no doubt! My act of sheer desperation will undoubtedly be heralded as my greatest endeavour at self-preservation and survival. My vision absolute, my hope eternal and my need undeniable. Silence and solitude are now my constant companions, as I endeavour to rekindle the fire of life, my life, a life that was once good and can be good again in time.

So, to begin I recall the dates and numbers that are significant in my life thus far.

THE POWER OF 1. FOR ME MY LIFE IS NOW AS CLICHÉ as the song 'One Day at a Time' because that is the only way I can cope. Truthfully, there are days where it is hour by hour. My grief and sadness are so debilitating that the sheer act of living is a struggle. I have an ache in my heart that is indescribable. It is so intense there are times that I heave in pain as I rock back and forth in an effort to self-soothe, like an unsettled baby. In retrospect, my understanding of the meaning of heartbroken was so underestimated. The term 'heartbroken' has now been exulted to a different level for me. The intensity of my malaise is off the Richter scale. Truthfully, there are no words sufficient enough to describe this pain. It has to be experienced to be believed. My empathy for anyone who has lost a parent is now experiential, and I hope so many of you are spared it for many years to come. I knew my Dad was dying. We had had our conversations, said our goodbyes and yet the reality is so different. I feel ill prepared for the gravity of this situation, dazed like a deer in headlights. Death is so final. Loss is undeniable and so profound and its reality cannot be refuted. However disengaged I am with my world now, I am still brutally aware of the disrespect I am showing to the life I have. Where is my gratitude? How can I follow through on my promise to Dad to live my best life when I am grappling with my own will to live? How could I be so disingenuous? Shame on me. I know how blessed we all are to be alive and well at this time. I also know that there are no promises or guarantees to rely on in our world. I am brutally aware that 'today is forever and tomorrow is never', and yet it is still only 'one day at a time' for now.

As I struggle with my loss, I cannot comprehend the loss my Mother must feel after losing her partner and best friend of sixty years. Their beautiful union has been crushed. Their companionship annihilated, their earthly bond severed forevermore. Two have now become one. My Mother's new status of 'widow' has a lonely tone to it. There is no melody to make it sound any sweeter. In a cruel twist of fate, we lost Dad and a few days later the country went into lockdown, meaning that my Mother's loss was even more catastrophic. Dad was gone, I moved home to be with my family, my brothers did likewise, there was no visitors, no neighbours, no grandchildren, there was no one! The void created by Dad's passing in the midst of Covid-19 was even more exaggerated now. My brothers and I moved home to nurse Dad for his last two weeks of life. It was a huge privilege for us as it was Dad's wish to die at home. For a brief moment in time we were back to our childhood days, 'The Quinlan 5'. Undoubtedly, it was the most special of times and yet the saddest of times, but it gave my Mom a false sense of security. Now my Mother's solitary life was even more profound. It only reiterated to her the intensity of her loss. A loss compounded by the restrictions of the Covid-19 pandemic. A loss that now really gave new meaning to 'table for one', because that is what her new life had become.

In reality, her cocooning was essential to safeguard her health and well-being. We could not cope with losing another parent and will not jeopardise her in anyway. However, there is little comfort to her in knowing this too shall pass as her daily lonely life of 'one' is exasperated by our new world. A world where isolation is our greatest show of love and solidarity for each other and the world we now live in. A world where 'one for all and all for one' is now synonymous with our Covid-19 survival kit. Unfortunately for those of us dealing with the loss of a loved one, there is no PPE (personal protective equipment) to help protect our broken grieving hearts at this time.

Introduction

With reluctant anticipation, I anxiously await the milestones that lie ahead. The many firsts that will be celebrated in Dad's absence: birthdays, anniversaries, graduations, Father's Day, Easter and, the one I fear most, Christmas. I already envisage the anarchy that will ensue both in my head and in my heart, the deafening silence of absence, the acceptance of reality and the acknowledgement that it is only by living well with the people in our present, that we can truly honour the people in our past, especially our Dad.

THE NUMBER 3. I HAVE ALWAYS BEEN ACUTELY AWARE of the power of three in my life because as siblings we were essentially 'The Three Musketeers' always. Their motto of 'all for one and one for all' reflects our unity as a family, especially as we cared for Dad. He always had the utmost of respect for institutions, for the collective power of minds, and for the hierarchy that existed. He appreciated it when and if he was a benefactor of such greatness. Well in the end, he frequented hospitals nearly as much as he had entered the house of God in his lifetime. In retrospect, the outcome of entering these institutions lead to the same end – that of death. However, there was care, compassion, comfort, life, hope, healing, suffering, and a promise of better days ahead either in this world or the next. Dad was resolute in his gratitude for his companions on this journey. He was quick to acknowledge that he was, in his eyes, a truly blessed man. As he said he had 'the perfect trilogy', the unconditional love and support of family and friends, the best of medical care and, last but certainly not least, his tremendous faith. In hindsight, I know that it was all of us that were truly blessed. I'm sure anyone who was lucky enough to know him would agree. We were the benefactors in all of this. We witnessed what true contentment in life and ultimately death was. Dad was the epitome of a man that knew he had everything, wanted for nothing and, as he said himself, his only regret ever was that he just did not have a little more time. He was a gentle soul. A quintessential gentleman. His gratitude was palpable. His love astounding. His faith unwavering even as he faced his impending demise. He was essentially ahead of his time. He was an anthropologist of sorts, as he had an insight into humanity that surpassed his formal education. It was as if it was part of his genetic code, a code that may have even had a sixth sense built in, as ironically, he had revealed to me that he had an uneasy feeling about the world he was leaving behind. A world he felt had lost its way, lost its moral compass, lost its value for family and for human life itself. A world where only by sheer virtue of a catastrophe was there any chance we could revert to living a pure life again. Only a man of true faith could have such a premonition of sorts. A man who with every fibre of his being believed in the Father, the Son and the Holy Ghost. He was a true believer whose inherent faith was enough to give him solace, knowing that eternal salvation was his. A faith that made his morning and night time rituals pivotal in his life. He never left our home nor ever went to bed without the ritual of laying his hand on three of his prized possessions: a statue of Our Lady, a picture of the Sacred Heart and a House Blessing that hung proudly in our living room. It was by their constant presence in his life he remained connected to the true meaning of life, living each day as if it was his last. By honouring his past, living in the present, he was preparing for the future. His passage to the next life was only bearable because he knew what was waiting for him on the other side when life ended here on Earth and eternal life began in Heaven. Imagine the joy of rekindling that sibling bond with your two precious sisters that had gone before you? Surely there would be an epic reunion, one that could only be bittersweet as they remembered their earthly brother Sean. Heaven and Earth separated by distance but connected forever by the belief in the unspoken, the unseen and of the omnipresence of the knowledge of Dad's love in our hearts and minds. The warmth of a physical connection now and forevermore replaced by memories that shuttle as if on an intergalactic expedition. A mission that brings nuggets of hope to all of us here on Earth.

THE NUMBER 13. THE 13 JULY 2018 – IT WAS THE BEST of days; it was the worst of days. My weight loss journey was long and arduous, and my relationship with the scales was tenuous at best. The scales were either friend or foe depending on its number. It was my index as to how I fit in to society. It would determine how my day would actually unfold. It essentially defined me. Well on this day we were bosom buddies, as I had reached my target weight. I had an elusive number in my head. It was a number that when and if I ever reached it, I knew that this was my magic number! Without question this was the day that essentially, I would be enough in the world. The day all my problems would evaporate into thin air. The day my life would be so, so very perfect. I walked taller. I now had a purpose in life. I no longer needed to make excuses. I would be accepted by all. Life would now be the fairy-tale that only little girls would dream of. Today was perfect. I was perfect. My world was perfect. It was as if this number obliterated all the anguish that had consumed so much of my adult life. The self-berating dialogue and self-sabotage that were my constant companions on my life's journey had disembarked. We had parted ways and this conscious uncoupling was liberating to me. Truthfully, I felt so alive that fateful morning. This feeling of exuberance and joy washed over me like a warm summer breeze. I was so bewitched by a state of grace that I was nearly levitating. This could not be a better day. It was epic to me.

Alas, this state of euphoria and giddiness lasted all of two hours. The warmth of joy that flooded my body was soon to be replaced by a frigidity that I now know was related to pure shock. In my deluded state when the phone rang and it was my brother, for a moment I thought well he must know that today is my special day. I thought how nice of him to acknowledge this. Telepathy must be alive and well among siblings as close as us. Maybe he was calling so we could celebrate this, after all this was noteworthy for sure, newsworthy even, as today was the day that my number reiterated my legitimate place and worth in the world. How that number soon became so insignificant. It had quickly lost its imaginary magic powers. It could not change our new reality. It was null and void in the scheme of what today was now all about. My self-professed perfect day lasted all of two hours and it was replaced by the start of a journey that has led to my new world – a world that will never ever be perfect again, regardless of my weight on the scales – because I am now in a world that no longer has my precious Dad in it! My brother was not calling to arrange a parade for me, rather his news rained heavily on my parade and has never stopped since. It was as if he was permanently cancelling all future celebratory family events for us. His news was devastating. The sunshine and joy that was in my world that morning had now been replaced by a foreboding darkness of uncertainty and fear in Dad's world. For those two hours it was as if I was living in a kaleidoscope. The colours of life's exuberance after liberation from the shackles of the scales were magical. The brightness intense. The vibrancy contagious. It was enough to exult me into euphoria. Yet, as Dad woke all he saw was nothing: a bleak abyss, sheer darkness, a void, as if some malicious villain had banished him into a world devoid of colour. My Dad had suffered a stroke. This was a pivotal moment in time for all of us, but now for all the wrong reasons.

In retrospect, I now realise how utterly idiotic I must appear. I was an educated woman who believed in the magical power of numbers. Was I still in my innocent childhood state? Was I having my Peter Pan moment? How utterly deluded was I? How much of my life had I wasted waiting to start living when this number was reached? How many days had I essentially wasted? How many opportunities had I missed? How many excuses had I made? I was existing day by day, waiting to start living, and now my Dad was living day by day waiting for his own existence to stop. Where was the justice in that? The enormity of this day was one that irrevocably changed me. A part of me died that day, the part of me that believed in magic, the child that believed her Daddy would always be with her. This was the day that I realised the number on the scales had lost its power forevermore. Forevermore.

THE NUMBER 19. WE ARE NOW LIVING IN A WORLD that will forevermore have a reference point of pre/post Covid-19. The number will have so many connotations associated with it. I foresee a future where its mere utterance will provoke projectile vomiting. Its sound will burn the inner ear and render us deaf. Its observation will scorch the eyes from its socket resulting in blindness.

Can we not lobby to have it obliterated from our world, just as it did to so many precious people who lost their lives because of its virulence? Can we demolish and banish it into oblivion as it did to our pre Covid-19 world? Can we reconstruct a world where 19 ceases to exist? So 18 now becomes 20. It is not unthinkable. It is necessary for self-preservation. Can we now legislate that we socially and physically distance from 19 in solidarity with humanity in an effort to safeguard our physical and mental health? Can we just crush and annihilate it as it did for so many who not only lost family and friends but also their livelihood, their life's work, their identity, their sanity, their loved ones and their freedom? Retribution is now part of our armour going forward. The scars of the Covid-19 pandemic's virulence will be forever engrained in our DNA. We carry these with us every day. Is that not enough of a punishment? We are neither alive nor dead. We are as if living in a forever lockdown. We are in our own purgatory. We are living in a forever hell, as we are taunted by the existence and freedom that is still bestowed on everything that is 19! It should not be afforded a stay of execution, rather it deserves the death penalty.

As many of our over seventies cocooned in an effort of self-preservation, there was no escape for all those men and women who were victims of physical and mental torture because of Covid-19. The plight of those with mental health issues was exacerbated by the isolation that was now our new norm. However, regardless of where these vulnerable individuals took shelter, their nemesis travelled with them. Their demons lived and resided full-time in the bricks and mortar of their own mind. No change of address would alter that. They struggled with uncertainty, fear, anxiety, isolation, loss, lack of control and with their own mortality. How after such trauma can they emerge into a world where 19 still has the freedom to roam free? The same freedom that was stolen from them – these people are forever tarnished and scathed by such a turbulent time in their lives and minds.

Unfortunately, food at times like this is either friend or foe, and when fear is all-consuming self-destruction is never far away. When we are rendered oarless on our own raft of life, we can easily succumb to erratic behaviour. We can fall into an abyss where food is in control of us rather than we are in control of food, leading to emotional eating and the so-called 'COVID stone' weight gain probability. However, where our control has been removed by others too often, the vulnerable among us will succumb to under-eating; desperate to regain some semblance of validation for their own choices in life, the visceral need for control restored by their control of what passes or more likely doesn't pass their lips. These are victims of the utter power of numbers: namely a number on a scale. How then do we think that they can live freely in a new world where they are forever confronted by the symbol of their own self-destruction?

IN AN ACT OF SOLIDARITY AND PROFOUND LOVE, WE separated from the ones that needed us most in exchange for the hope and promise of being reunited again with them. This gut-wrenching separation was felt by all, but for those of us grieving it was an act of inhumanity on humanity. Personally, I was crushed by it, my spirit annihilated and my perception of life forever altered. I have nothing but utter distain for the number 19. It is toxic to me. It is virulent. It cannot be redeemed. It is forever more banished from my world. Essentially, I needed to excise it from my life, as if it was a malignancy. I needed to try to regain some control in a world that seemed so out of control. My new world, maybe imaginary to me, is 19 free – so in some small way peace is restored!

20-03-2020 at 20:40

This was the date and time that my Dad departed our world to take residence in his new forever abode. It was a night like no other. The sky looked as if it was on fire. It was awash with the vibrant colours of magenta, crimson, violet. It swept above us as if painted by an artist's brush. Its intensity symbolic of the gravity of this moment for us. The celebrations had begun in earnest in Heaven as the festivities were in place to welcome home one of its most precious sons. This was a glorious day indeed for them, as they were going to be reunited with our Dad. I was entranced by the fire in the sky, transfixed even as I imagined the bonfires, the buntings, the fireworks and the exuberance of this happy occasion as their long-lost brother was finally home and would be reunited with his long-lost family. I imagined the welcome he would receive, the warm embrace of so many, a gentle kiss from his Mom. How so many stories would be relived, how a life so well lived would be commended. I knew Heaven's gain was most certainly our loss.

Dad once said to me that if life was different, maybe I would not have been born. Tragically my parents' first born, Margaret, died only after a few short days with them. The following year, I was born. I was loved and adored, and even revered by some as I was seen as a blessing in my parents' life after what they had endured. Dad said I was sent from God to mind him while he was on Earth and when he went to Heaven he would be reunited and minded by his other daughter Margaret. This was the calibre of man that my Dad was: insightful, pragmatic, stoic and essentially at peace, and was an eternal optimist even at the end.

I am haunted by Dad's final few hours where his struggle between life and death was so torturous. He was essentially in an abyss with one foot on either side. The battle between life and death was real. It was like an epic boxing fight. How many more rounds did Dad have in him? His pedigree undisputed. His calibre unmatched. His sportsmanship unrivalled. His integrity undeniable. His popularity momentous and yet his rival was undefeated. The odds were stacked against him. He was not the bookies' favourite, but Dad was never the underdog in any sport he played – that was until today.

Dad got momentary reprieve from his struggle, when he was revived by the blessing of holy water, it was akin to the boxer being douched with cold water in an effort to reinvigorate him. A temporary reprieve but a reprieve none the less. As I wept and held tightly to his hand, I caught sight of a dent on the wall. I smiled remembering days gone by. This was the evidence of the ingenuity of a determined child. This was remnants of my devilish childhood days. In an effort to wake my Dad who slept next to me with Mom, I would rock my cot back and forth incessantly. Hence the dent in the wall, and when that did not work, I would empty the contents of my night time bottle on Dad's head. Yikes! Imagine the warm smelly milk? Yet, I would be greeted by loving eyes, a warm smile and an even warmer embrace. The milk, however, has now been replaced by holy water. The elixir of life has now become the elixir of death. No matter how much we douche Dad this time he will not wake up. He will not greet us with his kind loving eyes or his warm smile. He has made peace with life, accepted death and is ready to retire from the game of life. He will not be victorious this time, regardless of his valiant efforts. His fan club, namely Mom, my brothers and I, have always been his greatest supporters and admirers. He knows that we have always been there for him, his greatest cheerleaders, cheerleaders in life and now cheerleaders in his impending death. He has made peace with his life's journey. He did not give up on life, rather he conceded to the stronger opponent this time: death. As he struggles with his last few breaths, he inhales as if to bring some of our life's breath with him to his new home. So that in death we will be forever with him, as we were in life. Essentially our breath is a symbol of hope, a symbol of life, a symbol of our eternal connection, a symbol of the promise of a good life in the future for all of us, where love of family will be paramount. Where we will honour Dad's legacy by living our best life.

AND FINALLY, AS HE EXHALES ANY MALAISE that resides in his body, regret, sadness, suffering, is released and then with his last breath he is eternally at peace, content, happy.

The game of life is over. Death is victorious: LIFE 0 / DEATH 1.

In that moment Dad's spirit left his body, and I envisaged the collective breath he inhaled from us acting like pallbearers carefully transporting the precious cargo of his soul on his final journey home. To be reunited with his dearly departed loved ones.

DAD IS NOW RESTFUL, PAIN FREE, A WAVE OF contentment and utter serenity overcomes his face. It is remarkable. Dad lived and died as he wanted to, with dignity and with his precious family, we were all five of us in Mom's and Dad's bedroom once again. But this time five had become four. Our family dynamic was irrevocably altered forever.

Warm tears fell heavily from us all, we held each other, whispered our last goodbyes to Dad. We wailed and lamented that this was it. Dad had gone. May he Rest in Peace Forever.

THE DATE: 21 MARCH. THE DAY THAT I WAS WITH DAD and he received his terminal diagnosis is a moment in time that I wish I could erase forever. It is as if I became allergic to life that day and from then on, I was repulsed by smell, recoiled if I was touched, was irritated by sound, and I was uneasy in my own body. It was as if I was suffocating under the pressure of my own skin. I had a constant itch that even with the force of my incessant scratching and the onset of blood there was no relief. I literally wanted to stand under a shower until my skin melted, my bones crumbled from the pressure, my organs failed and poof as if by magic my pain and suffering was over. But I was not the one that was ill. I was not the one that was dying here. But I felt as if I was. My Dad and I were kindred spirits. We had a love, connection, respect for each other that transcended the father-daughter dynamic, as though we were one, separate beings but being nourished by the same heart and soul. In retrospect, as Dad was dying, I was ultimately struggling to survive. Each day I was alive meant we were one day closer to Dad's death, the struggle was excruciating, the reality stark, the future bleak. I had no precedent to assist me with this. There was no paradigm for our situation. As days morphed into night, I longed for the soft caress of my pillow, a chance to lay still, to disengage from the reality that haunted every waking second of my day, a time where I would be actively unconscious from my life. However, I was not afforded this luxury because as I closed my eyes I was startled by the recurrence of this date 'March 21'. It was as if tattooed inside my eyelids. It was my constant night-time companion every night since my Dad's diagnosis. I was confounded by this, confused even. I trawled through my diary, my calendar, and asked my family if there was significance to this date. But we all literally drew a blank.

In retrospect, blank was what our life had now become as we now have a life without Dad. Well my Dad went to his new home just a little over 3 hours before March 21. Yet, it was on this date that his death appeared in print media and online. Now this date that had haunted me for so long finally made sense. It was official as the death notice now confirmed my Dad had died! I am not a clairvoyant, however I am somewhat comforted by my own premonition, as it reiterated the undisputed bond and connection that was exclusive to Dad and I. It was ours and ours alone. In a cruel twist of fate now when I attempt to sleep, I am haunted by this incessant ringing in my head, it is the ringtone of my phone. I have this recurring nightmare that Dad is trying to call me for help. I struggle to answer in time and even when I do there is silence on the other end. Dad cannot hear me. I keep telling him I am here, not to worry, everything will be okay. IS HE OKAY? My distain for night-time is palpable as the desperation that overcomes me is incredibly real. Ironically, this is not exclusive to the night-time hours. I have been startled by the intensity and the longevity of this ringing tone on a daily basis since Dad's death. However, this is only in my head. It is eerie, unsettling and enough for me to question my own sanity. I know I am not crazy. I am only demented by sheer and utter sadness and loss. In my current state of distraction, I can only empathise with the experiential nature of death, of loss and the aftermath of such. In the clarity that only time and healing will provide I hope to rationalise this some more so that I can become more engaged and invigorated by life rather than my current fearful even neurotic perception of my new reality. In time, I can only hope that I will be less haunted by death and more excited about the prospect of life.

OTHER NUMBERS: 24, 49, 82. THESE NUMBERS IN isolation are important but when combined they tell a bittersweet story. As I woke on 24 February another year older, I knew without question my 49th birthday was ultimately the last I would share with my Dad. Ironically, this was an age that I thought was elusive to me, as I have always felt I was going to die young. This is a burden that I have always carried with me. As convoluted and irrational as that may sound, it is real, raw and was ever present in my subconscious mind. An undercurrent of resistant anticipation accompanied me always. So much so that in an effort to be transparent, I disclosed this to my now husband, essentially giving him a way out, warning him of what may lie ahead, a chance to run so he could avoid the heartache of losing me too soon. As I write this, I feel there are those among you that feel an asylum and straight jacket is what I should have foreseen rather than my demise from succumbing to cancer. The reasons for this are twofold. Firstly, the prevalence of this demonic plague, the aforementioned cancer, that is ever present in our lives and claimed so many of our loved ones, including my Mom's sister Ella and my other beautiful aunts Kate and Betty. Dad's sisters both taken from this world too soon and now Dad had succumbed albeit reluctantly to its death hold too. Secondly, the narrative of a life less lived. 'Only the Good Die Young' played constantly as if on a loop in my brain. There was an ache that was omnipresent in my Mother as she was forever marred by the loss of her own Mother, shortly after her birth and the loss of her first child, Margaret, who died a few days after her birth. The complexity of life and death resonated with me, and somehow as if by osmosis seemed to alter my genetic code. It made me uneasy in life and uncertain, as if preparing for the worst because ultimately the worst was inevitable. So, the mindset of a child morphed into that of an adult. My comprehension thwarted by my interpretation of death, my interpretation of life, my sense of entitlement, my mortality uncertain, my validity often questionable. This was the perfect storm of sorts that laid the foundation and lead to my own inherent fear and certainty of my own early demise.

As we celebrated my birthday: 49 years on Earth. I felt like such a hypocrite, an imposter. Here I was celebrating life when Dad was facing impending death. My internal dialogue was turbulent; retrospection only lead to anger, self-analysis gave a definitive diagnosis of a 'life less lived'. The conclusion was unequivocal: I had wasted so much of the life that I had taken for granted. How could I claim to be so like my Dad, yet our approach to life be so utterly different? After all we shared the same genetic code. I was technically 50 per cent Dad. But as he marvelled at life and enjoyed every breath he took, there was so many times where I held my breath so long that there are lapses in my life that are totally unaccounted for. It is as if my motherboard had a short circuit and now needed rewiring to ensure longevity and a positive flow of energy again.

Was I just a fraudster? A dilettante? Was I just living an inauthentic life? Was it all a façade? In my working life, I was an exponent of living your best life by accepting you were 'perfectly imperfect' and being the best version of yourself and nobody else was all that mattered. My eureka moment was as profound as it was prolific, because I knew this newfound knowledge was only powerful if I was willing to apply it to my own life going forward. The scientist within me knew the theory, accepted the equation and on extrapolation of the data came up with a hypothesis that if not respected would totally belittle my version of the theory of evolution, namely that of my own. I had concrete evidence with the formula for a life best-lived, courtesy of my Dad. But unless this teaching moment was respected and revered, then it was a missed opportunity of epic proportions.

My regard for life was arbitrary. My conviction weak. My approach fickle. I had compartmentalised my life as an investor does with its portfolio of stocks and shares. The peaks and troughs that are par for the course for any investment echoed the trials and tribulations in my life's journey. However, I must have missed the memo on staying the course when times are tough and instead, I panicked and withdrew my investment missing out on so many opportunities. I was weak in my resolve and did not understand the prerequisite of perseverance and perspective for those that are the fully pledged investors. The people that are serious about getting the best return for their time. Just like my Dad! In essence the time has passed. I am still 49, but I have missed out on the opportunity of my investment maturing to its true value. In reality my time on Earth has not rendered me the best return on my investment and my portfolio is a reflection of this – a life less lived for sure!

However, all is not in vain as today is a new day, a chance to start again. In my journey of life thus far, it is fair to say the first two legs of the relay have been below par but now that I have the baton, I can visualise the finish line. I know that the best is yet to come – a sprint to the end – I owe it to my Dad's joyous celebration of life to teach my daughter that we should never give up in life or give up on life as I had; we may falter, even fall, but perseverance and faith will get us through. I want to emulate the hero that was my Dad, an iconic specimen of humankind, a true believer, a man that loved life, lived life and exuded life each and every day he was alive. His eighty-two years on this planet could equate to five lifetimes for the rest of us mere mortals!

I pledge to make the rest of my life the best of my life as a tribute to the man I call my Dad.

No more excuses, no more pretending, no more façade.

Introduction

MY RECIPE FOR LIFE GOING FORWARD IS:
LIVE each day as though it's your last;
LOVE unconditionally and unapologetically;
LAUGH at every opportunity and then LAUGH some more
and repeat until your last breath in this world is your first
in the next.

IN REALITY MY DAD'S DEATH HAS AFFORDED ME NOT
only a new perspective on life but also a new view. If I am
totally honest, I can now see meaning and symbolism in
almost everything within a five-mile radius! Truthfully,
I have a new insight into my environment and if I had
boundless energy I could keep writing forever. The reality
is my reserves are low, but my resolve is clear and this
exercise was one of a cathartic nature at its very core
for me. There were no resources at my disposal to help
me cope: no self-help book, no checklist, no real points
of reference that amalgamated the reality of death and
loss in conjunction with a worldwide pandemic and social
and physical isolation. In retrospect it may not even have
helped as I am sure how each person deals with death is
as unique as the individual themselves. That said, this is
my personal journey spanning the first month after Dad's
death. I now realise that there is no chronological order for
how we grieve, what emotions takes precedence or how we
extrapolate them. The fifteen emotions I write about are
specific to me and my experience. They are my catalogue
of the feelings that transcended and consumed my body

after the loss of my Dad. I foresee a future where they will always be present, some more than others, in isolation or as a deluge especially in my times of weakness. I can only hope that over time my RESILIENCE and strength will have fortified sufficiently so as to afford me the luxury of a more peaceful and less tormented existence. A life where my attitude of GRATITUDE and HOPE will colour my world enough to dilute the SADNESS and GRIEF that is synonymous with my mere existence after Dad had passed. A life where my DESPERATION and my ANGER are weakened by the presence of LOVE in my life, the love of oneself, the love of others and the sheer love of life itself. A world where ISOLATION is now by choice and a form of meditative expression rather than a requirement and prerequisite for survival. A world where my FEAR and my ANXIETY is no longer my Achilles heel rather the impetus to challenge myself and embrace my VULNERABILITIES and be open to a world of opportunities. A world where I no longer am disengaged and I am not so utterly NUMB to life itself. Instead I have embraced a new world where I have relegated the suffocation inflicted on me from the omnipresence of GUILT and replaced it with the exuberance of PRIDE. A world where I can now say that I am all woman, a woman who was not afraid to falter, a woman who accepted who and what she became, a woman who was resilient enough to reinvent herself so that she could be the woman she was meant to be, a woman that shows pride in who and what she is and what she has become, a woman whom her Dad was always proud of. A woman who can stand tall with the greatest of pride and shout from the rooftops that she is so proud to be the daughter of the one and only Mike Joe Quinlan. A woman who can say that she has lost her Dad and in losing him she has found herself. A woman who will never lead a life less lived again!

Sad

THE FEELING OF UTTER SADNESS IS RUNNING through my veins like a new blood supply. I even feel that its intensity has sucked my body dry of its own essential blood and now it is what is fuelling my body. The strength of this emotion is overwhelming. SADNESS is everywhere I look. It is in the eyes of my bewildered Mother, who is trying to make sense of her new life without my Dad – a life that now has to go on without the man she has spent nearly sixty years with. I see it in the emptiness in my brothers' eyes, that yearning for just some more time with Dad, hoping that this is only a nightmare that they have not woken up from yet. I see it in my uncle's vacant gaze; a look that he is lost in thought reliving a life that was well spent with a brother who was that and so much more. He was brother, friend and neighbour, and now he is gone. I see it in the angelic eyes of all Dad's grandchildren as they now realise the only place that they can see their beloved Grandad is in their dreams or when they close their eyes and daydream of all those wonderful days spent in his company. There is a SADNESS to them that they cannot give Grandad those vitally important hugs anymore; towards the end, words were few but the hugs were many. Now those hugs are only memories. In time these precious children will replace their SADNESS with gratitude and with the realisation of the time well spent and the privilege they all had to be such a part of Grandad's life. I see SADNESS in my daughter's eyes. She is nearly fourteen, neither child nor adult, and yet here she is trying to make sense of this loss. She is SAD for the pain she sees in me and she is SAD for the loss of interaction with my family due to the restrictions because of Covid-19. Ultimately though, she is SAD because she knows all her life's milestones and achievements can only be shared with her Grandad in her memories. He was her greatest supporter and loved nothing more than to hear about her basketball games, how school was going, how her life in general was. The biggest SADNESS I see is in my own reflection in the mirror, and this is only when I allow myself to look. I see a woman ravaged by turmoil, SADNESS, hurt, loss, desperation. I see a woman who bears the scars in her heart and on her face. I see a woman who looks older: browbeaten, downtrodden, hopeless and lost. I see ME!

SAD and Dad are both three-letter words. For today and many days to come in our foreseeable future, these two words to me will be interwoven.

I often feel that words are misused and so diluted in their context. However, when we as a family say we are SAD that Dad is no longer with us, it is a powerful word. A word that nearly brings you to your knees, as if you were punched in the stomach by a champion boxer.

I can hear the word SAD uttered on numerous occasions towards the end of Dad's life. Alas, this was a word uttered by him. As I write this, I weep as I recall my many conversations with Dad. When we got Dad's diagnosis, I was alone with him, and because his hearing was so poor he did not hear the Oncologist give him his projected life expectancy. So, it was my job to be the bearer of this most tragic of stories. The SADNESS that overcame me in that small private room was immense, yet I knew I had to compose myself and literally be the parent in this scenario, as if protecting a child from the villain in a story. It took every ounce of courage and resilience I had to do it, but I did it to the best of my ability. It truthfully was one of the hardest things I have ever had to utter to my Dad, the next was when I had to tell him he might have only a few days or a week at best to live.

Until a person experiences this, there are no words that can describe the pain that ensues after such utterances. When I speak of SADNESS the most intense of all was that in my poor Dad's compromised eyes. He often said that he had no regret in life but that he was truly SAD that he would not be around to see all the grandchildren become adults. He imagined great fun when they got older and he was curious to see how they would all look out for each other; he also was SAD when he thought that maybe the younger three, Amelia, Ava and Jack, would not remember him. I reassured him that they would never ever forget

46

him, and as a family we would never ever let that happen. The burden of this has truthfully taken a huge toll on me as whether by choice or by design, I took charge of Dad's doctors' appointments, and I was always first to get the bad news. I partly did this for Dad as he relied on me and had great faith in my ability to talk to the doctors as well as to understand what they said. He knew I was essentially his 'Wing Woman' or his 'Health Advocate' to the bitter end. Another reason this happened was that I possibly became the preordained Matriarch of the family, albeit prematurely, even reluctantly. In my own way I was trying to protect my Mother and my brothers from being on the front lines, so to speak. To me this was like a war with many battles and even though we won some battles, we ultimately lost the war.

I think the SADNESS in Dad's eyes will forever live with me. I cannot extinguish the SADNESS I saw when I told him that he had cancer and that his time remaining on this Earth was short. Obviously, my delivery was with the kindest heart imaginable, but my own SADNESS was palpable. As I uttered the most terrible of words, tears of pain streamed down my face and fell on our clenched hands – oh God how heartbroken I was. How I would not wish this pain inflicted on any soul on Earth. However, when I can take a breath and realise it now there is gratitude in my heart that it was me that told my Dad. I saved my siblings and my Mom from this terrible ordeal. I was essentially the human buffer in this, and I know that the experience in itself has to be a life lesson that can only make me stronger. Thus, allowing me to help others by imparting the wisdom and resilience that has come from my own trials and tribulations on my journey in life.

When I recall the man that delivered us Dad's news initially, I am actually grateful that Dad's hearing was as poor as it was because his callous and matter-of-fact delivery of Dad's prognosis was nothing short of barbaric. Dad's shortcomings in hearing and sight were a blessing in disguise in this instance as it allowed me to be the vessel to impart this life-shattering news to him.

I was bemused the other day when I overheard a girl say she was so SAD they did not have her favourite crisps in the shop. This was a travesty to her, but for me in my own mind I am thinking that she does not know the meaning of SAD. But then I thought life is all about perception and perspective and in her world, this was truly a SAD event.

All I know is that true SADNESS is so intense that it makes your heart and body ache and wakes you in the middle of the night with a pain that is so ferocious. This SADNESS is only understood when it is felt. It is a SADNESS I hope that so many of you reading this will be spared for many years to come. Yet, if it is something that you have experienced already, I can only sincerely empathise with you. It is a small word, but a word nonetheless with the power of a juggernaut. It is an emotion that seems to maybe dissipate from time to time, but truthfully, once it is experienced to the level I have experienced it, it is one that is never too far from your next breath.

Sad

UNDOUBTEDLY THERE IS A VEIL OF SADNESS THAT umbrellas our world at present. We are SAD because so many of us have loved and lost precious people in our lives. We globally have lost ultimate control of the world and lost the world as we knew it. We are all united in SADNESS, and must be resolute to also be united in heralding the new and glorious future that awaits us, as we emerge in solidarity from the epic SADNESS that will ultimately be synonymous with the pandemic of our lifetime. If we were to encapsulate this SADNESS and keep it forevermore, it would demolish our life going forward, like the most virulent contagion. For me, I know that my Dad would be eternally SAD if I was not resolute in my attempts at redeeming some semblance of a better life in the future. My hope is that in time my utter SADNESS will wane enough for me to engage in life again. I will always be SAD for what might have been, but I cannot allow myself to become a SAD creature that wallows in self-pity, in regret, in the past when there is life to be lived, love to be shared and laughs to be had with our nearest and dearest.

Numb

I SEE THE IRONY IN BEING ASKED HOW I FEEL AND MY answer is 'NUMB', as NUMB conjures up a state of feeling no pain! How can the most traumatic heartbreaking time of my life be described by saying, 'I am NUMB'? I cannot explain or justify it – all I know is that it is real. It is like an out-of-body experience. I am aware that I actually am alive, I know I am breathing as I see my chest move in and out, I am standing up, I am even having a conversation but still I feel dead inside – just totally NUMB! The death of my Dad is so real to me, but the reality of it also seems incredulous. I know he is dead. I saw him struggle to take his last breath. I felt his cold body as we laid him to rest. Yet, here I am standing upright but feeling dead. I am for all the world like a dead woman walking!

I have always lauded myself as a cosmopolitan woman, who had a heart of gold and one of my greatest skills was my empathy with people. My heart had a way of connecting with others, making them feel safe, giving them comfort at a time when they needed to be listened to, understood and certainly not judged. But now how can I appear so null and void, devoid of emotion, even heartless? Could it be I buried my heart with my Dad? I know that seems ridiculous, but could it explain my complete apathy for life, my distain for the here and now?

NUMB would never have been on my repertoire of emotions prior to this tragic loss in my life. We have all experienced shock and sadness in our lives, but to me this has been so life-altering, I feel like it has in some way altered my DNA. However, the scientist in me knows that this is not possible. Yet, here I am alive and yet feeling dead! With every passing day I struggle to make sense of it all. By nature, I always need to know my facts, I am a problem-solver, and yet this problem to me has no solution. It is like a theory that yet has not been solved, even though the greatest minds are collaborating in an effort to find a solution that will appease us all, especially me. In the cold light of day, all I know is that the chill in my body and the coldness that surrounds me is symbolic of my NUMB state. Outside the sun is shining, yet I am quivering in my boots with the cold, and I feel NUMB! Can it be that my heart is frozen in time in an effort to protect it? Is it nature's way of protected me from my own self-destruction? Is it my body's way of saying that this time of self-imposed inertia is necessary so that I can actually survive? Survive so that I can live to see another day? Is this my own version of protecting a species, namely myself so that I do not become extinct? There is obviously a reason that I feel nothing. I feel NUMB, I feel dead inside, but it is foreign to me. I am self-aware enough to be bemused by it. I take umbrage at the fact that this is my new reality, that I am culpable in this scenario, even angry to a certain extent that I am letting myself down. ME! The girl that claims to be gentle, kind-hearted, a nurturer. Is this just another of life's lessons teaching me that I got it so wrong, yet again? Now doesn't that sound just like self-pity and martyrdom? Honestly, I feel like this is an out-of-body experience. It is as if I am actually floating over my body, looking down. I know it is me on the outside, but I am dismayed at the sheer apathy I appear to be showing. All I want to do is shake myself, scream and tell myself to get a grip, let it all out, just start crying! I know it is me, but what has happened to me? I know that if I do not accept what has happened and actually allow the deluge of sorrow to release from my body, it will fester and erode my body like a cancer. Seriously, is that what I want? Hasn't there been enough destruction from that Beast in our life? I am screaming at what looks like me but wonder why there is no reaction.

As I write this, I feel as if a warm familiar hand lays on my shoulder to comfort me. Is this my Dad sending me a sign of hope? Is this the start of me starting to feel again? Is this really the start of the thawing of my body or is this just a momentary lapse of lucidity? I know that melodrama and I are not truthfully friends. If I am honest, I feel that melodrama tends to steal the limelight and overshadows what is really happening. In this scenario, I wish that I was a Drama Queen and that I was only performing, acting out so to speak, but alas this is not so. I do feel the need for an understudy, because the strain of the leading role as the 'NUMB Ice Queen' seems more than I can bear. I feel ill-equipped for the role, not mature enough for the mature role I must play. I feel like a child cast in an adult role. I am actually miscast in this scenario. Oh wouldn't that be great to know that this is all just pretend, even though I am in the starring role, it is only a rehearsal, only playtime.

Reality check: this is no dress rehearsal. This is real life and there is no understudy here, only me to play me, only me to be me! So, with the reality that I now most certainly face, I must address this conundrum of being NUMB. I know I cannot and will not allow my life to continue with this feeling of apathy and disconnection from life. Is there a book I can read? Or a person I can visit? Someone to help me? I know that only time will defrost me, and only by thawing can I heal. Only by melting can I expose what truly lies beneath and only by being exposed to the elements can I truly hope to flourish again.

My NUMBNESS is not an apathy for life. It is an emotional detachment from reality in an effort to protect myself. It is an escape from the reality that I do not want to be real. It is a deferral of the pain that I know I have. It is a way of stopping the deluge of sorrow that can only escape once my heart opens up again. It is an effort to build a reservoir of stamina to help with the impending grief that is in my future. It is my body's way of protecting me. It is a friend when I need a friend the most. However, in this battle, I believe the foes will outnumber the friends, and so then and only truly then will my wows be revealed.

Oh can I perpetually be frozen and just always be NUMB so that I will not feel the pain? I cringe, I shrink and recoil as if I am about to be attacked, but it is my beautiful heart that is going to war. It is going to war with the 'Gods of Sorrow' whose aim is to flood my heart with such emotion that I will feel so weak that I wished that I too had died with Dad. How can that be so? I vowed to always honour my Dad. I promised him that as a family we would continue his legacy. We would do him proud and never let him down – no matter what we would always be there for one another. How can I as the so-called Matriarch of the family fall at the first hurdle? This would be such a dishonour to the man we all knew and loved. I need to slowly try to become less NUMB each day so that I can feel and truly heal. It is then and only then that the strength that I know lies within me can be revealed. I am nothing if not resilient and that I know. My temporary NUMBNESS is like a momentary lapse in time as if to get my troops ready for battle. A battle that will have many struggles along the way, but a battle that will eventually be won as extra cavalry will be called upon. Undoubtedly in the game of life, we face many battles, some we lose, some we win, but we learn from all. Culminating in the realisation that when we love we lose, and when we lose we learn to love again. When we love again, we love the people we have lost even more. Which all leads to a more fulfilled life and ultimately a triumph in the game of life.

Isolated

I HAVE ALWAYS PRIDED MYSELF ON THE FACT THAT I was proud to be myself. I did not feel the need to conform to be 'cool', or to be liked by others. I was even a bit of a trendsetter wearing runners with dresses – before it became fashionable. Obviously I jest, but little did I know the self-imposed ISOLATION I had encountered because of my ill health and my hibernation after my business had closed was going to become a necessary way of life for the world to deal with the pandemic.

Six months prior to the pandemic, I had a complete burnout that literally had stopped me in my tracks. It left me with a general apathy for life, a complete malaise of body and mind. It was then and only then that I allowed my being to catch up and listen to the outcry from my inner soul that it had had enough! It was time for a change. It was time to refocus, redirect, prioritise and cop on. What I did not realise at the time is that my self-imposed ISOLATION would give me a rude awakening to the shambles my life had become. A life that I had allowed to disintegrate, a life where I was too busy being busy to realise that change was necessary. Not alone was change necessary, it was crucial for my existence going forward. Martyrdom looked good on me, I carried the shield so well, I was a fully-fledged member of the organisation and as such that excused my inaction in my own life. Being a martyr is the most awful attribute as it allows you to dismiss who you are, where you are and how you are. The fragility of life has been brought sharply into focus by the Covid-19 pandemic, and it took this global event to get us to wake up to ourselves, our constant excuses for not living life to the full, and our utter misuse of our time.

When I recoiled into my own hibernation after my business closed, the loneliness I felt was crippling. I thought in my own naivety that I would be inundated with 'well-wishers', people who cared, people who were genuinely concerned about my well-being and the welfare of my family. The stark reality that this was not so, was one of the most life-altering realisations I have ever experienced. It was not that I had an inflated sense of self, rather that I truly believed I mattered to more people than I actually did. The resulting disappointment and loneliness that I felt was indescribable. I began to question my worthiness and started to ask, What is wrong with me? How did I get it so wrong? Had I been lured by all these people into a fall sense of comfort and security? Was I just a stupid fool that was an easy target? Was I so unlovable? Was it even worth being alive?

The shame and dismay I felt at thinking that was enormous. The sense of not even injustice, but the confusion at my judgement, or lack thereof, totally zapped me of any confidence or self-worth that I ever possessed. I now was less than a person, only a statistic, a contact on someone's phone, a person that was of no more use, a person who used to run a successful business, a person who used to be good to know. Now I am just a nobody! A recluse that stayed at home with her phone on silent, her pyjamas on, her door locked; her heart pounding worried about what each day could bring. A person who was afraid to go to sleep and even more afraid of waking up the next day. A person who was somebody once but now is just a nobody, just like a shadow or a distant memory for all she once knew. I was alone. Lonely. Alive but literally grappling to stay that way.

Fast forward four months and here we are. A worldwide pandemic, with the words 'cocooning', 'lockdown', 'quarantine', 'physical and social isolation' now a part of everyone's vocabulary. Not just mine. The difference to me now is that I am united in this universal ISOLATION with everyone across the globe. It certainly does not dilute its impact, but the empathy I feel for them shadows in comparison with the loss and utter grief I feel for myself. Here I now am having lost my beautiful Dad to cancer. I am now at home less than six miles from my childhood home, and I am unable to visit and comfort my poor grieving Mother. I am unable to hug my nieces and nephew. I am unable to cry with my brothers at the emptiness we all feel that the colossus that was our Dad now lays in the local graveyard. A graveyard that I now cannot even visit to try and come to terms with the heartache I feel. To just talk to Dad's spirit. To lament with him that he had to go away too soon. To thank him for giving me life and to reassure him that in time we will all be okay. In reality I felt less alone and disjointed from my family when I lived in America!

How can I literally live less than ten minutes away and still feel that it is a journey that with all the will in the world I will not complete for weeks. A snail would probably crawl quicker and raise the victory flag at Dad's graveside sooner than me. I'm the daughter that promised to never let him down, never forget HIM, to look after his precious family – what a great job I am doing – just proves that all those people who did not contact me when my business closed were all right. I am a failure, not worth the effort, a waste of time and space, a hypocrite for even thinking I was anything more.

As I write this I am comforted by the chirping of the birds and reminded of new life, of hope, of springtime. How I wish I was a bird so that I could fly to see my Dad that I could sing to him and comfort him. How I could chirp and the chorus with all the other birds would keep him company, how my presence would ease his pain at losing all of us, how my sound would ease his broken heart in knowing that there was joy in our future and that the sounds would somehow echo and remind him of greater times ahead. If only I could be with him. When I close my eyes, I see him in my mind's eye. My heart flutters at the thought of him and my mind floods with all our memories – and then suddenly I shiver as if the universe reminds me that this is all I can have. Do not be greedy. You had a charmed forty-nine years with your Dad, now you must just deal with your reality and move on. I have felt this shiver since the night he died. It is a stark reminder of the chill of loneliness; the coldness we feel when we are not comforted by the warmth of an embrace. The chill that comes when your heart breaks and your world cracks as if it's a vessel dripping and losing its life source. Maybe it's the chill of death, the chill of loss, the chill of loneliness, but it's the chill of my reality at the moment. This is a catastrophe in my life as I feel like a prisoner of war, in a cold cell, alone, etching the days on the wall to prove that I have survived another day and that I am one day closer to ultimate freedom and life beginning again. A life that will be marred by what's gone before, a life that will never ever be the same, a life where the scars of the past will dictate the direction of the future. I am like a prisoner who laments what they once had but never will again and resolves to make amends when ISOLATION ends and life begins again.

Truthfully, words seem inadequate to describe the pain and anguish that I feel now on a daily basis. This morning when I awoke, I actually woke crying, and sobbing. I was totally unaware that I was crying, but my day started in despair knowing that today would be no different. Each and every day since Dad's passing, today, yesterday, tomorrow, is no different. It is like living in 'Groundhog Day' every day. Today was just another day where I would not get to be with my extended family and one more day where I could not visit my Dad in the graveyard. It would be remiss of me to not mention that even though I feel so alone, I share my home with my husband and my daughter. However, instinctively I want to protect them from my desperation because they are grieving too. As well as their own grief, they are acutely aware of the shambles I have become, and the self-imposed hell I am living in. They are coping and doing damage control as much as they can considering their ISOLATION is as real as mine. The mother in me also wants to shelter my child from my own inadequacies and my weaknesses, whilst still being transparent enough that she knows the importance of showing your feelings without being judged. She and her Dad are amazing, their unwavering love and support is my only lifeline at the moment. I hope that our resilience, our love, our cohesion as a family and our sheer coexistence will be the cement that keeps our family unit glued together in the future.

Hearing others who – on the surface – seemed to have fewer struggles than me complain about their ISOLATION is frustrating at times. Not that I would wish my experience on them, but it only reinforces how everyone's problems are relative to their actual perspective in life. Perspective and reality do not always coexist. However, if I were to view my life from the outside in, I can only perceive that others would empathise with my plight as a tragic repercussion of my current situation. I am certainly not asking for a universal cry of pity, but I just need the loss I feel to be acknowledged as real; the pain I feel to be justified and the ISOLATION I feel to be warranted for the greater good. My Dad would have always lived his life with the best of intentions and with the respect of family, friends and neighbours foremost in his mind. In some small way I am trying to justify my plight by echoing Dad's mantra of respecting others and treating others the way you would like to be treated yourself. He had the greatest regard for life, the people in his life and his love of the world we live in. To compensate for my lack of connection, I am trying to make sense of the motives we have for ISOLATION. It is truly an endeavour for the greater good of the world and the people that live in it. It is an effort to safeguard our loved ones, with that in mind I try to look within for the answers that might give me some peace and even clarity at this time.

If I truly want to make sense of these two worlds that are currently overlapping but are essentially parallel to one another, I think of the love that Dad had for himself and his loved ones. Then I can equate that to the love the world has for its inhabitants. Just as Dad loved all of us unconditionally, we too must now show the same love to the world we live in. I need to refocus my energy towards the greater good. The reasons why. The outcome. The result. The ultimate prize after all these sacrifices. Can I honestly say I have made peace with this? No, I cannot, but I am trying. Dad was never held back by his fear of anything. If anything, I am not sure he truly ever really felt fear. He might have felt it, but his own self-awareness was enough for him to use this feeling, to harness it so that he could catapult himself forward to a world that had greater opportunities, experiences and ultimately a better life.

We so often hear the term 'location, location, location' in the world of real estate. Well in my world, the location I am in is only prime real estate if I can use my imagination and know how to look at the end result. In the cold light of day and to the untrained eye, my location at present is bleak, undesirable, ISOLATED with little curb appeal, but if I am willing to invest my heart, my soul, and commit to where I want to go, the end result is worth it. My vision and patience will eventually pay dividends when my life is as valuable to me as any prime real estate is to an astute investor. So, for all of us lamenting where we are now, we must visualise where we truly want to go and not only manifest it in our mind's eye, but make it possible by our daily commitment to ourselves. We must make each and every day count. For me, a day without learning is a wasted opportunity and, if we allow ourselves, each day we are working towards a PhD in life that is invaluable. However, knowing is not enough, we must apply what we know. The universe is not teaching us these lessons only for us to discard them when our busy lives resume. The trials and tribulations that the world and I are facing are the most intense crash course in human fragility and resilience ever taught. Even though I respect the process, I am still struggling each day with my loss. I am humbled by how insignificant I am in the scheme of things, but yet I respect the fact if we were to dismiss our actions as insignificant, then we would not commit to global healing by coming together as a community. We might seem insignificant and ISOLATED in SOLITARY ISOLATION, but we are invincible when the world unites in GLOBAL ISOLATION.

> My wish for all of us is that in time our hearts
> will heal,
> Our bodies will feel the embrace of our loved
> ones' arms,
> Our eyes will greet the people we love face to face,
> Our smiles will be contagious,
> Our laughter will be deafening,
> Our tears can be those of joy not sadness,
> Our loved ones can be reunited,
> Our life can be fulfilled,
> We can live, love and laugh and when we are
> finished, we can repeat the process.

Once our ISOLATION is lifted, I will possibly fly like a bird to see my Dad. I will talk to him and tell him all that he has missed. I will reassure him that I was gone but he certainly was not forgotten. I will promise him that I will endeavour to live my best life, so that when my day eventually comes, people can say Majella was an example to us all. She loved life. She had a joy and exuberance for life and her loved ones that was contagious. She had no regrets and was so content with her life just like her Dad. We wish we could be more like them!

Lesson learned for sure.

Guilt

I AM EXPERIENCING A NEW FEELING, THAT OF NAUSEA.
Ironically normally associated with the promise of new
life, yet mine is attributed to death. I am GUILT-ridden
on so many levels, because with every waking moment
the narrative in my head is on a constant loop. It taunts
me. It chastises me. It berates me incessantly. A loop that
starts and ends with me unable to complete my Dad's final
wishes. I had promised him that his 'send off' would be
epic! A celebration of his most accomplished life. I had
promised him it would be a cathartic experience for all
of us on our quest to healing. I promised I would execute
this as well as I had executed his medical care, and yet my
promises are as weak as the cheap paper they were written
on. Even if his wishes were scrolled on embossed paper
by a calligrapher, the outcome would be no different.
The restrictions of the pandemic took precedence over
my Dad's request. How can I be consoled by the reality
of this when I am inconsolable? Yet in retrospect I know
that I need to be grateful for the participation of my
family in Dad's funeral, regardless of the fact that we

were small in numbers. The promise of a deluge of people was replaced by a mere trickle. People whom by their presence showed their solidarity with us and their love and devotion for Dad. Each of their faces will be etched in my memory for time immemorial. Their gracious gift of love and support is a true reflection of the calibre of man he was and coincidentally is reflective of the unity and collaborative power of humanity in our current pandemic world. Our devoted neighbours lined our driveway in my Dad's 'last goodbye' as he bid a fond farewell to what had been his home for eighty-two years. They bowed their heads in silence, their compassionate gaze an acceptable replacement for the customary comforting embrace of sympathy. Their silence was golden for sure. In lieu of a church filled to capacity with standing room only, only the front few pews were occupied. I took deep breaths in an effort to remain composed, trying to not allow that gruesome GUILT crush what was left of my soul. Was this really happening? It was like a party where I had forgotten to send out the invitations. A party that Dad and I had painstakingly planned together with every final detail arranged, and I had fallen at the last hurdle in my execution. Oh, how could I have let him down so badly? I got a momentary reprieve from my crushing GUILT, as I was consoled in some small measure by the fact that I was able to honour my Dad in my eulogy as I had promised him I would. A eulogy painstakingly written by me, words from my heart to his, but the echo of the emptiness in the church merely echoed the emptiness in my heart – our loss so profound and my GUILT so suffocating and relentless.

As we emerged from church, we were greeted by Dad's companions and colleagues from his sporting life. Their respect was profound, and their loyalty and love palpable. Their presence was equivalent to the greatest present that Santa ever gave to a beautiful child. Their show of solidarity was consolation to me, an effort to ease the turmoil I was being taunted by. Few could really understand the internal battle that was alive within me. Its existence and death's hold on me was as real as the death of Dad.

The people-pleaser in me was even more vulnerable than usual. I became more self-berating and self-critical than normal. I was so consumed by GUILT and resentment that I was beyond reproach. It festered within me like the most treacherous disease. I resented a world that had allowed this to happen. I resented that we had lost our beautiful Dad. I resented what I had allowed myself to become, a shell of my former self in spirit, a beguiling figure of regret, a scorned woman of sorts, a woman that was insightful enough to know that something had to change, namely ME!

I knew I had to make peace with the GUILT and resentment I was harbouring. The insidious nature of my shame and GUILT was undoubtedly excruciating. It was suffocating what little life was left in me. I now knew I had to make restitution. By accepting my own imperfections and inaction, I became more resigned to accepting that I was not at fault. As they say, it was 'extenuating circumstances'. A complex word, for a truly complex situation. Maybe the GUILT will never go away, only wane; maybe I will never totally forget this anguish, rather I will learn to forgive myself in time with the knowledge that Dad knows I truly did the best that I could do!

However, the turbulence within me was only confounded by the GUILT I saw when I looked in the mirror. I saw this pitiful creature staring back at me. I loathed what I had allowed myself to become, because I have succumbed to my inner demons, my Achilles heel: emotional eating! The self-soothing I had engaged in for months has left me with a body that I was now ashamed of. My inner dialogue reminds me I should know better. I am tormented by my mental nemesis, the one that has berated me all my life, telling me I was never good enough, smart enough, thin enough. I was never enough! Now, that nemesis had the upper hand. Just as Dad had lost his battle with cancer, I too had lost the battle with myself. I essentially had lost control, so now food was in control of me, rather than me in control of food. GUILT consumed me. GUILT confronted me. GUILT suffocated me and GUILT made my life unbearable. The voice inside me screams in disbelief that at a time like this I am so self-consumed: how can I even think of myself? Now GUILT spreads through my body like the virulent virus that is consuming our world.

As I agonise over my plight, I have an epiphany. I am confounded by another sinister consequence of this pandemic world. The reality that as parents we have a responsibility to shelter our children from the carnage of our collapsing world, and to reinforce resilience and self-acceptance in them for the new life they are ultimately facing. What am I teaching my daughter? I am by virtue of being her Mother the vessel of wisdom that should enrich her life, not belittle it because of an onslaught of negative emotions, primarily that of GUILT. The same GUILT that is working overtime in an effort to annihilate what is left of my already fragile spirit. My realisation crushes what's left of my soul. I am brutally aware that no matter how hyper vigilant I am I cannot always protect the ones I love the most. By virtue of the way I conduct my life, there is a domino effect on those in my inner circle, my nearest and dearest. My aura, my demeanour, my words, my actions, my thinking have all been tarnished by the gruesome GUILT I am harbouring. Unless I halt its virulence, I will endanger my daughter's spirit too. My unmonitored GUILT will spread like a malignancy unless decisive action is taken.

Even as I write this I am overcome by guttural GUILT. I am alive, breathing, above ground and yet my focus is on the negative, on my visceral need to control what's out of my control. It is a futile exercise and an injustice to the blessing of life. GUILT is like an expenditure on a balance sheet, in this case the 'balance sheet of life', and when incurred in excess it can tip your accounts into the red. In my wisdom, I should know better, but in reality, I am just a little girl who feels she disappointed her Dad. A little girl who made a promise that she did not keep. A little girl who just wants one more chance to do better, press rewind and not disappoint the Dad that she so adored. A little girl who is riddled by the onslaught of relentless GUILT and suffocating shame. A little girl who misses her Dad and is now just so terribly sad.

Grief

GRIEF HAS BECOME A TREACHEROUS ADVERSARY IN my daily life. It is as deadly as any spider that cocoons its prey in its continuous web. Each and every strand ensuring that impending death is closer. For me it is the death of life. The death of my soul. The death of the spirit that defines me. The death that is abundant the world over. The death of my Dad that has now become synonymous with my own existential battle between life and death. My helplessness is only confounded by my fear. It is as if the ordeal itself has rendered me useless in my own defence. My efforts futile against such an adversary when I am not even a proponent of my own willingness to live. I am paralysed by utter GRIEF. I am rendered a shell of my former being. I feel hollow, ineffective and very alone. Societally, we GRIEVE alone, but it is by mourning that we can accept death and attempt to heal. The need to GRIEVE is absolute. This is a privilege not afforded to me at present. I am confined not only by the imaginary walls I have built around myself but also the bricks and mortar of my home.

Grief

GRIEVING or trying to GRIEVE during the isolation of a pandemic is a crime against humanity. It is the cruellest punishment for an offence that I never committed. I have a hankering for the warm embrace of family. I have a visceral need for my compassionate friends. I am yearning to recall the stories of my Dad with the people who knew and loved him. I am shackled and unable to GRIEVE and mourn with dignity. I feel guilty that I am dishonouring the most honourable man I ever knew. My struggle is real. It is intense. It is affecting me on the cellular level. All 50 billion cells I possess are tarnished by this. So much so that I am very aware of my deficiencies when it comes to my own cognitive skills. It feels like my mind is perforated by holes, even craters. The most mundane of tasks, like getting dressed, are taxing and challenging to me. It is exhausting. I am always enthusiastic in my quest for knowledge but how can such an inferior, ineffective brain like I now possess be of any use? In some strange way, did my brain die along with Dad? I am exasperated by its dysfunction which only further exhausts me. I have a lethargy of mind and body that is similar to any cadaver in the morgue. This fatigue is confounded by my inability to sleep but also the sheer effort that goes into daily life or rather daily existence. My overall health is compromised by my Dad's death but is confounded by the 'sleep debt' that has followed. I have always been an exponent of the virtues of sleep, and yet it is now elusive to me. It is as if I am in the Sahara dying of thirst and the mirage I see is only another test of my resolve. It is only real in my mind's eye. There is no oasis to revive me. My eyelids struggle to stay open as if crumbling under the pressure of GRIEF, yet when I close them I am electrocuted by the intensity of the loss I feel. I relive Dad's struggle to stay alive. I relive the moments where I was the one. It was me that had to tell Dad that his time left to live was short. He was dying. My basic need for sleep is replaced by a feeling of suffocation that consumes me when I try to close my eyes. Dreams are replaced by nightmares. I wake up with the salty crust of tears on my face, my pillow harbouring the evidence as well. I often have the imprint of my nails on the inside of my palms, which reminds me of the desperation of our Lord on the cross. This echoes the helplessness I feel: the pain, the anguish and the guilt that I was not able to save my Dad. My complexion's ashen pallor is a reflection of the greyness of my cognitive skills. Both wavering between the vibrant colours of life and the darkness of death – a true reflection of the GRIEVING soul that I have now become.

My Dad approached life with a 'glass half full' attitude and that resulted in a life best lived. Yet I feel that with every breath I take I am inhaling toxic fumes. Fumes that are compromising my life and suffocating my thoughts, that are darkening my soul and making my very core as toxic as the fumes themselves. This negative state is like a poor-fitting garment: unattractive and needs adjustment and alterations. I have become a depressive recluse. Even as I write this the neurons, the few that still feel like they are functioning in my brain, fire up in an effort to shock me into submission. Shock me back to life. To get my heart functioning again so that I will no longer just exist as if in the 'Intensive Care of Life'. I will be given a second chance at precious life. Such a privilege cannot be wasted. This is essentially a new season in my life with each new season it is out with the old and in with the new, so to speak. It is a matter of decluttering and streamlining my thoughts as we would our wardrobe. Just as our hefty winter coat would burden us on a glorious summer day, so too would the wardrobe of negative thoughts be rendered obsolete in my new and less encumbered life.

In my utter GRIEF, is it okay to feel some hope? Even though, my utter distain for life is palpable at present. I need to unburden myself – if I have any hope of survival. This is a selfless, yet necessary, exercise in self-preservation. My current demonic thoughts need to be discarded as you would any toxic acquaintance. These thoughts are the 'energy vampires' of my life, destructive in nature and capable of penetrating every aspect of my sheer existence: spiritual, physical and social. Such an existence is debilitating and exhausting as it results in me flipping from one state of GRIEF to another several times a day, even several times an hour. In moments of lucidity this is all apparent and my resolve to accept my reality and be grateful for all that I was blessed with offers me a glimmer of hope. Yet this state of 'Nirvana' is a rare occurrence at present. In truth, my sanity and my will to live ebb and flow like stocks and shares on the stock market. As with any investment, the prerequisite for patience, perseverance and progression are to be respected. I need to respect the volatility of GRIEVING and trust that the investment of my time will render the best return for me. My bereavement and my journey are mine and mine alone. I cannot repress the reality of my present lonely state, nor can I deny it, or else I run the risk of prolonging what is already an excruciatingly difficult chapter in my life.

GRIEF is a multifaceted emotion and how it affects me may be totally different to others in my family. Yet as I move forward, I do so with trepidation, unnerved by the impact that it will ultimately inflict on all of us. However, I am certainly not alone and when we are allowed to partake in so-called 'normal life' again maybe then and only then can we all begin to GRIEVE collectively rather than in isolation. Such an outpouring of GRIEF will inevitably be a cathartic experience on a global platform and for me personally I can only hope it will allow healing to begin in my broken heart. A heart that has loved and lost in equal measures, but now has an unenviable melancholic disposition. A heart that I now guard like a hypervigilant gatekeeper, knowing its vulnerability. Intrinsically, I know that by its very nature GRIEF will organically morph and flow forever in my life. Even though it has visited my home and overstayed its welcome like an uninvited guest,

Grief

I am under no illusion that I need to respect its presence, otherwise it has the potential to tarnish all future events in my life. I long for days where the presence of a smile and the existence of contagious laughter is as natural, unencumbered and as real as the love that I shared with my Dad, days where GRIEF is not the emotion that consumes my existence.

Vulnerable

I WOULD NEVER HAVE SEEN MYSELF AS VULNERABLE.
To me the word alone conjures up the idea of a weakling; someone who is unable to fight their corner. Someone who makes excuses and takes the easy way out. In reality, this is unfair because I must have inadvertently seen VULNERABILITY as a choice, whereas VULNERABILITY is actually the end result of a set of unforeseen circumstances. In my world at present, my VULNERABLE state is as a result of my trials and tribulations endured over the last six months. Namely my struggle with ill health, my business closure and worst of all my Dad's diagnosis and ultimate passing. These events in isolation would have certainly weakened my resolve. However, these events in quick succession was enough to actually make me contemplate whether life was actually worth living at all! I feel ashamed to have thought like that when in actual fact so many people are struggling to survive and stay alive in the current climate because they are genuinely in a VULNERABLE category.

Vulnerable

It is certain that this pandemic is preying on the most VULNERABLE in society. How can I utter the words, 'I feel VULNERABLE', when the meaning has such catastrophic consequences? My VULNERABILITY is VULNERABILITY of the heart and soul, which is as valid in my world as all those poor innocent people who are victims of this woeful disease. Their enemy is invisible to the naked eye, but it is just as deadly. For me I hate what I have become. I honestly can say that I don't want to feel like this. There are reasons and many of them that make my plight a real struggle to survive at present. The fragility of spirit I am experiencing with every breath I breathe, I can only equate to the struggle someone experiences where their body is truly weakened and compromised.

VULNERABILITY is not something we aspire to. It is difficult to witness the VULNERABILITY of those we love and the ability to gently accept our own VULNERABILITY is rare and valuable. As I reflect on my Dad's struggle to live in his last few days, I realise it was then and only then that I saw the VULNERABILITY of his existence. His body was still strong in appearance but weak in its ability. His pallor now more grey with every day. His eyelids too heavy to open, even though his heart was still beating to stay alive. His eyes were closed but his heart and ears were open to all the love that surrounded him. His hands responding to the touch of his grandkids' little warm hands and the familiar loving caresses of all of us who cared for him. His apparent strong body only camouflaging the true struggle that lay beneath. His body was only masquerading the real turmoil that lay beneath his skin. I now know that Dad's attempt to be strong, to not complain, to accept his outcome was his way of protecting us. He knew of our VULNERABILITY. It was his selfless act of unconditional love for us. To the very end Dad was thinking about us more than himself. He masked his own pain and suffering to shield his VULNERABLE carers. He knew that when he succumbed to his body's own VULNERABILITY it would be then and only then that our own VULNERABILITIES would emerge. However, I cannot justify this feeling. I loathe what I have become. I actually feel like an inanimate ceramic object. I recall painting an old-fashioned ceramic jug, plate and fruit for a still-life exercise in art class. It was not very good, but I fulfilled the brief to the best of my ability. I was just average at art, if the truth was told. Ironically, isn't this still true? Here I am feeling average at the Game of Life. Though I am alive still. Still alive ... but only just!

There is a parallel of sorts in all of this. How can I be alive, but still? Still in that I feel stuck. I feel like my life is just a puzzle. Do I move left, or do I move right? What do I do? Is there any point in doing anything? Moving ... I am certainly breathing and I am alive, but I am not living. My VULNERABILITY has weakened my own resolve and exuberance for life. These negative emotions have invaded me like a virus and conspired to make me question my own existence and my worthiness. How can a woman who once was so accomplished and took such pride in all she stood for now feel as if her greatest days are behind her and what lies ahead is doomed to be a life less lived? In my eyes when you are as weak and VULNERABLE as I feel, all that you are entitled to is a mediocre life at best. How Dad would turn in his grave if he knew that this is what I have allowed myself to become. He never attempted the most menial of tasks and gave it a mediocre effort, so why then would I? He never ever settled for anything but the best. If I truly am to be a woman of my word and look after our family and endeavour to live my best life, well then I must enter negotiations so to speak with the other side of me: reason. I must reason with VULNERABILITY and resolve to come to a resolution that will allow normal life to resume.

So often we are too proud to admit our shortcomings, but it is only by self-awareness and acceptance that you can truly make amends. I stand up to my weaknesses. I acknowledge them. I do not dismiss them, rather I work with them and through them, so I can indeed come out the other end possibly wounded and scarred but grateful enough to admit that I have survived and will never be the same again, but ultimately I will be okay. With self-care such as this, it would be arrogant of me to think that I am immune from this again. If I become complacent with my body, mind and spirit undoubtedly my VULNERABILITIES will be undermined. When negativity abounds and your resolve is weakened it is then that you are susceptible again. I truly feel negative emotions are like a virus that lies dormant, ready to re-emerge and pounce when given an opportunity, when our guard is down and we are at our most VULNERABLE. Here's hoping that next time I am faced with my emotional fallibility, my emotional immunity and stamina might help me fight the ravages of such.

I do believe there is a universal cry of dismay at the moment because we all realise how insignificant we are. How menial our life has become, how materialism has been relegated to the background. How susceptible we all are regardless of status in life. Our world crisis has levelled us all to humans. There is no difference among us, only that the more VULNERABLE you are the more harm you potentially face. So as I live in a world of uncertainty, where I am uncertain of who I have become, I can only hope the insight I am now gaining on my life's journey will make me more resistant and less VULNERABLE to the emotional weight that often can tarnish our most precious life.

Lesson learned.

Lesson earned.

Lesson to be shared with others.

Desperation

AS I OPENED MY EYES TO GREET THE DAY I RECALLED the DESPERATION in my Dad's eyes when he realised his time on Earth was drawing to an end. My own utter DESPERATION is such that I have become utterly consumed and rendered powerless by it. I struggle with the thought of a 'designated duvet day' where I could recoil into the foetal position and just be still. However, this is short-lived as I realise this would be an injustice to the beautiful child lying next to me. It is theorised that it is by our actions rather than our words that our children learn mostly from us in times of crisis, so even in my state of DESPAIR I was still aware of this. Molly sensed my unease and I tried to explain my recent distain for life and my vulnerability to her. I attempted to apologise for the ineffective role model and the disengaged shell of a woman that I had morphed into. I reiterated to her that I was engulfed by such acute grief since Grandad had died that I had become completely disorientated and detached from life. I was remorseful for my actions as in truth it was incongruous with the mom I truly was and I wanted to be for her. We spoke openly about feelings: the fact that feelings are not problems when they are acknowledged and surrendered to. The problem only arises when feelings are denied and fester, and therefore have the potential to corrode our inner being and slowly erode our potential for joy and exuberance for the blessing of life. We both giggled when we visualised the explosion that would result if I was ever to self-combust!

All of this openness and transparency allowed me to explain my recent vulnerability, DESPAIR, and apathy. I needed Molly to know that my utter DESPAIR and the domino cascade of emotions that evolved from it were as a result of my acute grief. However, I promised her that I was hopeful that in time we would all acknowledge and adjust to our new norm and the acceptance of life without Dad would indeed bring solace and healing to our broken hearts. The last thing I wanted was to tarnish the fragile soul of my beautiful child with the transference of my own feelings and DESPERATION. I needed her to know that even in my apathetic state, the lines of communication were always open and regardless of my despondent and dishevelled attempt at living, I was always there for her. After all Molly is and will always be my beacon of hope and light. We both snuggled like we have never snuggled before, where the warmth of our embrace conveyed our eternal love and devotion to each other. In that moment I felt alive, sad but alive and hopeful that in time once we all acclimated to our new life, we would remember Dad with more love than pain and live accordingly. Until this happens I must learn to honour the living whilst mourning and grieving the dead, realising that excruciating grief is the price you pay for loving someone so much. This parent–child hug was cathartic and poignant in equal measure as it is reminiscent of the many glorious hugs I shared with my precious Dad, who I so DESPERATELY missed – even more in that moment.

IN AN ATTEMPT TO RESCUE THE DAY, I KNEW I NEEDED fresh air. I see disappointment and DESPAIR everywhere. I cannot attempt to manifest a better life when there is that visceral gut-wrenching war going on within my soul. In my former working life, I would be like a pundit proliferating the merits of a so-called 'Makeover Monday' and in my current reality I feel like I am living instead what feels like 'Massacre Monday'! Regardless of being in isolation or not, the days are no different, each one is a struggle irrespective of what day it is. We now live in a world that is obsessed with compiling data, examining it and finding a solution to numerous problems. Unfortunately, there is no solution to my problem. Life cannot be restored. I cannot go back in time and what once was can no longer be again. My Dad is gone and is gone forever!

Oh, if only I could be granted a high dose of anti-depressants or could be anaesthetised so that I could become immune and even oblivious to the turmoil I was embroiled in. Could this act like the 'mega dose' of radiation received by Dad in an effort to stop his cancer metastasising and consuming his body?

Would options like these thwart my pain? Would they ease my DESPAIR and my utter despondency with life?

I am disillusioned with the battle between Good and Evil. How could a man as virtuous and good living as my Dad be overcome by the demonic evil of cancer? We are in the midst of Easter and for me the Easter buntings are replaced by buntings that symbolise death and darkness. Wasn't one of the lessons of Easter that of suffering and resurrection? Does that mean in some twisted way all this suffering is for the greater good? All I know is that the nails on the cross and the noose of DESPAIR that hangs around my neck are one and the same. I certainly do not have any false exaggerated sense of self, but at present the struggle to stay alive and keep my head above water is real and nothing short of DESPERATE!

Normally people are excited about Easter fashion, the bright colours and the lighter fabrics are a promise of better days ahead. This year my Easter bonnet has been replaced by a black mantle – a fashion accessory that does not look good on anyone. The deferral and cessation of life is not just confined to me. It is universal. It is as if life as we knew it has never and will never be the same again. This pandemic can only make sense if all the lives lost will make the lives that have to be lived more enriched in some way. As I write this, I do not mean to belittle those beautiful souls that have succumbed to the virus because I know how life-shattering this is for all their families. If I were to allow the catastrophic nature of our world to become real, I feel the weight of its burden would crush me. I feel I am incapable of viewing the crisis all around me as I am barely coping with the crisis that is within me. How unchristian of me to think of me and only me. Wasn't I raised better than that? Wasn't I taught to always think of and respect others? Shame on me and shame on what I have become.

As if by design I was made aware of the fact that I am alive by the greetings of a gentle, 'Good morning. Isn't it a great day to be alive?' As I looked up from the road that seemed to just magically move beneath me, I saw a kind face, gentle eyes. There was a lovely country woman across the road. She remarked that everyday felt like Christmas Day, where we had all day to do nothing and there was the sense of uselessness that now seemed the norm in everyday life. Wasn't that so true? So, it wasn't just me that seemed lost? Maybe there was hope if this woman who appeared to not be burdened by any apparent crisis was having some struggles herself. I knew I could not go on if I succumbed to the DESPERATION that was my new norm. It was a most unattractive trait; nearly as ageing as my greying roots and my ashen skin. Time and circumstances had cast their wicked spell and now my physical appearance was more like an ugly sister than Cinderella. If there was to be any hope of redemption or resurrection, then wasn't it time that DESPAIR was replaced by hope? Or at least diluted enough so that I was not just a physical shell of the woman I once was. I knew that my DESPERATION was certainly exacerbated by the isolation I felt from the separation from my family, as well as my separation from my Dad. I know in time I will see my family again, but the same is not true for Dad. I can only see him in my mind's eye or in my dreams. I can feel him in my heart. Yet the reality of this is even too much for me to bear. There are those among us who revel in playing the victim. They love the 'woe is me' scenario. Have I now become one of these degenerate souls? If that is the case what is all this suffering for? I have to believe that this struggle is a lesson in life. A lesson in what it is to have loved and lost and a lesson in learning how to love again. I have to believe in the resumption of my life after my DESPERATION eventually dissipates. I have to believe that this too shall pass, that my suffering can only lead to the resurrection of my own life. That I will be a better partner, mother, daughter, wife, sister, aunt, niece, friend and role model after this life experience. I have to believe in myself, because only when I believe enough in myself can I manifest what is meant to be: a future where even though I am scarred and somewhat broken I will endeavour to make the most of every day I am blessed with. Some days will be dark; some will have shadows and some will be illuminating. But regardless, I will participate in all, respecting the journey, acknowledging the process and being willing to learn along the way.

Anger

ANGER IS SUCH A NEGATIVE EMOTION. IT CONJURES up an idea of a person out of control, misguided, maybe even disillusioned and irrational. Yet these are all words that I can now associate with on a daily basis. As I walked today, I found myself even more ANGRY than I have been in recent weeks. Maybe because the actual act of walking was enough to somehow dislodge my emotions and thus allow them to inhabit my body and become real. I heard some birds chirping. They were perched high upon some trees and the chorus seemed unbearable to me. What was, in reality, a beautiful birds' chorus was only noise and turmoil to me! I was irate that these birds were in essence more privileged than me. They were allowed the luxury of the company of their family and friends. And they had the audacity to be gathered together – certainly not two metres apart! How could such a mundane and yet glorious part of nature irk me so much that I actually felt violent towards them? How was it that as I stood beneath them, I nearly wished a plague to wipe them out so that I could resume walking and not be taunted by their God-awful chirping? Ordinarily I would marvel at the sounds of nature, at the beauty of the world, and the privilege of living in the countryside. However, in my current state of mind I only felt distain for such life. How could life go on when our life stopped when my Dad died? I was ANGRY to the point that I was nearly foaming at the mouth. I could feel my palms sweaty and my face flush. I never truly lose my temper, but I was close, so close. I was desperate. I was ANGRY. I was missing Dad.

As much as I love the country, it now is only a stark reminder of what we have all lost. Ironically, it was Dad's love of the outdoors and his joy at the beauty of the land that seemed to be what put me over the edge. It was as if nature was dismissing him, forgetting him, moving on without him. All I know is that as I stood there all the ANGER that had been welling up inside me since his diagnosis came to the surface like a volcano ready and waiting to erupt.

Wouldn't that be some headline? 'Woman self-combusts whilst out for a walk'. It would be a mystery to all except me. I knew at that moment this was symbolic of all the feelings I had been repressing for months. I had tried to be strong for so long in an effort to protect Dad and buffer everyone else in the family. All the while the ANGER was festering inside me like the cancer that had eroded Dad's body. I was ANGRY that cancer had decided to visit us again. I was ANGRY that my Dad had to suffer. I was ANGRY with God that he would inflict such a burden on a kind, gentle soul like Dad – a man that always strived to just do his Christian best. I was ANGRY because we had to live without him. I was ANGRY because I could not make Dad's pain go away. I was ANGRY because I was ANGRY too.

ANGER is a substantial emotion. It warrants attention, but unless it gets the attention in time it can become so unreasonable and destructive that it leaves a wake of devastation in its path. As I stood looking up at those birds on the treetops, who were oblivious to the lunatic peering up at them, I felt a release. It was like a valve had been released at some pressure source, slowly to ensure a gradual release and not an explosion. It was as if the floodgates to my heart just opened. I stood crying initially but then shuddering and eventually sobbing to the point where I had to rest my hands on my knees in an effort to support my aching body. It was as if the outcry from my heart was too much to bear and my torso had become too weighty for the rest of my body to support – the support I had given to others had taken too much out of me. The façade was over; the pretence no more. I am now just here all alone on a country road: broken, raw and vulnerable with the outpouring of all the emotions I had suppressed all along being released. It was as if I had shelved away my ANGER, because I did not have the time to deal with it – my energy had to be redirected elsewhere. There was time in the future to deal with that foreboding ANGER – I guess today was the day for that!

In some way, I wonder was this Dad's way of getting me to deal with his loss? Was it his way of getting me to stop pretending, accepting my fallibility and by doing so I would be able to move forward, albeit without him? I had promised Dad I would be okay, but I also told him that when he was gone, I would most certainly fall apart. He knew I was strong when I needed to be, but that strength came with a hefty premium. The strength I displayed when needed was so intense and often maybe overpowering to others, but it was also only a coping mechanism. It was so necessary and dominant that it prohibited me from truly allowing myself to accept and acknowledge my sheer ANGER. There is always a lesson to be learnt and in my walk today, or in my persecution more like, I now know that today may be 'Day One' of my healing journey. I actually realised that my connection with nature will unravel me, yet it will cocoon me and allow me to deal with my pain and sorrow.

The seasons we experience in nature will echo the seasons of my grief. There will be growth, development, blossoming and death. I now think that it will be my openness to be at one with nature that will allow my ultimate healing. Ironically, we are in the spring/summer of the year which is not usually synonymous with death, but rather with the hope of new life. I need to see this time of year as a beacon of hope where ANGER will wilt and exuberance for life will bloom again. It is as if the negative emotions of my being are the weeds that will soon be replaced by the bright colour of beautiful flowers. Colour will replace the dark; joy will replace sadness; acceptance will replace ANGER and a smile will replace my tears!

Anger

The ANGER the world is now facing in the light of the pandemic and its death hold on our people is the same ANGER I can equate to the demon that is cancer. 'Cancer' and 'corona' are both six-letter words that embody the ugliness of what the world can do when evil prevails. I am ANGRY that the world has to experience pain and suffering like it is. I am ANGRY that so many people have to die needlessly. I am ANGRY that so many people died alone. I am ANGRY that Dad will not get to see his precious grandchildren grow up. I am ANGRY and my ANGER is real and now not hidden anymore.

As I made my way back home, I was bombarded by an array of emotions. My display and acceptance of my horrible ANGER had in some way given permission for so many other emotions to attack me. It was as if I was experiencing a pollen attack, but this was so severe I was almost in anaphylactic shock. By acknowledging the ANGER, I now seemed even more vulnerable to all the other negative emotions that were hidden in every orifice of my being all the while I was masquerading as the strong one. The one that was holding it all together. Wow the joke's on me because it is now that the carer needs to be cared for more than ever before. So, am I not justified at being ANGRY? I am now admitting my vulnerability and my outcry for help ironically cannot be heard because we are now living in a world where distance from your loved ones is the new norm. Distance, albeit physical, is our greatest show of solidarity for the ones we love the most. So, at a time when I need the comfort of a physical embrace, or a warm familiar hand to gently cradle mine, or the comforting smile of a loved one, all I am resigned to is connection by phone.

ANGER then is a very hard emotion to dissolve because it is like an ice cube that melts and thaws only to be solidified again once the cold temperature of reality takes over. So, as my ANGER has peaks and troughs, just like my blood pressure, I truly know that this too shall pass, but unfortunately it will not pass anytime soon. Rather it will linger and lay dormant like the virus that now infects our world. There may be times when we think we have conquered the beast, only to awaken to its deadly grasp again. I have often heard of patients being prescribed 'ANGER MANAGEMENT', and in my naivety I would have thought that these people must have a genetic disposition to such ANGER or that they were degenerate in a way that prevented them from being part of civilised society. I might even have thought that they were narcissistic in some way. But now I have fallen into this category – not by choice, but by circumstance. I am ANGRY that I have become part of an elite club. A club that I do not want to belong to, a club that I am eligible for, because I have lost a parent. If only I could forfeit my membership. But no such luck. There is no going back. There are no real benefits or merits to this God-awful club. Once you have membership you have membership for life. I am ANGRY because I never ever wanted this. I am too young for this membership. Yet here I am. ANGER has now become my middle name!

Anger

I now have a greater respect, awareness and understanding to the ferocity of the loss of a parent. Undoubtedly, in the past when I offered my sympathy and condolences to those bereft, I did so with respect and intent. However, in the future my compassion and empathy will be borne from my own personal experience. Even in my guttural state of grief and ANGER, I am brutally aware of the experiential nature of losing a parent, and I am cognisant of the disparity that exists between sympathy and empathy when it comes to such. The truth is until you lose a parent you cannot comprehend and will never understand how your heart aches and how you are irrevocably changed forevermore, as the only source of knowledge for this is the actual experience itself.

Even though I cannot share or unburden the grief of others, I am by my own affiliation humbled by the enormity of their foreboding sadness.

The enormity of my ANGER is a direct result of the enormity of my love for my Dad and the enormity of the loss that I now feel. I am ANGRY that I am so ANGRY, and even feel that my ANGER is ANGRY too, such is the world we now live in.

Love

LOVE IS NOT JUST A FOUR-LETTER WORD THAT IS synonymous with Valentine's Day. LOVE is the elixir that our world survives on. This may seem trite to some but to me LOVE is the Holy Grail. To have been LOVED by a man like my Dad was a true blessing, and the extent of his LOVE was not just confined to within the four walls of our happy childhood home.

My Dad's LOVE of all was just that. He had a LOVE of us, a LOVE of life, a LOVE of his friends, a LOVE of his neighbours, a LOVE of the land, a LOVE of the great outdoors, a LOVE of sport, a LOVE of his faith. He was unapologetic in his LOVE of all things great or small. He was blessed with the foresight to see that the more you LOVE what you have, the more what you have LOVES you back!

The coexistence of LOVE and loss is even more profound because the LOVE we knew in Dad was so immense. I am grappling with making sense of my loss, and the more I grapple, the more clarity emerges. My Dad's LOVE of life and everything in it cannot be compartmentalised. That is why now in his wake I see his presence in everything. As we are now in Covid-19 isolation our grieving is somewhat delayed, even interrupted. We are smothered by the loss of contact in the aftermath of Dad's death. The contact of people that my Dad so enjoyed. His LOVE of life and our inability to show our LOVE is making my loss even more profound. To truly cope I am really trying to convince myself that this isolation, apart from being the greatest show of solidarity, is the greatest show of LOVE for each other and for the world we live in that humankind has ever seen.

I would never regret a moment of LOVING my Dad or being LOVED by him, but in my new reality the intensity of this love is the reason I am struggling so much. The intensity of my LOVE for him and his LOVE of his life is only making the loss more persecuting.

As I look at my daughter, I struggle as I know how deeply he LOVED all his grandchildren: Molly, Chloe, Lily, Abbie, Jack, Amelia and Ava. How he marvelled at every aspect of their lives, how he LOVED every idiosyncrasy that made them unique.

I lie here holding my beating heart remembering how in his last few days, his heart was beating frantically to keep breath in his body because his LOVE of all he had was too unbearable for him to leave behind. I feel the lack-lustre beating of my own heart is in stark contrast to the intensity of his. How can a dying man's heart beat stronger than mine? Maybe because his definition of LOVE was greater than mine? Whereas someone like me had lost sight of the sheer joy of living, the joy of LOVE and the joy of LOVING being alive!

My epiphany has been hard earned. My life has been rattled by loss on so many levels. However, I now am humble enough to realise that I was truthfully on the wrong path and was misdirected by nobody but myself. I know that the last six months has taught me to accept LOVE more dearly and see LOVE more clearly. The lesson Dad taught me was that LOVE is free, it costs nothing but if it is not available to you freely it costs you everything. What I mean by that is if you are like Dad and LOVE everyone and everything in life, you have a complete, content existence. Whereas, if you are damaged like me, you see strings attached to LOVE. Therefore, you become so blinded by the pitfalls that you miss out on all that is right in front of you to be LOVED. In reality we as a world collectively have been too busy LOVING in isolation and maybe LOVING with a prejudiced mind, and we have deprived ourselves of the real joy that lies all around us and all that we have to LOVE and all those we have to be LOVED by.

I firmly believe that anyone who was lucky enough to cross paths with Dad was blessed because he had an aura, a charisma that seemed to affect us all by the sheer company of his presence. I smile when I recall as he was about to leave hospital before Christmas. He had a line of well-wishers to bid him a fond farewell and wish him a happy Christmas. The staff were unanimous in their collective admiration for Dad. They all reiterated how special and kind he was. How he made each and every one of them feel appreciated. He had an innate sense of making you feel like you were worthy and that he was so happy that he was in your company. There was a unilateral show of LOVE and support for the man I was lucky enough to call my Dad. To me this was a sign of Dad's LOVE of humanity and one that is often lost in the fast-paced world that we are all trying to escape from … just as we all are now.

The LOVE that Mom and Dad shared had spanned sixty years. For my Mom, the LOVE in her life is now replaced by cocooning, isolation and the uneasy silence at home. A home that has a place for everything and has everything in its place, except my Dad. In the cold light of day, and especially at night, it is far from perfect, as it is missing her one true LOVE: my Dad. His chair is empty – his place no longer there. What words are there to comfort her? What people are there to ease her pain? All I know is that the guilt I feel for not being that warm embrace, that shoulder to cry on has eroded at my inner being. I LOVE my Mother, but I am totally worthless to her at this time. One can only hope that the knowledge of LOVE is enough at times such as this. There should be no doubt in her mind of the LOVE we all have for her. Our distance is a sign of LOVE for her well-being, nothing else. It is not symbolic of our own need to grieve our loss in isolation. It is from a LOVE of the family we still have and do not want to endanger or lose, that we are keeping our distance.

It feels weak to say, 'Distance makes the heart grow fonder.' For me it just prolongs the pain in my heart and postpones the grieving that hangs over us as a family like a storm cloud ready to explode. When it does all the LOVE in the world will not be enough to deal with the wave of sorrow and despair that will follow. I know undoubtedly that when I emerge from this current stage, somewhat broken but healed, my experience of LOVING my Dad will give me more LOVE in my life and life in my LOVE, so maybe it is worth the pain and heartache at the moment? The experience will gift me the ability to accept LOVE like Velcro rather than repel LOVE like Teflon as I would have in the past.

Often people talk of 'verbal diarrhoea' where the spoken word can be trite, excessive and ridiculous. Even as I write this, I feel I am such a hypocrite. My head is prompting me to type my inner thoughts, but my heart seems to be on a different trajectory. I know that in essence I mean what I say, even though I may not always feel what I say. In reality I applaud Dad's LOVE of life and everything he stood for, yet here I am vehemently berating myself for the mess I have become. The blob that greets me when I am brave enough to look in the mirror. The LOVE that oozed from every orifice of Dad's being is only equalled by the distain I feel for what I have allowed myself to become. How can I truly accept LOVE, know LOVE, when the lack of LOVE for myself is so intense?

Shouldn't I honestly know better? Here I am a forty-nine-year-old woman who has got this far in life with a body and mind and soul that is unique. It is mine and mine alone. Shouldn't I LOVE the body I am in rather than covet the one I want? Has Dad taught me anything? Dad was never jealous of anyone. If anything, he was always happy for people when they did well. He was not materialistic and he would always see the good in any situation or in anyone, no matter their shortcomings. If Dad were here, he would applaud my bravery in dealing with the current crisis. He would acknowledge the mind I have. He would say how proud he was of the daughter, mother, wife, sister, aunt, niece, friend and role model I am. He would express his LOVE for me. His unconditional LOVE of a woman so imperfect in her own eyes, but utterly perfect in his. My solemn wish for myself is that I can salvage my own self-esteem by emulating his LOVE of everything in his world and by appreciating all that I am without passing judgement. By allowing myself to become who I was meant to be, then and only then can I nourish my soul enough to actually allow LOVE to flow more freely in my veins, thus living with LOVE and LOVING living more than ever before!

Fear

WHAT CAN I SAY ONLY THAT I AM TRULY SAD,
heartbroken, shattered by the loss that we have just
experienced as a family. My Dad's legacy is eternal. His
impact on us will forevermore be felt in how we live our
own lives. His appetite for life was ferocious. His love of
everything was immense. His quest for new challenges was
unwavering. His contentment, the ultimate nourishment
for the fulfilling life he always lived, was so admirable. He
possessed a 'go for it' attitude that rendered him brave
and FEARLESS in every endeavour in his life. For me I
want to harness that exuberance for life and not allow
the shackles of my own FEAR be the reason that I do not
achieve my true potential.

There has always been an underlying current of unease
within me in the knowledge that I had not allowed myself
to reach my full potential. The truth was that I knew that
I was better than what I had allowed myself to become.
Not for a second do I have an inflated sense of self, rather

I believe wholeheartedly that I have the potential to impart great knowledge to others, if I follow my dreams and pursue my passions without allowing FEAR to undermine my resolve along the way. I believe that I am capable of changing the lives of so many. However, that is only possible if I am ready, willing and able to unshackle the FEAR that has been my antagonist for many years. I have always allowed FEAR to be one of the emotions that dictates my path in life or rather derails me from the path I should have been on. FEAR for me has been a constant companion, a toxic friend that has zapped the joy of the life that might have been. It has deflated the potential life that I could have lived, and it has held me back to such an extent that the primal FEAR that resides within me has stolen my *joie de vivre* from so many areas of my life.

As my Dad struggled in his last few weeks, there were many nights when our family recalled memories of childhood. Often, I would hear, 'Majella, do you remember that?' And honestly, even though I had a very happy childhood, there are so many memories I do not recall. Now as a nearly fifty-year-old woman, I realise that my FEAR throughout my life was so intense that it actually overshadowed the wonderful experiences I was an integral part of. In reality my memories have nearly all been suffocated by FEAR! It was as if the need to survive was primal in me. I needed to just do whatever to not be heard, or seen, just to be and that FEAR was the guiding force of my life. I felt great darkness in my struggle to keep quiet in order to live, to survive and I was willing to make many compromises in order to just be quiet so that I could live for another day without being a burden to others. As melodramatic as it may seem, this was how I felt as a child, this carried through into adolescence and adulthood. Trust me when I say I had a beautiful childhood, but it was my own inner thoughts and perception of my reality that exasperated this catastrophic state of FEAR – not the environment I was living in. However, with each decade the FEAR became stronger, a colossus that was my forever shadow wherever I went. I was acutely aware of FEAR in my life, but was also aware of my need to please, to be liked by others and not to let anyone down. Ironically, I wanted to be a perfectionist, which prevented me from trying anything new – in case I did not reach perfection. Yet, by never reaching for the stars, so to speak, I was limiting my own humanity. This was an epic fail, as my inaction lead to me failing miserably at reaching that elusive perfectionism I was so eager to achieve. How can you aim to be a perfectionist when you lead such an imperfect, unfulfilled FEARFUL life? What then ensued was a life less lived that was forever shrouded by a number of missed opportunities and the lament of what might have been.

The irony is that I always say with the greatest of pride that I am so like my Dad. But my Dad was never AFRAID of anything in his life. I cannot say he was even AFRAID of his impending death as he knew it drew closer and closer. He knew that there was life after death and as with any task he ever faced in life, he faced this without FEAR too. Maybe sadness but certainly not FEAR.

I vowed to myself as I accompanied Dad on the final stretch of his journey here on Earth that I would become more responsible in my own life. That I would harness the FEAR I felt and make sure that it was the fire that ignited the engine of my new life that lay ahead. As my precious Dad left this world, I had to believe that the best part of my life still lies ahead of me. That I would no longer be ruled by FEAR but rather be catapulted forward into a new realm where new opportunities were endless. I had to believe that this life lesson was one that was well learnt from the most learned scholar that I knew on the subject of living your best life without FEAR: my Dad.

So as I move forward, I move with a heavy heart as my Dad's loss is still so new and raw, but I move forward with a flutter in my heart for the excitement and promise of my impending and more fulfilling life ahead. Certainly, there will be challenges, but I vow that I will not allow FEAR to hold me back, I vow to be willing to make mistakes, I vow to never stop trying, remembering 'forward always forward' is the only way. Wholeheartedly, I vow to make my Dad proud.

I ultimately vow to start living my true authentic life: FEAR out and freedom in is the way forward! However, it would be remiss of me to think that I am invincible and by some miracle I will never feel FEAR again. I know I will experience FEAR daily, but in future I will have to use this as an accelerant to my life's fire rather than a fire hose that could quench it and I will epitomise the saying, FEEL THE FEAR AND DO IT ANYWAY – a legacy that my Dad had certainly taught me.

I recall my Dad's lack of FEAR as we start to live each day now without him. As my Dad struggled towards the end, my family and I spent Dad's last ten nights back in our childhood home, together, safe and cocooning. As if protected from, and even immune to, the outside world. As we struggled to accept that Dad was dying within the confines of our own four walls, the outside world was bracing itself for the new world that was emerging. In truth, we were oblivious to what was happening. We were so consumed and desperate that we could not unleash the burden that existed outside our home onto ourselves. It would have been more than any one of us could bear. It was as if our door was locked, we were safe and as long as we did not open the door, we were protected from the virus and the fragility of life that existed outside!

SO THE FEAR WE FACED AT LOSING DAD, WHICH existed inside our home, was cemented by the FEAR of our own fragility and mortality when Dad died and we had to essentially play 'catch up' and wake up to what had been happening in the world without our knowledge. They say ignorance is bliss, well our life was far from blissful and we had enough of a pandemic in our own world without the knowledge of the outside world's one!

Truth be told, when Dad died and we were enlightened as to what we were facing, our FEAR factor went off the Richter Scale! Certainly for my brothers, I think they became overwhelmed by the FEAR of losing someone else that they loved and so they endeavoured to do everything possible to safeguard their families, and rightly so. For me, I actually think I was a little slow on the uptake because I was so numb from the trauma of Dad's loss. I felt that I was too weak to acknowledge or accept the fragility of my immediate family's life as I knew it. Ultimately, I might have even been frozen by FEAR unknown to myself, but now I think it all makes sense to me because all I really felt for the first ten days after Dad's death was nothing. I was numb, numb to emotion, numb to loss, numb to FEAR! Ironically my body had a chill in it that no matter what clothes I wore I still was frozen. Whether it was from shock or FEAR I am not sure, but I believe that these feelings coexisted and, in some way, maybe their coexistence was a survival technique for me. If I really acknowledged the severity of what was occurring in the world, like my brothers did, I believe I might just have crumbled under the pressure. As the days went on and the numbness thawed somewhat, my acceptance of the global tragedy awakened. I became acutely aware of our mortality, the fragility of life. The subsequent FEAR was real and intense for me. I am not a hypocrite. As I said earlier, I vowed to not let FEAR hold me back, but in this instance, I think I needed to feel the FEAR to actually begin to feel alive again.

This feeling of FEAR was a necessary catalyst to allow me to start loving being alive again, and to make sure that my inner covenant with myself, to not allow life to pass me by, was genuine and reinforced. The FEAR that I was feeling was a collective worldwide genuine FEAR. It was not the hysteria of a woman who was AFRAID of making a mistake. Rather, it was the cumulative acknowledgment from the world that we had made many mistakes and now we needed to refocus and readjust our life as we would move forward. FEAR without action is worthless as all it does is diminish your soul. FEAR needs to be felt. FEAR needs to be respected. FEAR needs to be acknowledged, then FEAR needs to be harnessed and acted upon for the greater good. On a personal level this means self-development; on a global level this means accepting our inadequacy, our mortality, our fallibility, then growing and moving forward so that we can go back to where and what we were before: a community of people that looked after each other above and beyond all else.

This FEAR is here as a life lesson in our own resilience and as a wake-up call to show us how off course we truly were. So, after this FEAR we are redirected to where we will find our original destination. Hopefully, we are on course to a global rediscovery of the true meaning of life. Where we have what we need rather than need what we want. We want to reacquaint ourselves with ourselves, our families, our friends, our neighbours, our co-workers, our community. We need to have a 'vision' and a 'mission statement' for our family and life as much as we do for our business. We need to nourish our roots so that our tree of life truly flourishes.

In a world where FEAR is real, how sad would it be if we did not allow ourselves to learn from it? I have always believed a day without learning is a wasted opportunity.

All these days we have spent at home in isolation are to me like a crash course in the University of Life. Whether we graduate with distinction or flunk is entirely up to ourselves. Let us not be AFRAID to feel the FEAR and do it anyway! Life has to be lived and lived here and now. When we change the way we look at things, the things we look at change. We can be either driven by FEAR or consumed by FEAR: the choice is ours.

As my Dad was ready to pass on to his new home in Heaven, he truthfully was not AFRAID because he had faith in what awaited him. This was only made possible by the fact that he was a man that was so content with his life. He never allowed FEAR to get in his way. I can only aspire to be more and more like my Dad every day from here on in. I vow to be FEARLESS just like he was. He was FEARLESS both in life and in death. This is the legacy of the great man that he was. His FEARLESSNESS was an essential component for the prototype for a life well lived.

Imagine going to bed tonight knowing that our best life has yet to be lived!

So, feel the FEAR and do it anyway. Good luck to all!

Anxious

IF ONLY THERE WAS AN ANTIDOTE FOR THE EPIDEMIC of ANXIETY that is suffocating our precious world at present. This global emotion is just as prevalent as the catastrophic pandemic. There is not a human among us – man, woman or child – at present that is immune to feeling ANXIOUS at varying degrees. This phenomenon has resulted in so-called 'pandemic paralysis' that has violated our core existence and weakened our resolve, thus contributing to many of us feeling paralysed.

Personally, my long-established history with ANXIETY has rendered me somewhat obsolete, redundant somehow, unable to decipher reality, perception, even the difference between fact and fiction. Ironically, I would have thought my intimate relationship and my overexposure to ANXIETY would have afforded me immunity. Alas, the reality is it has only made my ANXIETY more catastrophic in its personal vendetta against me.

My Dad's death unveiled how raw I felt and how vulnerable and susceptible I had become. I was an easy target. In my previous life before Dad's death and

Covid-19, my existence was akin to that of a perpetually ANXIOUS child. A child that lived as if irritated by their own existence. As if their skin was an irritant. Being afraid of almost everything, even their own shadow. A child that was haunted by the 'Boogeyman' and feared the night, the darkness, and noise. A child who basically feared everything! Even the shriek of other kids unnerved them. A strengthening wind was often enough to bring tears, as the onset of a catastrophe was inevitable in everything that surrounded them. Life was a challenge because with every breath there was uncertainty: the fear of the unknown. ANXIETY was the only fuel I knew. It was as if it was the only food I had been weaned on. I never ventured far from home because it was inevitable that the impending doom I felt constantly was around the next corner. So, it was no surprise that as a child I never ventured off the so-called 'LONELY STEP' at school. A step, with room for one and one only. A step that was a prototype for the isolation that is now our new norm. A step which was a safe haven. A shield from the dangers of the real world. I was so paralysed by fear, afraid to step off the step onto the schoolyard, in case I was confronted by the schoolyard bully. This was a natural state of existence for me. I was unknowingly debilitated by fear, so consumed by my own ANXIETY, yet always aware of its constraints. This was my normal everyday life!

IN MY NEW REALITY WITHOUT DAD AND LIVING IN A world crushed and engulfed by a pandemic, my ANXIETY has exploded and reached levels of epic proportions. It is as if my nemesis – the schoolyard bully – has morphed into an army. Ironically, paralleling the way in which a virus grows and multiples. It now feels like one has become many. My already compromised and vulnerable inner child now stands alone, shivering, paralysed by debilitating fear. My body, uncontrollably flooded with 'survival' hormones, is overwhelmed, simultaneously stuck in quicksand and alert for impending danger.

Our ancestors used these 'survival' hormones to outrun the predators that roamed the Earth. We still live in a treacherous world where it is essentially survival of the fittest, but our greatest threat is not visible to the naked eye. How can something so small be so deadly? As we ponder on Darwin's Theory of Evolution, we can only surmise that survival is only afforded to those who are willing to adapt and modify to face their new world. We are truly living in a jungle of predators. Yet the ferocity of any wild animal is no match for the 'pandemic paralysis' that is threatening our mere existence. As we lie in wait for ANXIETY to recoil, we contemplate our own existence, our validity, our mortality. This overwhelming emotion is building momentum, pulsing through our veins. ANXIETY is now and will forevermore be ingrained in our collective memory of this era. It will be remembered as an emotion that was ever present, keeping everyone on guard and aware of the need for survival. But this emotion needs to be rationed, validated, even consolidated and used efficiently. It's an emotion that could be channelled into something positive.

I know that the roller coaster of life is mirrored too often by the roller coaster that life becomes because of the ANXIETY that most certainly accompanies us on life's journey. Essentially, it's one of the most contagious emotions and has the potential to either make or break you. It can bring out the best of you or reveal the very worst of you. If it's acknowledged and dealt with using the right coping mechanisms, it can be the impetus for change, for growth, for self-development, and you can be driven by it rather than being paralysed because of it.

FOR ME, I KNOW MY ANXIETY, WHICH I HAVE NOW become accustomed to, has exasperated my OCD. It is an unattractive trait at best. Yet, I need to respect it enough to acknowledge its power over me, and therefore work on using it to my own advantage. As much as I may validate its presence and prevalence in my life, this does not make me bulletproof in any way to its virulence. In its presence, I too need validation for the tumultuous mess my life has become whether in reality or in my exaggerated version of reality.

I have become brutally aware of my mortality since Dad's passing and with the onset of the pandemic. I now know that the more I become exasperated by my shortcomings – namely my unproductive, unaccomplished, unstructured life – the more ammunition I am giving my ANXIETY. In the past six months I have lost my livelihood, my Dad, I nearly lost my sanity, ultimately I lost my way. Just as the world authorities are formulating a survival plan so too do I need to create my own 'life plan'. A plan in which I respect my own fallible nature, but implement enough change and structure so that real growth and survival ensues. I need rituals that enrich my life so that my escapism is meditative rather than melodramatic and catastrophic in nature. There is a worldwide call for reinvention. Its impetus crucial for our future survival. I need a 'vision', a 'mission statement', a 'Manifesto', not only for my business, but for my greatest project to date: myself. My future life and existence in a post-pandemic world depends solely on this and my willingness to implement it. One key formula for my own personal survival is:

REALITY + PERCEPTION = LEVEL OF ANXIETY

I know that my interpretation of this is crucial to my well-being and state of mind.

My eternal hope is that our world will not allow itself to become paralysed by collective ANXIETY. That we will rely on fact, not fiction, to be our guiding light. That we will gain more empathy for the vulnerable and be less judgemental of others. That we will have more tolerance for others, and will be more robust. But, above all, we will know that our mindsets matter. We need to acknowledge and validate our insecurities, our idiosyncrasies and have an acceptance of such and to not allow an epidemic of ANXIETY be the reason we are not living the best life we were meant to live.

Anxious

A wise woman once told me:

Never trouble trouble
unless trouble troubles you,
because when you trouble trouble
it troubles others too!

So as my life's journey continues, ultimately without my Dad. I know to truly honour the man that he was and his legacy, I have to become the woman he knew I was, even before I did.

The ANXIOUS little girl, paralysed by her own ANXIETIES can now become the woman who acknowledges ANXIETY and harnesses it to catapult her forward on her onward journey in life.

Gratitude

TRUTHFULLY, IN THE COLD LIGHT OF DAY AS WE reflect on my Dad's life and death we have so much to be GRATEFUL for as a family. We were truly blessed to have had the opportunity to spend so much time with Dad in his final few months. There were weeks on end spent in hospital where we collectively as a family never ever left Dad's side for a minute. We executed his care like the most proficient relay team you have ever seen, seamlessly handing over the baton from family member to family member. Dad loved us all dearly and this gave him such tremendous comfort. Our constant presence in his life was the greatest present we could have ever given him. He expressed often his GRATITUDE and pride at our solidarity and love. He never missed an opportunity to tell anyone how lucky he was to have 'one of his own' always looking after him. But where else would we be?

Well the answer for most of us would be work, yet for me that was no longer the case. Did I ever think that losing my business of fifteen years would be a blessing in disguise? When the trauma unfolded after my business closed, I must admit I thought I had hit rock bottom. I thought this was a tragedy of epic proportions. This was the worst thing to have ever happened to me. Little did I know what was about to transpire. I only had three weeks to nurse and grieve the tremendous loss of my livelihood, my identity, my purpose in life before the universe unleashed its powers of destruction on my heart, on our family, on our life and on our world as we knew it.

In retrospect, I am eternally GRATEFUL to have had the luxury of the time with my Dad – unadulterated precious time. Dad was resolute in his conviction that this was possibly the best thing that had ever happened to me. Initially, I thought this was in an effort to placate and comfort me. But now I know that he knew that my work was ruling me rather than me ruling my work. So his opinion was an insightful one. I had become a victim of myself. I had fallen into the same trap as many other self-employed perfectionists: I was busy being busy! Ironically it was my mismanagement of time and my disrespect of it that had left me living a life that was well below par. In hindsight, I am beyond GRATEFUL that this loss allowed me the freedom to be with my Dad and not be stressed and exasperated about keeping my business open.

For me the time I spent with Dad was priceless, precious, invaluable. Time that money could not buy. We lived every day with purpose, love, GRATITUDE and eternal hope. Each day enjoying the little things in life, not realising in our time of grief and reflection as a family that they would be the big things that now give us solace. Dad was ever the optimist, and so it is only fitting that he was the benefactor of the serendipitous outcome of my business closure. The freedom of time it afforded me was fortuitous in equal measure to both of us. Yet, greedily as they say 'much wants more'. If only I could just have one more day.

However, in retrospect, the gift of time that was ours is not a luxury afforded to everyone. In the present reality of Covid-19, there is a human tragedy that is profound the world over. There are so many families that are robbed of a final goodbye. The sanctity of life and death interwoven in time, a time that cannot be relived, rewritten or rewound. With each passing day we are more aware of how blessed we were as a family to have had such uncensored access to Dad at the sunset of his life. This heralds even more GRATITUDE in my lonely being as I recall that on the eve of a two-week stay in hospital, Dad was fortunate enough to be facilitated by two very kind audiologists, who fitted him with new hearing aids. These were two of my most memorable weeks ever with Dad. The increased capacity to hear gave him a new lease on life, a chance to speak, a chance to be heard – for us as a family it was truly glorious. It was a gift like no other. Before this Dad had sometimes become a little disengaged from life because of his profound hearing loss. It was as if he recoiled so as not to draw attention to his shortcomings. He was frustrated by the frailties of his body; his absenteeism was lamented by all of us and yet his desire to be part of everything was still absolute. I was euphoric with the boost of life this afforded Dad and benefitted all of us, too. However, the downside to this was that there were many more open and honest conversations. While we were in hospital Dad and I had many the tearful chat about life, death, his funeral, his wishes, his bucket list, his concerns, his loss. As difficult as this was, it was my privilege to do this for him. He knew I was the strongest of all of us, when it came to the reality that was our life and his impending death. He knew he could rely on me because I was essentially strong like him. He recalled the resilience and stamina of character of his own Mother, Molly. He reiterated my uncanny likeness to her with the greatest of pride. He knew he could burden me with the trappings of his death and I would execute this to the best of my ability, while somehow protecting everyone else. In reality, my brothers were still in denial and Mom, even though she knew, was masquerading as the innocent bystander – all the while wishing this was not happening. He knew my strength but also knew my vulnerability. I told him I was honoured and GRATEFUL to do this for him, but told him that my GRATITUDE would be overshadowed with pure sadness when he was gone. For me I can now live knowing that I have no regrets regarding my time with Dad; only that it just was not enough. I am eternally GRATEFUL that there was nothing left unsaid by either of us. What a blessing that was for both of us.

One of Dad's greatest fears was dying in hospital, even though he never missed an opportunity to thank all of the wonderful doctors, nurses, dinner ladies, cleaning ladies, porters and chaplains that were responsible for his care. He always had one foot on the floor ready for the road that would lead him home. Dad was a huge man of faith, and whilst in hospital in December he begged me to work my charm to get him home for Christmas. He wanted to be with his precious family for Christmas dinner and he also wanted to go to Christmas Mass. Both were achieved with success. As I sat beside Dad at Christmas Eve Mass, I sobbed incessantly knowing it was our last. As I did, I was comforted by a warm hand from a friend. A lady similar to myself, whose Dad was also ill, there were no words spoken, we were kindred spirits united by our love of our fathers and the privilege of shared moments in time. That kind gesture is one that I will be eternally GRATEFUL for.

On Dad's last visit to the Palliative Care Unit I had the unenviable task of telling Dad his time was short, he had a few days maybe a week at most to live. I still feel the ache in my heart as I remember speaking those words. This was an existential experience of mind, body and soul, and the most harrowing experience of my life to date. The enormity of such, undeniable. The execution was only made possible by the comfort and support of the gentlest of souls, my Dad's palliative doctor. All I can say is that in the twilight of your life the palliative team are like a beacon of light sent to guide you home. Their professional accolades only superseded by their humanity. The feeling of love and compassion that exists in that Palliative Unit is exuded from every human and inanimate object housed within its four walls. As we left that day, I knew I would not see these people again, well not with my precious Dad by my side.

As we prepared for home, our final journey as such, Dad's doctor embraced me. It was a warm, comforting embrace, just like that of a mother pacifying and soothing an unsettled and perturbed little child. With tears in her eyes, she told me she had never witnessed a love like Dad and I had shared. She professed how remarkable it was that it transcended the normal father–daughter bond and resided in a more gracious and elevated state of connection and love. She said it was truly beautiful and special and that her life had been enriched and even enlightened by it. She reiterated the blessings of love, the luxury of time, the bond that was ours and ours alone. She spoke to Dad with the respect and love that was befitting of him. Her standard of care was exemplary and her tone as pure and calming as the angels in Heaven. The angels she knew that were waiting to greet him very soon. We said our last goodbye. Our soulful sad eyes locked, a melancholy gaze exchanged, drowning in tears, knowing what was inevitable in the next few days. I could not ask for more from her, unless a miracle perhaps! I am eternally GRATEFUL to them all.

My Dad was a man of great faith. What gave him great peace was knowing that his new world was awaiting him. What I know now is that all angels do not have wings and the angels in Heaven sent a guardian angel in the guise of his night nurse, Carmel, to prepare his passage for him. In the darkest of times she was a shining star for us as a family. She was what Dad deserved. He was the best and so only deserved the best, which he got with

Carmel. I was so overwhelmed by the reality of what was to come but I was SO GRATEFUL that her expertise and sheer compassion enabled us to keep Dad at home. I had an old-fashioned school copybook with all Dad's wishes, not that I needed it as they were all engrained in my brain anyway, but it was a great pleasure to know that our collaborative efforts enabled us to grant this wish for him. With the best will in the world our family could only do so much. Carmel had a gift of preparing us for each step, her actions pre-emptive in nature, but her mission was absolute. She would facilitate Dad to leave this world with dignity, in comfort and all the while bolster us so we were engaged and involved in every decision. Dad was aware of her prowess and he trusted her. Even on his deathbed he made us all promise to look after her for him when he was gone. What a selfless man he truly was.

The framework of support was immense for us and Dad. The help we received from our daily visits from the doctor and nurses and our nightly rendezvous with Carmel was invaluable. They gave us a beautiful gift of time with Dad. Time that had allowed us to truly say goodbye. Time for the grandkids to administer the tonic of their daily hugs and time for them to get used to the fact that Grandad was going to Heaven. Soon. Just too soon for all of us, including him!

In a world of uncertainty all that we are truly certain of is death. The more certain we were that Dad's death was near, the more GRATEFUL we became for the luxury of the time we had with him. It was not enough and if it was up to us, we would never have enough time with Dad. In the end, the struggle to stay with us – his precious family – was just too much for him to bear. On Dad's last day, we were GRATEFUL for the humanity all his carers showed and the gift of Fr Brendan's presence in his last few hours. This was pivotal in Dad's release from this world in order to go to the next. Essentially, this gave Dad the 'green light' to go. He knew the full-time whistle had gone. There was no extra time. The game of life was lost and the game of death was won all in the same breath, but in true Dad style, Dad did it his way, the way he wanted to go: surrounded by his precious family that he loved, Mom, me, Joe and John. We were all five of us, 'THE QUINLAN 5', together for the very last time in Mom and Dad's bedroom. The same bedroom that held such fond memories of our childhood; the laughter, the giggles, the snuggles, the kisses, the love. The innocence that was synonymous with our childhood now annihilated by the stark reality of death. This was the finale of Dad's life. These were our last hugs, our last kisses and now five became four, and our life would never be the same again.

The reality of death now emphasised by the stark reality of our new world. We had been oblivious to anything outside our door. Our world had been exclusive to the confines of our home. Our focus, our energy, our resources, our love, our time all reserved for Dad. We were now waking up to the reality of the Covid-19 pandemic and being shrouded by restrictions rather than our relatives and friends. We were confounded by it all. Now we were entering a new world where Dad's death would take on a new meaning. Little did I think I would express such GRATITUDE at the timing of Dad's passing. A moment in time pivotal to us all and, by virtue of its timing, it granted us all the ultimate gift of participation in his funeral. All his precious grandchildren played such an active part in honouring and remembering the man he was. I had the privilege of giving the eulogy and describing my Dad in my own words. It seems strange to say we were GRATEFUL Dad died when he did, but if he had died a few days later there would have been no gifts, no readings, no eulogy. It literally would have only been a ten-minute Mass. I believe that a Mass like this would have annihilated my soul and damaged me irrevocably forevermore. I am already struggling desperately with the emptiness and lack of formalities. On a personal level, I find the lack of a traditional Irish wake and the lack of connection with people who wanted to pay their respects leaves a huge void. I needed the celebration of a wake and the connection of sympathisers to truly allow me to grieve and ultimately heal, but that was not possible. It violated my core values, my intrinsic need for people and the guttural desire I had to honour our Dad the way he deserved. My existence was tenuous enough and now was only harassed by the helplessness I was consumed by. The farewell Dad received from friends and neighbours lining our driveway and the guard of honour outside the church will be etched in our memory always. If Dad lived a few more days that would not have been his reality. Never did I ever think I would utter that I was GRATEFUL Dad died when he did!

Gratitude

AS EACH DAY NOW MORPHS INTO NIGHT, OUR LIVES GO on without our Dad. At night, the silence is often deafening, yet can also be enlightening, as it provides time for reflection. During the day, the sunshine is a beautiful reminder of hope, of better days ahead, of life, of remembrance, of love. My Dad was GRATEFUL for everyone and everything in his life. His attitude of GRATITUDE a template for a life best lived, a life where contentment was bestowed upon him because he knew how truly blessed he was. Here's hoping our post-pandemic world will render us all more GRATEFUL, so that we too can all know the virtues of living a more content, fulfilled and GRATEFUL life with the ones we love and who love us back, where we want for nothing and what we need we already have. A world where instead of always getting ready to live, we are actually living and so are ultimately GRATEFUL for the privilege and blessing that life truly is.

Resilience

RESILIENCE IS NOW A PERMANENT RESIDENT ON MY repertoire of character traits. It is undoubtedly a necessary prerequisite for the survival and re-emergence of our new and improved world too. The crisis we are all currently living through will either make or break our society. Personally, I have always been resolute in my belief of the tremendous hidden power of our own inner strength. I believe that every crisis will strengthen and reveal our character rather than mould it. The challenges and how we deal with them have the power to reveal a different version of ourselves, unearthing the true RESILIENCE that resides within us. When life becomes unbearable – as it has for me in recent times – I had no option than to become more self-aware, more accountable and ultimately more self-accepting. Without this process, I believe I would have just shrivelled up and died. When I became resigned to the fact that the 'old me' was no longer a viable commodity, it was then and only then that I knew I had to make peace with the 'new me' and the new world I was emerging into too. This imperfect world without my Dad was now inhabited by the new imperfect me! The same me that had survived. The same me that my Dad needed, relied on, depended on completely. I was a caretaker to others' needs in lieu of my own and my own self-preservation. The same me that was such a beacon of hope to others, as I wilted into near oblivion myself! The same me that was utterly annihilated by sadness and regret. The same me that had to now accept myself as the imperfectly perfect version of me, if I had any chance to survive and thrive in my new world – merely survive now day by day, but hopefully, ultimately thrive later.

During my struggles, I felt I was in essence nearing my own extinction after Dad's life was extinguished. I felt I had no more to give. I was totally running on empty, existing on mere fumes. In retrospect, I was certain my own demise was imminent. My own end was near, a foregone conclusion for sure. It was then and only then I realised I actually had a reserve of fuel for emergencies. Undoubtedly, this certainly constituted an emergency of epic proportions in my world. This was enough to restart my engine, to resuscitate it, to give it hope, to relight my internal fire and my will to live.

Life has reiterated how RESILIENT I truly am. I am always on an endless quest to learn, but in hindsight this was never a lesson to be learnt from any book rather a life lesson in itself. It was certainly my most challenging curriculum ever, experiential in nature. Too often we look for others to impart wisdom to us. Truthfully, this is only a foolhardy exercise because, as I now realise, RESILIENCE cannot be delegated to us from anyone. Otherwise we relegate ourselves to a life less lived, a life where we are so consumed by regret that our past suffocates our future. It is only by acceptance of our own fragility and vulnerability that we can invoke our strength, that we can rely on the inner sanctum of our own core RESILIENCE, our God-given gift, one that is ours and ours alone.

I have weathered many storms and survived, dishevelled and battered but still alive. Yet the storms that ensued as a result of Dad's illness and subsequent death were like a tornado and tsunami combined – unmerciful, relentless and utterly cruel. It ebbed and flowed like waves of destruction, unapologetic in its severity. Its course and aftermath, a true reflection of my vulnerability, my battle between debilitating weakness and my utter resolve to survive. Such a struggle has been exhausting. It has been as challenging for me as it has been for those in my inner circle.

I have always championed empowering women: now it is time to do the same for myself. I knew that no matter what, I had the power within me to come through this. In essence, I knew that I would survive. I needed to nurture and cultivate the seeds of RESILIENCE as diligently as my Dad always had his glorious crops. He always reiterated that quality seeds when nurtured would flourish to a quality crop. If I am to grow and flourish and respect my own RESILIENT seeds, I need to replicate his actions. My duty of care is paramount, my actions essential, my resolve unwavering and myself belief crucial. My life, my work, my journey would essentially be a representation of self-love, self-acceptance, grit and determination and a template of survival for others. The experiential nature of life's journey is as personal and unique as our own DNA. How we interpret and utilise it is a choice that is ours and ours alone. To participate and learn from life's journey is crucial so that our life will flourish and mature like my Dad's crops, so that we can all essentially benefit from life's bountiful harvest. My hope is that I would become a beacon of hope for others. I would be a symbol of survival. I would stand for real women everywhere. I would be in a position to impart my wisdom as my empathy and experience, even though unique to me, was not exclusive to me. It is only by my self-awareness of my shortcomings that I am in a position of self-acceptance. It is only by learning from the past and looking forward to the future that we can make sense and live in the present. The possibilities are endless, if, and only if, we are all willing to dig deep within ourselves and, excavate our own hidden treasure: RESILIENCE!

However, I cannot help but wonder how long this process will take. When will my so-called theory become reality? I had made a flippant remark to a friend about my upcoming fiftieth birthday. I had an epiphany of sorts. I dreamt that this would be when I would have a rebirth of ME! A relaunch of the woman I was and had now become, the new poster girl for RESILIENT women everywhere. I felt that I would have healed my scars, mended my broken heart, rebuilt my confidence, redirected my energy, established my allies and refocused my goals by then. I also had a vision of donning a beautiful THEIA gown that would symbolise my metamorphosis. I knew that only such couture was befitting for the tapestry of my life – without the seams and threads – only the beautiful finished garment on display. The latter essential so the former can exude a life of itself. I knew I needed all my own threads and seams intact so that I could be whole again, complete, a unit, a separate entity. I know I may have many tears and many flawed edges in the future because of the rambunctious nature of life, but these can be mended, just like my broken spirit.

My heart yearns for a more fulfilled and rewarding life, not only for myself but for humankind. I yearn for the possibilities of the future, I ache for solace in my body and I hope that I will be accompanied by many more RESILIENT women who will accompany me on my life's journey. I have eternal hope for a more nurturing and content society. With the optimism that was omnipresent in my Dad, I look forward to a RESILIENT world inhabited by RESILIENT people, including a more RESILIENT ME!

Proud

IN THE AFTERMATH OF MY RECENT TUMULTUOUS life events, I am in a place of retrospective analysis. Each day there are new emotions, challenges and even revelations that unfold. I have become acutely aware of the emotive power of PRIDE. Especially now since I reside within the confines of my own home, socially and physically isolating according to the current guidelines. The consequences of such isolation, especially after the loss of Dad, have only reiterated the overwhelming PRIDE that I feel for our family, friends and neighbours. Not for a moment have I ever questioned our unity as a family. I knew our strengths, was aware of our resolve and had faith in our commitment to each other. I was PROUD of the cohesive nature that was the foundation integral to the heart of our family unit. I was totally in awe and overwhelmed by the dedication of my brothers to my Dad, especially in his last few weeks at home. My two brothers are honourable, kind, loving men. They are men of outstanding character. This is no big surprise as they are my parents' sons and, above all, they have Quinlan blood running through their veins. Our Dad was always so utterly and unashamedly PROUD of each of us. It exuded from every orifice of his existence. It was his own humility and lack of ego that made his display of PRIDE even more profound. My Dad had an inherent sense of SELF-PRIDE. His integrity and respect was of the highest calibre. He was a quintessential gentleman. Dad can now rest easy with the reassurance that his family will honour his legacy with the greatest of PRIDE as long as we all reside in this world.

PRIDE of family, PRIDE of place, PRIDE of oneself was always evident in how he conducted his life. Dad was a beacon of hope and light to us all. He possessed the prototype on how a life is to be best lived. He showed us all how PRIDE was an essential ingredient in the recipe for a fulfilled life. He was as PROUD as PROUD can be. For me personally, I am so PROUD to say I am my Father's Daughter. He was a man who showed PRIDE in his life. PRIDE in his work. PRIDE in his family. PRIDE in his sport. PRIDE in his country and PRIDE in his faith.

Did I inherit that same instinctive sense of PRIDE? Was this PRIDE guaranteed because of my ancestral line? Maybe PRIDE skips a generation? As I start to interrogate myself, I have to interrupt that internal dialogue that questions whether I did enough, whether I could have done more. It is then I realise I need to stop! Dad was so PROUD of his 'young one', as he often referred to me, especially to the doctors. He was PROUD of my intellect, my ability to converse and to understand. I was Dad's go-to person, his Health Advocate, so to speak, when he needed it most. To console my broken heart, I need to truly acknowledge this. The PRIDE he showed in me is disrespected if I do not reciprocate the same PRIDE in myself. He was so utterly PROUD of me. Why then do I struggle with a lukewarm sense of PRIDE in myself? I had a moment recently where I was walking and a passer-by said that I was 'walking with a purpose'. Those who know me know I have two speeds: slow and accelerated! Even though I am broken-hearted, my body is still trying to honour the fact that I am still alive. For the first time in a long time, I actually admitted, albeit reluctantly, that I was PROUD of my body. The body that was keeping me moving and playing caretaker to my broken heart. I pledge to be its custodian until I draw my last breath. In that moment I realised that unless we experience PRIDE in who we are, PRIDE in what we are, PRIDE in where we are, we are not truly living, just merely existing. I had fallen into this trap unknowingly. I had actually lost PRIDE in who I was, PRIDE in where I was, PRIDE in what I was! Cumulatively, that had led to my life being less lived, mediocre at best. I had succumbed to the insecurities that are synonymous with modern living: feelings of not being enough, not doing enough or not having enough. Where good enough just was not enough anymore! So, without having SELF-PRIDE, the reality was in actual fact I was living an inauthentic life. In truth, I was an imposter, but a good one. How now could I claim to honour Dad's life and legacy, if SELF-PRIDE was not on my agenda? I constantly reiterate to my daughter how PROUD I am of the young woman she has become. Yet I know that my greatest influence on her is by my actions rather than my words. My Dad was my greatest tutor, but along the way I had disengaged and by severing the ties to my inner core, I had weakened my ability to feel any SELF-PRIDE. With a diluted and misguided sense of PRIDE, I had deluded myself into complacency, a state that allowed me to live less consciously for sure.

The struggle and the turmoil I am experiencing at the moment is nothing short of exhausting. Yet, I am aware of the real struggle our entire civilisation is facing. We are questioning the attack we are under from this demonic virus that is ruthless. We are aware of our vulnerability, our own shelf life, so to speak, and even coming to the stark realisation that we are all expendable. This surely is the wake-up call that the world needs so it can recalibrate its priorities and re-emerge as a more robust civilisation that exudes PRIDE in its words, PRIDE in its actions and PRIDE in its thoughts. This is already evident in the humanitarian ethos that has bolstered our current compromised society. I feel immense PRIDE in the display of unconditional love we have shown for each other. Never have we shown such solidarity as a community as now. Ironically, we have never been more together by being more apart.

This is bittersweet for me, as my need for people in my life is superseded by my desire to protect the people

I love from the ravages of this pandemic. As humans, we are the sum total of nature and nurture. So much of who and what, we are, is decided by our genes and the rest by how we live, how we are raised and the people who raise us. For all of us living through this pandemic, it is certainly the worst of times, but it is also the best of times. It is in times as traumatic as these that the true calibre of the world's inhabitants is evident. This moment in time will teach future generations the definition of humanity. It will be an exercise in selfless love. It will exult our frontline workers into a new class of 'superheroes' and it will demonstrate how PRIDE of ourselves, PRIDE of people and PRIDE of place, how sheer PRIDE was the fuel that kept our world alive. As people without PRIDE we are nothing – but with PRIDE we are everything. PRIDE is and will be the elixir, the impetus, the incentive, that will keep our world vibrant, the reason we will not give up. The reason that every day we wake up is another day where we get up, dress up, show up and partake with PRIDE in the life we are blessed to have.

Oh, how my Dad would be so PROUD of the new and improved world that we are becoming and even more PROUD if his family were active participants in it. By sheer virtue of who I am, where I am from, whom I belong to and where I want to go, it would be remiss of me not to instigate a life where I can emulate the PRIDE of place, the PRIDE of family, the PRIDE of work, the PRIDE of oneself, that was inherent in the man I called my Dad. So, with the guiding light and wisdom from above, I must begin to live and love again. I must partake in self-care of my body, mind and spirit so that SELF-PRIDE can run through my veins and exult me to a place where I feel worthy of my Dad's unwavering PRIDE in his little girl … a little girl who is PROUD of the woman she has become!

Hope

WE HAVE ALL HEARD THE EXPRESSION 'HOPE SPRINGS eternal'; never ever has that been more appropriate than now, both in my personal life and in the world in general. In our darkest of days, unless there is HOPE, we are doomed to feel crushed by the foreboding reality that has consumed us. In a world of uncertainty, HOPE is essential to ensure that we can all catapult ourselves forward and start to live again. Such powerful words; however, I am bemused by them because my disposition does not always complement or correlate with what I write.

As I attempted to get motivated this morning, I was encouraged by my daughter's warm embrace. It was as if her touch was pushing my 'start button'. A paltry attempt to get me into the 'on position', so to speak. In my discombobulated state I was still aware that this was a day where I had to at least pretend to be alive, if not for my own sake, then for my family's sake. It was yet another day I had to HOPE would be better than the day before. As we snuggled and chatted, she proceeded to tell me a funny story that resulted in both of us actually laughing and me tickling her as I did when she was a baby. What ensued was truly magical, dare I say it was even HOPEFUL, where there was an echo of screams and giggles from both of us, so much so that there were tears running down both our cheeks. The difference was, however, that these tears were not the ones I had become so accustomed to in the aftermath of Dad's loss. Those all-too-familiar tears of loss and sadness. The ones that had been exacerbated by pandemic isolation. These were tears of HOPE, tears of joy, tears of the promise of what could and would most certainly happen again. When I would allow myself to engage in life and actually start living once more. The HOPE was real. The HOPE was tangible. The HOPE was comforting to me. Even though, I could not see my face, I saw the joy in my daughter's face. I knew that I had replaced that catatonic stare with a glimmer and glint of HOPE in my sullen eyes. That vacant stare that I had become so accustomed to was a reflection of the vacancy in my heart after we had lost Dad. It was a hole greater than any volcanic crater. It was an emptiness for sure, a void and an abyss of nothingness.

The giggles and laughter were a HOPEFUL sign that there was life in my home and life in my heart once more. Oh, how encouraging it is to know that I can survive this. I felt it was as if my heart was like a dead car battery that had been recharged by a trusty mechanic, thus injecting a new lease of life back into it. My heart had been resuscitated and given another chance at life. For me life and being alive equates to HOPE, and HOPE equates to a better life, for now at least.

My internal tug of war is a game without an end as I relive each day the battle between the 'impossible' and 'possible'. The internal battle between what I want and what I need. On one hand, there is the impossible of what I want, which is Dad to still be with us; on the other hand is what I need, which is to accept his loss. I know I need to be at peace with the fact that ME and ONLY ME is responsible for how I live the rest of my life. Until I accept this and add my strength and support to what I need, this internal tug of war will drain me.

I have recalled to all the terrible chill that has existed in my body for weeks now, irrespective of the sun in the sky. That is until today. Imagine my shock when I actually felt warmth on my face! I was aware of the sun's rays and even felt a flush in my cheeks. There was HOPE! Oh, was this a sign of the new life that was starting to begin? Was the warmth on my face symbolic of the thawing of my body and of the ignition of my heart? Oh, if so, this was nothing short of miraculous. Oh, there truly was a God. Now that God had a new trusted companion, my Dad, to help him in resurrecting me from the Hell I had fallen into. The warmth of the air was so refreshing. It made me think of the wonderful summer evenings we had as children when we frolicked carefree as little lambs in our fields. Oh, they were the best of times. It's interesting that in the worst of times we recall and lament the best of times. I guess the lesson here is, it is only then we can all truly appreciate what we really had, what we had all taken for granted and in our naivety assumed would never end. It is then and only then we can actually express our HOPE for what we can all have again.

As quickly as it came, the warm breeze seemed to go again as if quenched from above. I was startled in a way as I could feel the cold return and my surroundings darken and it was then that I saw that the sky had become overcome with dark ominous clouds. I had been so bemused by actually feeling alive, feeling HOPEFUL that I was oblivious to how quickly everything changed. However, as I steadied myself and placed my Dad's hat on my head (it was something he loved to wear and now brought me comfort), I realised there was HOPE on the horizon. Even though the storm clouds hovered over me in the distance, I saw a lighter sky and the clouds began to dissipate. The dark threatening clouds replaced by more encouraging and, dare I say it, HOPEFUL ones. They were like those created by an artist's brush. They were lighter in colour, fluffier in nature and even more fun to look at. This was a sign of what I was walking into. I was leaving behind the darker days in the HOPE of brighter ones. What I do know in retrospect is that my walk is like my life's journey. It will have sunshine, storm clouds, warm breezes and even a chilly air, but no matter what, just like the weather, it too shall pass. Dad was never put off by the weather, even though it really dictated his livelihood. Dad always said, 'Never let the weather deter you.' There was no such thing as bad weather, only bad clothing to protect you from it. So, just as Dad's hat gave me comfort today, I know that on my future journey I will not let those storm clouds deter me. There is always a glimmer of HOPE, as we all know that there is always sunshine after the rain. However, I will have to be resolute in my conviction to accept the existence of HOPE. I will have to reiterate this to myself daily and pledge to look for more rainbows in the sky. I love colour; even in my state of grief, I refuse to wear black. Each day I wear a kaleidoscope of colour in an effort to lift my spirits and honour Dad's love of life. For me colour is synonymous with life and with HOPE. As I approach my home I am greeted by my red door. I have always wanted a red door. I have always thought there was something inviting about it – and this has never been so true. Dad's favourite colour was red, and I recall as I kissed Dad for the very last time, I left the imprint of my red lipstick on his cheek. It was my way of saying goodbye, and to remind him I was always close by, living a life where colour, exuberance and eternal HOPE were alive and well. Now as I enter my home and close my red door behind me, I feel safe. I actually feel HOPEFUL, as I believe as life is resuming on either side of the red door, so too is life resuming in my heart. Colour means life and red to me means HOPE. As I close my eyes and lay my hands on my beating heart, I am reminded that WHERE THERE IS LIFE THERE IS ALWAYS HOPE. My beating heart symbolic of a beacon of HOPE for a new and better life to come, not only for me and for my beautiful family, but the whole wide world too.

Finally, my ETERNAL HOPE is the stimulus that will encourage me and give me the impetus to live a good life in the knowledge that I will be reunited with my precious and beloved Dad again one day.

A Day like No Other

For on this day a month ago our world fell apart,
For in just an instant it was so real that Dad had to
depart.
The sky was filled with splendour as the party had
begun,
Because it was all so evident, they needed to
welcome home their precious Son.
Our Earth has lost a treasure and Heaven regained
its son,
And in that moment reluctantly our new world had
just begun.

The truth is often bitter like a story seldom told,
Of a man who lost his life too soon and who was
known for his heart of gold.
He was the kindest man we ever knew. His smile
was full of glee,
For he was always happy with a bun and cup of tea!
There will never be another to replace a man like
he.

But our hearts will be forever open though, as he
holds the magic key.

In a world where life is everything, death is
forevermore.
We now have a home with such loss behind its door,
Replaced only by a postman with letters and cards
galore!
Our home is now so empty, a loss so profound
where the promise of time and healing words is
all that could be found.
No matter what one says to me, how pure and truly
kind,
I know there will never be such a specimen of
humankind!

I close my eyes at night with a hope of what the
new day brings,
But alas my heart is broken by so many small
things.
A tissue is of no comfort when all I want is a
warm embrace,
from the people who mean the World to me and I
get comfort from their face.

As I realise with each day passing what's done is
here to stay,
we cannot change the past per se, but just learn to
live day by day.

A Day like No Other

A life lesson like no other is what my world has now
  become,
Where we ponder on life's purpose and we examine
  all we have done.

If my Dad was our role model of humanity and
  humankind,
he would tell us all to love each other and always
  to be kind.
To always love your family and value friendship
  too,
and never let others' troubles be troublesome to
  you.
His faith would be his driving force, his resolve
  forever new,
He would remind us of the beauty in every day so
  new.

Love you, Dad, forever.

*Written by Majella Quinlan Duignan on 20 April 2020 to
honour her Dad on the first month anniversary of his passing.*